Christ in Focus

Christ in Focus

*Radical Christocentrism in
Christian Theology*

Clive Marsh

scm press

© Clive Marsh 2005

British Library Cataloguing in Publication data

A catalogue record for this book is available
from the British Library

0 334 02981 3/9780 334 02980 9

First published in 2005 by SCM Press
9–17 St Albans Place, London N1 0NX

www.scm-canterburypress.co.uk

SCM Press is a division of
SCM-Canterbury Press Ltd

Printed and bound in Great Britain by
William Clowes Ltd, Beccles, Suffolk

Contents

Preface

What do Christians mean when they say 'Jesus is here'? What does the attempt to be 'Christ-like' actually amount to? What does it mean to claim to be 'in Christ', or to say that 'Jesus Christ is with us'? What sense can be attached to the Church's identification of itself as the 'body of Christ'? And is the Church the only 'body of Christ' in the world today? These, and questions like them, have given rise to the research project out of which this present book, and its forthcoming companion volume *Christ in Practice* (to be published by Darton, Longman & Todd), have emerged. I have simply wanted to get to grips with what Christians actually make of, and do with, the figure of Jesus Christ not just in belief, and not just in worship, but in theology, spirituality and ethical practice – in short, in all dimensions of Christian life. I also wanted to clarify the central importance of these questions for Christian faith and practice. For the shorthand expressions of worship (Christ is here) and ethical reflection (what would Jesus do?) veil a complex reality: Christology is the primary way in which Christians do their God-talk, and this God-talk affects, even shapes, the way in which Christians behave and relate to other people. Moreover, adjustments to Christology should have effects on practice (and if not, then the Christology is not worth much, as it is not being 'lived'). The practice of daily life, and the relationships of which it comprises, should also be having an impact on Christology: to confirm and accentuate it, to challenge it, to ask questions of it. In this way, the adequacy of what Christians say about Jesus

Christ, and do on the basis of their belief, is constantly re-examined.

In this present book I first explore the 'Christocentric' character of Christian thought and practice. In Part One I take a close look at how theology works, and emphasize the inevitable centrality of the figure of Jesus Christ in Christian theology. Recognizing that to speak of a 'centre' is sometimes unhelpful, I nevertheless argue for Christology as Christian theology's main theme. In distinguishing the 'focus' from the 'starting point' of theology (Chapter 2) I note that Christian theology must maintain a clear emphasis upon Christology. There are, however, clear dangers to such a radical Christocentrism, and Chapter 3 spells these out. Even when located within a trinitarian framework, Christocentrism is not to be diverted from its primary task: to live and proclaim the gospel of God as known in and through Christ.

Two questions arise from this. What does a contemporary Christology capable of sustaining such a Christocentrism actually look like? And what does this 'living and proclaiming' mean in practical terms? The second question is addressed in *Christ in Practice*. The rest of this present book addresses the first question. In the three chapters of Part Two, I expound an understanding of Christ in three steps, using a different conversation partner in each case. In Chapter 4 I enter into dialogue with the theology of Friedrich Schleiermacher (1768–1834). In the dialogue, I probe especially the interplay between Schleiermacher's christological emphases and his clear concern for what I call 'Christ-piety'. One of Schleiermacher's main concerns was to identify who the Redeemer is, from the perspective of those who experience communally the Redeemer's influence upon them. This means that his thought forms the basis for exploring a contemporary, corporate Christology.

In Chapter 5 I move forward a century to enter into dialogue with the work of the German-American Baptist, Walter Rauschenbusch (1861–1918). Known as the theologian of the 'social gospel',

Rauschenbusch proves an ideal conversation-partner in the task of clarifying what it means to speak of Christ in socio-political terms. In examining Rauschenbusch's prophetic exploration of Christ as social liberator, I speak of his commitment to 'Christ-society'. Rauschenbusch's concern was to ensure that whatever is made of Christ, this must influence the way in which human communities are structured. A corporate Christology linked only to the social reality called 'church' will prove inadequate. Rauschenbusch's attempt to place the Kingdom of God at the centre of theology and ethics proves profoundly instructive.

In Chapter 6, I draw on the contemporary Asian-American feminist theologian Rita Nakashima Brock's exploration of 'Christa/Community' in order to investigate one of the leading edges of current christological thought. Discussion with Brock provides an opportunity to test where and in what form ideas implicit in Schleiermacher's and Rauschenbusch's work take shape in the present. Brock's concern is to explore a contemporary, communal meaning for 'Christ', one not consumed by attention to the past, male individual Jesus of Nazareth.

The findings of Chapters 4 to 6 set up the two simple questions which Chapters 7 and 8 address: what? and who? is Christ today. In Chapter 7 I explore the fact that despite their talk about the presence of Christ, Christians too often leave ill-explored the form of Christ in the world today. If 'Christ' is clearly not present as a first-century Palestinian figure, then what is it that we are actually talking about? Finally, in Chapter 8, I draw together the consequences of the exploration for the task of expounding a contemporary Christology: in the light of radically re-asserting Christocentrism in Christian thought and practice today, what can we actually say about Jesus Christ?

This book and its companion volume have been part of my life for over a decade, across three different jobs: one in higher education, one in the Methodist Church, and one in theological education within the Church of England. I dread to think how many people there are that I should be thanking, and whose roles in its production I might have forgotten. It has been through many drafts and its content has been tried out in many different forms before reaching the present two manuscripts. That it has finally 'made it' into published form is, however, due to the help of many. Ann Harvey typed most of the very first version, not only 'doing her job' as my secretary at the time, but also admitting, when typing 'beyond the call of duty', to enjoying hearing and thinking about what she was typing. Ann, I thank you for all that typing. You'll still see some of your words in here, even if not as many as you or I might have expected.

Paul Badham, Meg Davies, Gavin D'Costa, David Fergusson, Richard Kirton, Robert Morgan, Paul Murray, Peter Selby and Haddon Willmer have all read part or all of earlier drafts. That this book has emerged at all is due in no small part to their various critiques, even though some of those readers may well be horrified at where it has ended up. Jill Marsh and Ruth Nason were my final critical readers. I cannot thank both enough, as they both dared to ask the hard questions ('what do you actually mean?') of near-to-final texts, which then proved to be not as final as I'd have hoped. Any unclarity which remains is all down to me.

The Church Army Training College, where I taught from 1989 to 1995 (first in Blackheath, London, and then after its move to Sheffield), proved a great place to work and teach Christian doctrine, for what we explored in our classes together clearly mattered to those who studied there. I value greatly my time at the College, and am grateful for the stimulus of students and staff and the sensitive management which enabled me to keep identifiably academic work ticking over so profitably. A period of study leave in early summer 1994 proved invaluable. I am grateful, too, to the College of Ripon and York St John (as it was then called) for support for trips to libraries from 1996 to 1998 and for the granting a period of partial study leave during 1999–2000.

For all of the book's life I have been among Methodists, and one of 'Mr Wesley's Preachers'. I wrestle with Methodism from the inside, valuing especially the way it has enabled me to piece together various bits of my own spiritual journey (Christian Brethren piety, Liberal Protestantism, socio-political concerns, and more than a hint of Luther). It will not take a reader too much insight to see how all of this has influenced the study that follows. Conversations with Methodist colleagues, many of which – in recent years – have taken place within the British Society for the Study of Theology, have informed the book's content. Membership of the Society has forced me to engage with movements in theology I might have chosen to ignore, and I am grateful for that. I hope, somewhat mischievously, that this book might encourage some of the Society's members to listen to movements in theology they themselves might sometimes be prone to ignore. I also acknowledge a debt to various sections, groups and seminars within the American Academy of Religion, whose joint meeting with Society of Biblical Literature I have attended regularly since 1989. Papers on Ritschl (1989), Tillich (1991), Schleiermacher (1993) and the Historical Jesus (1995) could be regarded as working papers for the present book. During the course of writing, it has proved delightful to renew contact with the Revd Peter Francis, Warden of St Deiniol's Library, Hawarden. Two very enjoyable week-long stays there have been crucial at various stages in the writing process.

Finally I would like to thank my immediate family. Jill, Philip and Hannah are wonderful companions. It is proverbial, but nonetheless true, that I owe them so much. In an age of the mistaken idolization of the nuclear family, and in the midst of such a network of loving relationships within our wider family, it is a hard but important lesson to learn that families are not everything. Learning what it means to be 'in Christ' takes us, after all, beyond our immediate families and friendships. I dedicate this book to them nevertheless, knowing that our roles in relation to each other, and the nature of our relationships with each other, will go on changing over the years.

Clive Marsh,
February 2005

Part One

The Path of
Methodological Christocentrism

1

Centres and Margins

What lies at the heart of theology? God, obviously. What lies at the heart of Christian theology? Again, God, obviously. Or should that be God in Christ? Or even just Christ? And, anyway, would it not be better to ask who, rather than what? These simple-sounding questions and answers have given rise to this book. For any obvious answer to the question 'what lies at the heart, or centre, of Christianity?' only raises many further questions. References to 'God' or 'Jesus Christ' remind us that faith and theology work with words and images, which have to be interpreted when the sense of the presence of God, or Christ, is explored. '*What* lies at the heart of Christian theology?' is therefore as important a question as 'who?'

This opening chapter examines the notion of centrality in Christian theology. Is it right to ask about a centre at all? For the notion of a centre implies margins, and a centre and margins could easily be equated with major and minor, more and less important. And who would decide what is central or marginal about God or Christ? Furthermore, if Jesus Christ was, in an important sense, a marginal figure, then his centrality for Christian thought and practice needs close scrutiny. Centrality and marginality in Christianity need to be carefully related. I maintain that identifying what is central is an important part of the theological task: it is important to know where emphasis is being placed in any attempt to articulate the content and meaning of Christian faith in any age.

In order to address the question of what is central, and to begin to explore the relationship between centrality and marginality, I shall first examine *how* theology is done. Then I will explore *by whom* it is done and finally I will specify *where* theology is done. I offer a christological case for each step of the argument.

How is Christian theology to be done?

Christian theology is done at all because of Jesus Christ, and so Christian theology is bound to be methodologically Christo-centric. Christian God-talk is reflection on the presence and action of God, but always as God is known in Christ. Christian theology is thus reflection on the presence and action of a God who is assumed always to be present and acting in a Christ-like way. Answers to the questions 'by whom?' and 'where?' Christian theology is to be done are also affected by this methodological Christocentrism.

Christian theology draws on many sources and resources and comprises a number of sub-disciplines. Which are the most important, and does it matter?

Sources and resources

Theology is usually said to operate with four main sources: scripture, reason, experience and tradition. In Christian theology, scripture means Bible, though which particular Bible (Protestant or Roman Catholic canon) depends on institutional, confessional factors. In the past, 'reason' included all aspects of human sub-jectivity. The fact that the term has needed to be supplemented in modern and postmodern times by the concept of 'experience' indicates that 'reason' has come to mean rationality alone.

'Experience' is a difficult term. It may mean either specif-ic religious (or spiritual) experiences or 'life experience' more generally.[1] 'Tradition' is just as problematic. It may denote a limited number of generally accepted texts (for example, the classical creeds) or confession-specific material such as the Thirty-Nine Articles, for Anglicans, or Wesley's sermons, for Methodists. More broadly, 'tradition' may be used for the more complex way in which theology is carried. So, in addition to specific writings, a 'tradition' also comprises an ongoing set of practices (e.g. liturgical, ethical) and cultural products (e.g. art, literature, film), which communicate theology without necessarily having any official status. Within 'tradition', we can therefore distinguish between primary 'sources' and other 'resources' (a wide range of interpretative materials which feed off scripture and 'official' tradition). In the latter, broader sense, 'tradition' begins to sound like another (over-used and ambiguous) word: culture.

The boundaries between scripture, tradition, experience and reason are unclear and porous. Not all scriptural texts are useful, nor do they all function equally authoritatively. In practice, elements of tradition sometimes carry greater weight than scripture. Experience (of whatever kind) sometimes proves authoritative over both: faith has to be lived, not thought about. Rationality's role is to prevent Christianity from becoming wholly irrational, even while it must be acknowledged that many of Christianity's operations are not wholly rational. The interplay between the sources is, then, a crucial factor to explore and evaluate.

In this study, as I shall show in Chapter 2, I adopt an understanding of theological reflection which is profoundly experiential, yet heavily tradition-related. I shall conclude that it is not possible to do theology on the basis of experience, reason,

---

1 I have already explored the place of 'experience' in theology in two studies: 'The Experience of Theological Education: Maintaining a "Liberal" Agenda in a Post-Liberal Age' in Mark D. Chapman (ed.), *The Future of Liberal Theology*, Aldershot: Ashgate, 2002, pp. 139–59; and 'Appealing to "Experience": What Does it Mean?' in C. Marsh, B. Beck, A. Shier-Jones and H. Wareing (eds.), *Unmasking Methodist Theology*, London: Continuum, 2004, pp. 118–30.

scripture or even tradition, alone. My understanding of 'tradition' will, though, be very broad. Any christological enquiry demonstrates how multifaceted the image of Jesus is, and thus how theology inevitably draws on doctrinal tradition, biblical material and a vast array of cultural interpretations of Jesus/the Christ. So the interpretation of sources and resources, a task which lies at the heart of theology, turns out to be a complex exercise in (theological) cultural studies, to be undertaken with the deftness of an artist.

My christological argument for adopting an approach which seeks to be firmly experiential and heavily tradition-related is as follows. If Christian theology is reflection upon the presence and action of God (as God is known in Christ) in the world, then God in Christ has to be *experienced*. Experience of Christ never happens in a vacuum, but is recognized and becomes interpretable and communicable because of a *tradition about Christ*. Human experience/s can be interpreted in relation to this tradition, and be made comprehensible, be enhanced or be transformed by the interpretative work undertaken (theology). A tradition about Christ is primarily a *narrative*, carried in a complex way within a *culture*. Though the narrative surfaces in a particular and limited way in the form of doctrinal orthodoxy, the way in which culture carries an image or images of Jesus the Christ is complex: hence the need for respect for a broad understanding of 'tradition'. Attending to the oscillation between a human experience of God in Christ and the tradition about God in Christ (the 'infinitely concrete and yet infinitely variegated image of Christ' carried within a culture) renders Christian theology appropriately methodologically Christocentric.[2]

---

2 The quotation is from Ernst Troeltsch, 'The Significance of the Historical Existence of Jesus for Faith' in R. Morgan and M. Pye (eds.), *Ernst Troeltsch: Writings on Theology and Religion*, London: Duckworth, 1977, p. 194. Troeltsch appears again in Ch. 2 below, and the significance of 'the infinitely concrete and yet infinitely variegated image' will be teased out further in *Christ in Practice*.

Disciplines

Theology is a collection of disciplines. In interdisciplinary times, it is common to draw attention to the way that theology is related to other disciplines, including literary studies, philosophy, psychology, sociology, history and anthropology. In truth, theology has always been interdisciplinary, leaning on the work of literary scholars, historians and philosophers. What has changed in the last century or so – and particularly over the last four or five decades – is the range of disciplines with which theology has been conversing, and the ideological (sometimes anti-theological) base upon which the other disciplines rest. Theology has therefore been more severely challenged than ever before about its subject matter, by disciplines with which it may not share common methods or goals.

That said, theology has an identifiable task: to speak of God. This can be done only within given traditions, be they broad (e.g. Christian, Jewish, Muslim) or narrow (e.g. Baptist, Progressive, Shiite). Yet, although limited in scope, theologies are in constant conversation with readings of God, humanity and the world that are offered from outside the particular religious or theological traditions that fashion them. Christians are not Christians in isolation. Roman Catholics who try to speak of God in a Christian way without reference to other traditions are unwise to do so. The challenge of enabling traditions to speak to each other – even within a single religion – is a considerable one, however.

A Christian theology within any confession subdivides: into biblical study, doctrine, ethics, pastoral (or practical) theology and liturgical or worship studies, to name but the most obvious components. How these are taught and studied is crucial as far as the links between them are concerned, and the extent to which they are regarded as self-contained. Christian ethics taught without reference to the Bible and doctrine, for example, will be inadequately taught. Liturgy undertaken without reference to doctrine and church history is likely to produce poor Christian worship. Christian theology is, then, already a collection of disciplines.

All theology's sub-disciplines in turn have links with disciplines beyond theology. Biblical scholars are historians, anthropologists, linguists, philosophers and sociologists (and sometimes theologians too). Christian ethics needs sociology and philosophy as well as Bible and doctrine. Liturgists must attend to what psychologists and semioticians say. Christian theology is, then, not only already a collection of disciplines. It links to many other disciplines beyond it.

Further, how these disciplines come into play in life in turn shapes how they are constructed as disciplines.[3] The extent to which pastoral theology draws on psychology and counselling studies, for example, affects the degree to which participants are enabled to make interdisciplinary links and thus to identify the many dimensions of a pastoral encounter in ministry. Likewise, the extent to which pastoral theology (as practical theology) is socio-politically informed affects the degree to which participants view pastoral encounters in their economic and social context.

What, though, is the most important sub-discipline of theology? Is this even a valid question? Do we really want biblical scholars, pastors, systematic theologians, ethicists and liturgists squabbling over the matter? Perhaps, for the sake of theology's health, the argument is necessary. Perhaps all should continue to claim the relative merits of their sub-disciplines while knowing that each needs all the others.

In this book, *I begin from the assumption that practical theology is the goal of all theology*. By this I mean simply that theology in the practice of living is all that ultimately matters. The disposition and human interactions of the Christian believer are the true test of

---

3 I resist speaking here of disciplines being 'applied' in life. As will become clear, I do not think that the practice of theology can easily be divided into 'pure' and 'applied' aspects.

theology. But those dispositions and interactions are themselves subject to rich, critical enquiry, which is biblically, doctrinally, ethically, pastorally and liturgically informed. This book may admittedly be classed as a work of systematic theology. It seeks to clarify what should be said of Christ today. It offers a Christology, drawing on Bible, liturgy and the practice of human living. Its focus is doctrinal articulation. The complementary study (*Christ in Practice*) presses its practical consequences a stage further. However, it should not be thought in any simple sense that I have 'done' biblical, ethical and liturgical studies in this present book, and then 'apply' the findings of this study to practical theology in the second book. Theology does not work that way. All the sub-disciplines interweave.

The Christology to be expounded in this book, then, is already 'practical'. It is already caught up in the task of exploring what it means to identify, celebrate and participate in the presence of God as known in and through Christ in the world today. The book is a work of 'systematic' theology only because its primary task is to spell out features about *Christ* (rather than about the believer in Christ) which need articulating, and to do this in relation to other themes in Christian thought (e.g. Trinity and Spirit). The book then proceeds, in Part Two,[4] in quite a traditional way: through critical dialogue with theologians past and present.

Practical theology needs to be seen as the goal of theology for a simple christological reason. The goal of all Christian theology is the celebration and articulation of an experience of God as known in Christ. (In this sense, the best practical theology is also missiology: it spills over into a desire that the significance of speaking of Christ is recognized by others.) Systematic theology's heart, as we shall see in Chapter 2, is Christology. But systematic theology cannot rest content with careful articulation of an understanding of Jesus the Christ. It works in the service of

---

4 Chs. 4 to 6 below.

enabling people to *experience* Christ. A methodological Christo-centrism thus sees practical theology as the goal of all Christian theology.

By whom is Christian theology to be done?

Anyone who undertakes God-talk is a theologian of sorts. But not everyone engages in sustained critical reflection on their God-talk. The critical task is undertaken by relatively few: those paid to teach theology in some form, some bishops, some priests or ministers (though by no means all) and an assortment of others (deacons, preachers, layworkers, other enthusiastic lay people) who recognize that faith becomes richer if you think hard about what you and others believe. So one answer to the question 'by whom is Christian theology (in the latter sense) actually done?' is 'not by as many as would be useful for Church and society'.

By whom *should* theology be done, therefore? What would our methodological Christocentrism suggest? At this point I must make a detour to investigate the relationship between central-ity and marginality. For assertion of the centrality of Christ and Christology for Christian theology requires close attention to the social location of those who seek to articulate an understanding of the presence and action of God in Christ today. The work of the Korean-American theologian Jung Young Lee is instructive at this point. Lee's work *Marginality: The Key to Multicultural Theology* provides a helpful analysis and critique of much Western theology, whose preoccupation with 'centrality', he notes, often masks the desire and striving by Western theology for domination. His study offers a corrective to easy claims to identify a 'centre' for theology. Crucially, Lee's is a christological argument, offered as a challenge to customary Western appeals to 'centrality' in theology.

Lee begins his study autobiographically, reflecting on how,

through his own life experience, he discovered himself to be a 'victim of centrality'.[5] Instead of seeing from the start the inevitable interdependent relationship between centre and margins ('Without the center there is no margin; just as there is no center without the margin'), he observes how his identity was defined by those 'at the centre' of American life, who failed to respect Lee's Korean origins. He sees plainly how the centre functions as the focal point of action:

> Traditionally, we have learned to think from the perspective of centrality. We, therefore, think that the center defines the margin. When the rain fills the pond, the margin or the periphery expands; when the dry season comes, the margin of the pond contracts. Yet the center *seems* to be the same. Moreover, action takes place in the center. The margin *seems* to be receptive and appears to respond only to what happens at the center. The center is not only steady but is the origin of action. Thus, the center is attractive and seems to be a preferable location for us to be.[6]

In contrast to this, and without denying the importance of centrality, Lee then develops a multi-focal approach to theology which seeks fully to respect marginality. Indeed, he feels a need to stress marginality over centrality in order to correct an imbalance in the way the two concepts have been understood or implied in theology. Marginality proves to be the 'in-between' position:

> Marginality . . . is more than a boundary itself; it is many boundaries encompassing two or more multiple worlds . . . In other words, marginality has no separate existence of its own.

---

5 J. Y. Lee, *Marginality: The Key to Multicultural Theology,* Minneapolis: Fortress Press, 1995, p. 30.

6 Lee, *Marginality,* pp. 30–1.

It is always relational, for it relates worlds that oppose one another. So marginality is best understood as a nexus, where two or three worlds are interconnected.[7]

The christological grounding of Lee's argument is spelt out in full in his chapter 4: 'Jesus-Christ: The Margin of Marginality'. Here, the many motifs contained in the Jesus narrative (insignificant birth, contact with the sick and the poor, homelessness, the cross) become the bedrock on which Lee builds his case for 'a new center', a 'creative core'. This 'creative core' proves to be trinitarian. It is 'where the Son, Spirit and Father are present'.[8] It is, in other words, where God's presence and action in Christ are fully identified as the work of God. But this creative core is 'different from the center that people seek. The center they seek is the center of centrality, a false center.' In other words, if God in Christ is sought where cultures, churches or individuals identify the 'centre' to be, they are not likely to find the creative core. Instead, following Christ, they must look to the margins. This methodological Christocentrism leads people to the edge, rather than to the centre, of their worlds. Only by this journey will people have a chance of discovering who God is.

Lee's position makes 'marginality' central to theology, with telling effect. Without negating the centre (which, as Less recognizes, is necessary to locate the margins), Lee nevertheless relativizes the centre's importance.[9] His insights are, I suggest, crucial for the

---

7 Lee, *Marginality*, p. 47.

8 Lee, *Marginality*, p. 97.

9 Lee's drawing of a distinction between a theology of marginality and many forms of liberation theology is important here. He writes: 'According to a theology of marginality, the liberation of marginal people is not possible without the liberation of central-group people from their exclusive thinking. Liberation is, then, a mutual process'; Lee, *Marginality*, p. 73. I am sure that many liberationists would agree. Certainly many feminist theologians argue clearly for the liberation of both women and men. But Lee's point is nevertheless well made.

task of identifying who should do theology, and his concerns are echoed throughout much current thinking. Women, lay, ethnic-minority, gay and lesbian theologians have all found a voice in recent decades in a way that has not happened before. Those living in inner-city or in poor rural areas have also challenged the dominance of those articulating contemporary versions of orthodoxy from their urban or suburban contexts. Lee's insights invite us to respect the fact that methodological Christocentrism will require us to look at the margins, and at the points of intersection (the 'in-between' places), to see where God in Christ is. It is therefore at such points that we shall find the voices that must first (or most?) be heard: those who stand between Church and world, between faiths, between words and images, and even perhaps between orthodoxy and heresy. Such theology will listen to insiders and outsiders, to the outcasts as well as the in-crowd, to lay as well as ordained, and to people in many different forms of Christian ministry.

There is, though, a danger of romanticizing here. People who stand in such locations often do not have the time or inclina-tion to be theologians for Church or society. There are many urban church workers who are too tired, or too impatient with the sluggish inner workings of churches, to do the jobs that they consider well-paid bureaucrats are meant to be doing. Granted. Lee's insights therefore need to be heeded differently. Whoever is undertaking theology's critical task, from whatever social location, has to respect the margins, and be critical (and self-critical) with regard to their own centre. This is the inevitable result of Lee's critique.

In other words, whoever undertakes the task of theology will attend to the margins of Church and society if they make Christ central. This will entail listening to a myriad of complex and clashing voices. But it is only through such listening that the opportunity to listen to God as known in Christ will arise.

Where is Christian theology to be done?

All theology has a location. This is true in two senses, both of which are to do with place and people. Theology is contextual in so far as it is articulated *in and out of* a particular setting, be that geographical, an institutional location, or a specific group of people. Theology is also contextual in so far as it directed *to* a particular public.

Contexts out of which theologies are constructed are always ultimately very specific. An academic theologian may write theology as a piece of research, having undertaken detailed historical enquiry into a phase of Christianity's history. The intent may be to reflect critically on a past theologian's potential value and contribution to the task of contemporary construc-tive theology. But the academic may well write her theology in a cramped office in the context of a modern campus university, under the pressure of needing to produce an internationally recognized piece of scholarship. Alternatively, she may write her work in a quiet country retreat, while enjoying a period of extended study leave. Then again, she may write it in the context of domestic life, snatching odd hours between routine tasks of home and profession. Any of these concrete settings could easily influence the resulting work. She may also be fighting an illness, or in the best of health, struggling with loneliness, tense with the challenges of family life, caught up in a messy divorce, or hoping to have children. A serving minister may write her theology in short bursts, writing early in the morning or late at night between the responsibilities of local church life. Her work may be closer to journalism than scholarship, yet is no less theological for that.

As the author of this text I clearly have a context. I have writ-ten up elsewhere a version of the autobiographical background to my own writing.[10] To that account one major new factor should be added. I have recently moved from a largely white area

---

10 C. Marsh, *Christianity in a Post-Atheist Age*, London: SCM Press, 2002, ch. 1.

of a Northern English town to a multiracial area in a city in the Midlands. This is a crucial part of the setting in which my own work is done, as are the changing patterns of family life. The task of writing constructive theology is not exempt from the impact of such contextual factors. It is bound up with them, while not being reducible to them if it remains *theology*.

Theology undertaken within the parameters of methodological Christocentrism can respect such a close relationship between personal circumstances and theological construction for one main reason: the incarnation. If God was and is incarnate, then it is in enfleshed form that God in Christ will always go on being discovered. The claim that 'God was in Christ' (reconciling the world to himself; 2 Cor. 5.19) clearly demarcates a precise and decisive point in history at which God acted. But the claim does not confine God's action in Christ to that point in history, however determinative the events of Jesus' life, death and resurrection prove, and however significant the reflection on those events are for Christian belief. Christology always takes account of the *impact* of the person of Jesus Christ upon the respondent in the here and now. Any Christian theology is marked by the way the person who constructs it reflects on the impact that the person of Jesus Christ has had on them, personally.

Such an approach recognizes that Christian theology is dealing with the *real presence* of Christ. One key premise of this book is that Christ is not some disembodied spirit or mere mental construct. Christian theology offers an account of the real presence of Christ from within the complex context/s of daily life today. If it cannot do this, then it has lost its purpose.

Nonetheless, the institutional contexts from which Christian theology arises merit further consideration. David Tracy's influential exploration of the public character of theology is important here.[11] Tracy recognizes that theology relates to three

---

11 David Tracy, *The Analogical Imagination: Christian Theology and the Culture of Pluralism*, London: SCM Press, 1981.

publics: society, academy and Church. It is undertaken out of and for these three distinct, but overlapping, institutional contexts. Society itself comprises three realms: the techno-economic, the political and the cultural. The techno-economic realm is that aspect of society dealing with the allocation of goods and services. The political realm concerns social justice and the handling of power. The cultural realm comprises the arts and religion in all their various forms, in fact all aspects of a society that make up its complex symbol-system. Theology has a role to play in relation to all of these realms.[12] This accounts for the fact that theology is being done by chaplains and artists and in the context of the work of economists and politicians just as much as it is by ministers in local churches.

The practice of theology in the academy has undergone many changes in recent years. Often seeming to be squeezed out of higher education altogether, in favour of supposedly more value-free 'religious studies', the academic practice of theology is more usually associated now with seminary/theological college or course settings. In practice, the split is not quite as clear-cut as this might suggest. 'Theological study', in the sense of the study of belief systems and ideas, happens within religious studies. Complete disinterestedness is not possible, even when such study is not undertaken for confessional purposes (i.e. to support the practice of a particular religious or theological tradition). Equally, critique of traditions can happen in all settings, even in the context of ministerial training for a particular tradition. Furthermore, because of the requirements of educational validation, public scrutiny of all academic study of religion and theology is a prominent aspect of such enquiry.

In the light of all this, theology undertaken in a formal sense from and for the Church need not ghettoize experience of God and reflection upon that experience. Theology from and for the

---

12 Tracy, *Analogical Imagination*, ch. 1.

Church respects the Church as an important social reality and also the Church's role as a carrier of a specific theological tradition. But where society and academy, the other two publics of theology, disappear from view and the Church functions as theology's sole reference group, then an important aspect of the centrality of Christ in Christianity also goes missing. Without respect for all three publics, the significance of incarnation is underplayed, and Christocentrism is distorted into ecclesiocentrism.[13]

Methodological Christocentrism: a summary

Christ is at the heart of Christian theology, then, because Christ is at the heart of Christian belief, thought and practice. Christians only claim to know anything distinctive to say about God because of Christ. But who and what Christ is remains a matter for continued exploration. The claim that Jesus (of Nazareth) was and is (the) Christ locates a history and narrative in relation to which present-day experience of God occurs and contemporary exploration of God's presence and action in the world is undertaken. But because Christian theology always has the task of interpreting present-day experience of the presence and action of God (in Christ) in the world, Christology can never be focused on a past action of God alone, however decisive the (past) Christ event proves to be. The 'Christ event' goes on happening.

Furthermore, clarifying the identity and meaning of Christ entails finding out where Jesus may be found and includes reference to those, past or present, who have experienced the impact of the figure of Jesus Christ. Given the history of Jesus of Nazareth and the narrative about Jesus the Christ, the task of interpreting God's presence and action will draw interpreters to the margins of their own social worlds. For it is with reference to the narratives

---

13 On 'ecclesiocentrism' see further Ch. 3 below.

about Jesus found in the canonical Gospels that what occurs on the margins of society is instructive for the discovery of who God is and what God is doing. At that point, centre and margin interpret each other.

What will result is a practical theology with Christology at its heart. It will be a practical theology born of deep exploration of the experience of Christ in 'in-between' worlds. This experience will be critically examined in relation to the complex narrative of Jesus the Christ, as transmitted not only by the Church that bears witness to him but also by the many cultures in which his image is carried. To perceive Christ 'at the centre', and to locate Christology at the centre of the human task called Christian theology, means to be taken to the edge of social comfort, of experience and of language. It is to the construction of such a practical theology that this book and its companion volume *Christ in Practice* are devoted.

Identifying a 'centre', however, is not the same as clarifying where you start. And uncritical adoption of the concept of 'centrality' may itself distort the theological task ahead.[14] Chapter 2 therefore looks at the important distinction between 'starting point' and 'focus' in theology.

---

14 Since Lee's work, and in the light of post-colonial approaches in theology and the humanities generally, there has been a shift in discussion from 'marginality' (which requires centrality) to 'borders' (which are centre-less and can focus on the act of border-crossing). I have sympathy with the shift in so far as the purpose is 'decentering' and removing hidden powers from their thrones. But as will become clear in Ch. 2, I do not see how we can avoid owning up to where we put our emphasis, and what we deem to be important. If this is not a 'centre', then it needs defining in some way. And to have borders you need territories.

2

Starting Point and Focus

Where to start?

Theology starts with God. That is not in dispute. No one needs undertake God-talk if there is no God.[1] People who do theology believe they are not deluded, and that they are responding to a given: God. This is a vital premise for theology. But it does not get us very far. For theology is human work. It starts with God, but as soon as theology is recognized as a human discipline, then questions of method and procedure arise. Where do you start, as a human interpreter of the presence and action of God? Even if you have identified the appropriate thematic centre of Christian theology (Christ), from which all other theological reflection flows, do you actually start there? And what are you starting *with*: an experience of Christ, a tradition about Christ, a story about Jesus the Christ, or what? These questions form the substance of this chapter.

---

1 This is not, of course, the same as saying no one would undertake God-talk. ('If God did not exist, it would be necessary to invent him', Voltaire.) Room has to be left, of course, for non-realist approaches to theology which argue for the necessity of God-talk even while recognizing that there is no external reality, and that theology is wholly a human work. The possibility also must be mooted that all theology is mistaken. But here I start from the assumption that God-talk is undertaken because there is a reality – called in English 'God' – whom/which a great many human beings seek to describe and live in relation to, through a variety of particular and often incompatible channels (religions).

From Chapter 1 we have brought forward the insight that our goal is practical. We must seek to speak of Christ in a way that interprets the presence and action of God (as known in Christ) in the world today. We must do so in a way that will make sense to anyone who wants to ask questions about God, Christ, or contemporary living. In theory at least, all enquirers into the mysteries of human life should be able to access the results of the study. We have also brought forward the insight that while theology can be said to have four main sources (scripture, tradition, experience, reason), in real terms these four sources collapse into two: experience and tradition. The 'tradition' with which Christology works can be summarized as the collection of 'texts' (e.g. Gospels, but also icons) and traditions (e.g. doctrines, credal statements) about Jesus the Christ. If Christology is the thematic heart of a practical (systematic) theology, then the methodological centre of Christian theology is therefore the attention paid to the oscillation between experience of Christ and the tradition thus defined. How, though, does this methodological centre actually work? What does 'oscillation' mean in practice?

In order to address the many questions identified in these opening paragraphs I shall work through a series of examples of what it might mean to start from experience or from tradition. This allows me to tease out the strengths and limitations of each starting point, and the inevitability of needing to start from both ends (even if not simultaneously!). I shall then examine how the notion of a centre can be maintained in practice, if there cannot be a single starting point. Centrality will remain important, but it is also crucial to understand centrality in an appropriate way, and to identify the centre correctly. I shall distinguish between 'centre' and 'focus' as the argument develops. The distinction between starting point and focus is also important, for where you start may not be where you expect to finish. It becomes apparent that in order to keep Christ at the centre, many pairs of eyes are required to maintain an appropriate focus in Christian theology.[2]

Starting from experience

What might it mean to start theology from an experience of Christ? Don't you need some prior knowledge of who Christ is before you can even identify the experience as such? It is true that reflection on experience depends on the availability of tradition. Exploration of who and what Christ was and is happens in the context of reflection on propositions and narratives about Jesus the Christ. But if such tradition remained a fixed, controlled interpretation of the presence and action of God in the world, there would be no fresh experience of God in Christ. God could not be a 'critical friend', questioning our certainties and highlighting our shortcomings, or as a guide for life, opening us up to new wonders and fresh discoveries. God in Christ could not encounter and challenge us, in short, as 'other' in the world today. It would ultimately mean that *we* controlled the content of theology and were thus seeking to control God. We (whichever church is being referred to by that 'we') would have allowed the traditions to ossify and stifle fresh encounters with God in Christ. Any theological method has to know how it can encounter new truth. It must also work out how to do this in a way that ensures appropriate continuity alongside necessary change: that is, continuity with the tradition within which experiences are interpreted, and change brought about by the challenge to traditions that experience offers.

Starting from experience, then, means accepting that there

---

2 The 'many pairs of eyes' imagery is derived from J. A. T. Robinson, whose *Truth is Two-Eyed* appeared in 1979 (London: SCM Press). His argument focused especially on what Christology can learn from interfaith dialogue. With hindsight I can see that this entire book is in many ways a continuation of the train of thought begun in Robinson's essay 'Honest to Christ Today' in *The Roots of a Radical*, London: SCM Press, 1980, pp. 59–77, esp. pp. 71–2.

is an interpretative framework within which theology is done. Experience is not a blank slate. Reference to experience as one of the four sources of theology already locates experience within a particular way of undertaking reflection about human living, in relation to a specific body of knowledge about God and the world. So, when we talk of reflecting on an experience of Christ, we admit that we already half-knew what we were looking for in identifying a particular aspect of human experience *as* an experience of Christ.

Half-knowledge is by definition incomplete. This incompleteness is crucial for the way that theology works. The traditions and narratives about Jesus the Christ, which form the 'centre' of Christian theology, are incomplete. They are still being written within, and in the light of, the actions and the reflections of people who are shaped by these narratives and traditions and who seek to shape their own lives accordingly. Starting from an experience of Christ is thus a necessary strategy for all Christian theology, lest such theological reflection be merely second-hand, derivative, only cognitive, or dead history. Such experiences do not just clarify 'the' meaning of Christ, filling out what is already known about Christ. More, they contribute to a constantly-being-refreshed, new Christology, which must demonstrate how it stands in continuity with the old.

Four examples of such experiences of Christ can be given, to enable further exploration of what is entailed. First, an experience of Christ is often claimed to occur in personal conversion. A person moves from a situation in which they do not believe in God to a situation where they do, or from a stance in which they do not believe that they can be 'saved' to one where they believe themselves to have received forgiveness and/or salvation. It may not have been an instantaneous conversion. It will certainly have happened in the context of some familiarity with the Christian world of belief and thought, and this will have provided a language for describing the experience. Often such an experience is termed an experience of Christ. Believers talk of 'meeting Jesus' or 'encountering Christ' when referring to such major, often life-changing occurrences.

A second example draws on the experience of Christian worship. Every celebration of Holy Communion is an experience of meeting Christ. In the context of ritually enacted celebration, praise and thanksgiving, and through remembering and looking forward, the drama and impact of Jesus' life, death and resurrection are related to the lives of those gathered. Physically being with others who likewise relate themselves to Christ, the believer who takes part in Holy Communion *is* participating in Christ.

My third and fourth examples move beyond the Church. In keeping with the insights about centrality and marginality carried forward from Chapter 1, we must look at the margins of both Church and society, as well as at the heart of church life, to see where Christ is present. One example that brings both Church and society together, at the margins of each, is that of a playgroup for children and their fathers, run by a church. Often such community-oriented groups relate little to the church by which they are supported. They may have one or two personnel from the church (paid or unpaid leaders and helpers, for example), and a few people from the church may use the facilities provided, but the reality is that such groups tend to be rather like satellites of the church community. However, their theological significance can be immense. This is strikingly the case when a church provides a main community base for a fathers and toddlers group. In the area where I lived until recently, the contemporary crisis about masculinity was very apparent. Against a background of uncertain employment in a post-industrial age, macho culture, and high rates of early pregnancy for women, a major issue that arises is the social role and status of young fathers. A playgroup provides a space in which practical support is offered, and also a level of acceptance and understanding which might not be possible elsewhere.[3] The interactions that occur in such settings, offering dignity to those involved, *are* manifestations of the presence and action of God, as known in Christ, in the world today.

However, since this third example is from the margins of Church and society, it may be asked who would benefit from such an interpretation of dignifying human interaction. Would the Church simply be salving its conscience by being able to point to this as its mission activity? Or would the interpretation of the interaction as an experience of Christ be transforming for all concerned?[4] I believe the latter, and my whole attempt to refocus Christian theology appropriately christocentrically is undertaken to clarify how and why this is the case.[5]

The fourth example comes from political struggles for justice. Not every political cause is just. Not every political struggle is worthy of being identified as one in which Jesus of Nazareth might himself have fought. Nonetheless, the interplay between traditions and narratives about Jesus the Christ and people's quest and struggle for justice is a powerful example of tradition and experience at work in Christology. People who fight for a noble cause, whether Christian or not, are often inspired by the example of Jesus as narrated in the Gospels. The standing together of Christians and others in political protest – be that for fair world trade, freedom for political prisoners, or appropriate political change – is itself an indicator of where the presence and action of God in Christ must

---

3 I am not, of course, claiming that such support is offered by no other groups, or that church playgroups automatically offer the highest quality of pastoral care. I am simply observing that churches often do, in practice, identify social gaps and meet needs which fall through other kinds of 'safety nets' in social welfare systems.

4 It would certainly spill over into evangelism and the socio-political dimensions of evangelism. A church which does not declare what it thinks is really going on in the world is a church which keeps itself to itself. A church which behaves in this way has given up the gospel.

5 And the full development of the argument, I emphasize, includes the second book *Christ in Practice*.

be sought in the world today. The experience of such protest can thus be an experience of Christ.

What is to be made of these four examples? First, they confirm the insight that it is not possible to consider experience in isolation as a source in theology. The first two examples required, respectively, a Christian thought world and the context of Christian worship to make sense. The third and fourth examples relied on the memory of Jesus and his impact for such human experiences to be seen as locations of the work of God in Christ. Given what is known of Jesus the Christ, it should be *expected* that wherever people's dignity is respected, or appropriate justice is fought for, then God in Christ is at work.

Second, the examples make clear the incompleteness of God's work, and thus of what is to be made of Christ. Conversion is the start of a faith journey with a God who always moves ahead of the believer. Holy Communion is itself an anticipation of a messianic banquet prepared for all people. Seeking the recognition of human dignity remains a task so long as there are any human beings whose dignity is denied. The struggle for justice continues until God's kingdom comes. In a clear sense, then, Christ is not yet fully known.

The examples indicate, thirdly, that the contemporary Christian theological task could just as appropriately begin with any of these four 'cases', as with a more traditional source such as a credal statement. Liturgical theologians might work on the second example, political theologians on the fourth. Pastoral theologians are likely to dwell on the third example, specialists in spirituality or the psychology of religion on the first. But all would be examples of exploring contemporary manifestations of the presence and action of God in Christ in the world. All would be equally legitimate starting points in experience.

Starting points are not end points, however. A circular or spiralling movement (from experience to reflection/tradition and back) is indeed part of the theological task.[6] But I must stress that to start with experience in this way does not imply that all that can be known and should be said about Christ is simply contained in the experience. On the contrary, if the theological exploration is real, then something is also *brought to* the experience to enable it to be more fully grasped. My main point in this section has been to establish that human experience can truly be an experience of Christ. As such, it is new material for theological reflection and contributes to our understanding of the presence and action of God in the world today.

Starting from tradition

Starting from experience requires attention to a framework within which an experience can be understood to be an experience of Christ. This implies that tradition always comes first. Though this is true to an extent, it is misleading if the conclusion is drawn that theological reflection always begins by reference to 'the tradition'. Tradition comes first only in so far as the existence of a theological/doctrinal framework reflects the prior givenness and availability of the God without whom there would be no theology at all. It does not follow either that this framework is fixed or that its givenness means that it is the only place to start. In this section I explore more fully what 'tradition' means and supply examples of what 'starting from tradition' does and does not mean.

Tradition, in the narrowest sense, means Bible, creeds, liturgies, catechisms and confessions. More broadly – but still in an ecclesiastical context – it also means hymns, sermons, icons, murals, statues, architecture, stained glass, art, church reports, official speeches, synods and committee minutes. This is the stuff of

---

6 Clive Marsh, 'The Experience of Theological Education: Maintaining a "Liberal" Agenda in a Post-Liberal Age' in Mark D. Chapman (ed.), *The Future of Liberal Theology*, Aldershot: Ashgate, 2002, pp. 144–53. For a selection of users of the 'pastoral cycle' see p. 145 n. 7 of that essay.

churches' worshipping and political lives, within which their theologies are in practice contained. 'Starting from tradition' in Christology, then, means beginning the task of interpreting Jesus the Christ by studying such sources. A narrowly traditional Christology seeks to expound for the present what the Bible and creeds mean. A broader Christology may explicitly make use of other 'traditional' resources to expound the content of Bible, creeds, etc.

This exposition and interpretation do not, of course, occur in a vacuum. In the same way that starting theology from an experience of Christ entails reference to a framework of belief and thought, so starting from tradition always occurs in a specific experiential context. Examples make clear how this works.

An attempt by an individual theologian, for example, to interpret the person and work of Jesus Christ is never only an exposition of a gospel, the Gospels, a creed or a confession. Nor is it even just an interpretation of a combination of those sources as filtered through later doctrinal tradition within a denominational perspective (e.g. through Aquinas, or Luther, or the Council of Trent, or the Westminster Confession, or the works of John Wesley or Newman). Even if it professes to be such, it is also influenced by the theologian's participation in an embodied form of a tradition – that is, in a real community. It is affected also by their agreement or disagreement with aspects of the order and discipline of the church in which they stand. It is further influenced by personal circumstances and particular commitments, which may or may not be hidden and may or may not be consciously and explicitly incorporated into the work of Christology that results. It cannot be otherwise, if the writer in any sense wishes to expound the meaning of Christ for today, not only for him- or herself but for others.

Second, an attempt by any official, representative church group (e.g. a commission or working party) to articulate what it means to believe in Jesus Christ today is subject to similar, if different, influences. Church reports and statements written by a group of contributors are usually published anonymously. Mutual critique by other contributors as part of the writing process may serve to lessen the impact that individual writers' own circumstances have on the work. Even so, denominational tradition, or ecumenical endeavour, will still weigh heavily. Contributors have a specific interest to serve, be it the further development of a specific ecclesiastical tradition, or the clarification of common ecumenical goals. Starting from tradition is thus never simply the looking back to past, agreed texts that it may at first appear to be.

A third example of starting from tradition cuts across the first two examples and demonstrates the necessity of mutual critique even within an understanding of theological tradition in the narrowest sense. It can be argued that the Christian doctrinal tradition is summarized quintessentially in the classical creeds (especially the Nicene-Constantinopolitan Creed and the Apostles' Creed). But a moment's reflection indicates how inadequate such a doctrinal base proves to be in Christology. Neither creed contains very much narrative about the life of Jesus. The Apostles' Creed records: 'born of the Virgin Mary, / suffered under Pontius Pilate,/ was crucified, died and was buried'. The Nicene Creed reports: 'he was crucified under Pontius Pilate; / he suffered death and was buried'. There is nothing about itinerant preaching, teaching, the telling of parables, healings, the doing of miracles. There is nothing about who Jesus mixed with, his gathering of a following, or the trouble he caused in Jerusalem. Yet these are crucial features of the gospel traditions. They are related, indeed, to the very reason why the Gospels were written in the first place: the details of the life had to be set down so that the story could be earthed – otherwise the word about Jesus might have been reduced to a series of sayings, or his life consumed into a doctrinal statement about his divine significance.

Gospels are not enough. If they were, creeds would not have been necessary. Creeds sum up in a compact way what later doctrinal development sought to express. But creeds are not enough either, for they compress unduly. They need the Gospels as a corrective. Both in turn need to be understood within a broader doctrinal (patristic) tradition out of which the creeds came. And all of this will always be interpreted in the light of how these and other, later texts were and are received. In short, 'starting from tradition' is a helpful shorthand for the fact that there is a wide range of 'official' sources and resources upon which the contemporary Christian theologian must draw when undertaking the task of interpreting Jesus the Christ for today. But the supposedly fixed points themselves interweave in complex ways, and are always received in a very specific context.

Starting points: the story so far

It is time to take stock. Where does theology begin? With God. But where, as a human work, does theology begin? In Christian understanding it begins with a human experience that is interpretable as the presence and action of God as known in Christ (an 'experience of Christ'). It also begins with a grasp of the theological framework (doctrinal tradition) within which human experience can be interpreted in that way. In other words, Christian theology begins with Christology, understood as the intersection of experience and tradition. Neither is dispensable, even if, in the analysis, it appears as if one begins at one 'pole' or the other. In truth, 'poles' is unhelpful language. It would be better to return to the terminology introduced by Jung Young Lee and speak of the 'creative core' of the intersection between experience and tradition, located at the margin of each.[7] The starting point of Christian theology can be expressed in terms either of an experience of Christ or of a desire to rework the inherited traditions/narratives about Jesus the Christ. But both do, in fact, belong together.

---

7 J. Y. Lee Ch. 1, above p. 12.

What, then, are we to make of claims that theology can 'start from the Bible' or 'start from reason'? Or how are we to evaluate a claim that theology begins with an 'experience of the Spirit'? The position I am espousing enables us to see that appeals to the Bible are always appeals to *part* of the tradition. The Bible functions as a key witness to the figure of Jesus the Christ. But in Christian theological understanding its significance, while huge, must not be allowed to get out of proportion. Reason is employed in all theological discourse, but it cannot of itself provide theology's raw materials. And, as we shall see in a moment, though any other theme from systematic theology can be called a starting point, the methodological Christocentrism of Christian theology inevitably means that 'experience of the Spirit' is disclosed as an experience of Christ. All experiential starting points will, in Christian under-standing, inevitably be christologically shaped and construed.

Before moving on to draw an important distinction which will clarify matters further – between starting point and focus – one additional point must be explored: have we yet allowed our understanding of 'tradition' to be broad *enough*?

Starting out within culture: the question of a broader tradition

It is not only Christians who are interested in Jesus. Many accounts now exist of what people outside the Church have made of Jesus.[8] By no means all such interest is theological. Some pay attention

---

8 There is a sense, of course, in which much recent scholarly work on the figure of Jesus is 'outside the Church' in being undertaken 'in the academy'. I am, however, thinking here primarily of explorations of the figure of Jesus outside of a Western setting and/or not undertaken directly with reference to what Christians make of Jesus. Other religious traditions' and artists' interpretations of Jesus become important. See e.g. C. Bennett, *In Search of Jesus: Insider and Outsider Images*, London and New York: Continuum, 2001, esp. chs. 4–6; though also G.Parrinder, *Jesus in the Qur'an*, Oxford: Oneworld Press, 1995; S. E. Porter *et al.* (eds.), *Images of Christ: Ancient and Modern*, Sheffield: Sheffield Academic Press, 1997; and now esp. in J. L. Houlden (ed.),

to Jesus as moral exemplar or stimulating teacher. Even where a theological interest is present, this is not always compatible with trinitarianism.[9] Alongside such interpretations are many more deriving from people who are explicitly Christian, and from people who may have been Christian and consciously seek to remain in continuity with their past faith, even while feeling unable to share in it fully. Films are an excellent example of the broader interpretations that come from all these sources.

Four films across four decades show varying attempts to interpret the figure of Jesus in a contemporary form. None of the four counts as an 'official' Christian source, yet all have contributed in practice to the shaping of Christians' theologies and spiritualities, and to the encounter with the figure of Jesus within wider society. I am referring to Pier Paolo Pasolini's *The Gospel According to St Matthew* (1966; original 1964); Franco Zeffirelli's *Jesus of Nazareth* (1977); Denys Arcand's *Jesus of Montreal* (1990; original 1989); and Mel Gibson's *The Passion of the Christ* (2003).[10]

Jesus in History, Thought and Culture: An Encyclopaedia, Santa Barbara, Denver and Oxford: ABC-CLIO, 2003. The account of the quest of Jesus by journalist Charlotte Allen, *The Human Christ: The Search for the Historical Jesus*, New York: The Free Press, 1998, is Western in focus, but has the advantage of not being confined to the quest undertaken in the Church and academy alone.

9 As a complex faith subject to wide influences Hinduism, for example, might often seem more accommodating of Christian insights than happens the other way round. But despite deep respect for, and even devotion to, Jesus Hindus remain unitarian (see e.g. Wingate's comments on Rammohan Roy in his article 'Hinduism' in Houlden (ed.), *Jesus in History*, p. 345).

10 On the first three, see e.g. W. Barnes Tatum, *Jesus at the Movies: A Guide to the First Hundred Years*, Santa Rosa: Polebridge Press, 1997; Lloyd Baugh, *Imaging the Divine: Jesus and Christ-Figures in Film*, Kansas City: Sheed & Ward, 1997; R. C. Stern *et al.* (eds.), *Savior on the Silver Screen*, New York: Paulist Press, 1999; and the surveys of Jesus films by W. R.Telford, 'Jesus Christ Movie Star: The Depiction of Jesus in the Cinema' in C. Marsh and G. Ortiz (eds.), *Explorations in Theology and Film*, Oxford: Blackwell, 1997; and L. J. Kreitzer, 'Film' in Houlden (ed.), *Jesus in History*, pp. 288–92. Richard Walsh, *Reading the Gospels in the Dark: Portrayals of Jesus in Film*, Harrisburg: TPI, 2003, looks in detail at *Il Vangelo secondo Matteo* and *Jesus of Montreal*. On Gibson, see

I use these films as examples of the complex way in which images of Jesus are carried and explored within culture. We have arguably now reached a stage where more people in Western cultures watch TV and visit the cinema than read their Bibles or access theological resources regularly (via worship, in literature or via the Internet), but this does not mean that they are untouched by religious resources. Gibson's *The Passion of the Christ*, for example, will have been watched in the West by some Christians (though not all) and many others for whom it will have been the main stimulus for reflection about Jesus in many years.[11] However neatly churches may wish to define the boundaries of 'tradition', the way in which cultures carry Jesus traditions makes it very difficult to limit the range of sources called upon.

Cultures carry with them very diverse explorations and interpretations of the figure of Jesus, a complex mix of orthodoxy and heterodoxy. These both complicate and enrich the 'tradition' that Christians draw upon. Starting from tradition and starting from experience in theology thus become yet more complicated when it is considered how many people may encounter the figure of Jesus as a result of watching a Jesus film or interacting with a theological resource outside of the mainstream range of official sources. Whether or not people have such encounters from a faith perspective, the potential exists for the figure of Jesus to make an existential impact upon them, and thus they may participate in what Christians call an 'experience of Christ'.[12] I cannot develop

---

e.g. K. E. Corley and R. L.Webb (eds.), *Jesus and Mel Gibson's The Passion of the Christ*, London and New York: Continuum, 2004; S. B. Plate (ed.), *Re-Viewing The Passion: Mel Gibson's Film and Its Critics,* New York and Basingstoke: Palgrave Macmillan, 2004; and J. Burnham (ed.) *Perspectives on the Passion of the Christ: Religious Thinkers and Writers Explore the Issues Raised by the Controversial Movie*, New York: Miramax Books, 2004.

11 See works cited in previous note, though also C. Marsh, 'Why the Quest for Jesus can never only be Historical', forthcoming in Peter De Mey (ed.), *Sourcing the Quests*, Peeters: Leuven, 2006.

12 This is not to be decried or condemned. It is merely a recognition of what can actually happen.

the significance of the insight here through a detailed exploration of samples of such sources and how they work. It is, however,
vital to acknowledge this phenomenon within the way that theological traditions are carried and with respect to how theological
resources function. It is a further example of the centre being also
the margin: the creative core of which Lee speaks.

Christology as the focus of systematic theology

If methodological Christocentrism is to be espoused, does this
mean, in systematic theological terms, that one must always *begin*
with Christology? Systematic theology works with many themes.
In addition to Christology, it considers the doctrine of God *per se*
(especially the character and attributes of God and the doctrine
of the Trinity), Holy Spirit, creation, Church, ministry and
sacraments, human being, salvation and eschatology.[13] As with
our enquiry in Chapter 1, to seek to find a 'centre' in all of this may
be misguided. Or if the question must be posed, then the answer
may be felt to be straightforward: God is central, and the doctrine
of the Trinity is, in Christian understanding, as central as you
can get, being the distinctively Christian doctrine of God. Such
a line of thought has been followed very heavily in Western theology over the past twenty years or so, after an extended period of
relative neglect of the Trinity.[14]

Yet it is this line of thinking that I wish to challenge, in the
name of practical theology. As I shall go on to show, Christology
does lie at the heart of any Christian systematic theology. But this
means neither that Jesus 'replaces' God at the heart of Christian
thought or practice, nor that the Trinity is neglected. Recognition
of the centrality of Christology in a practical Christian systematic

---

13 Mariology can also be added to this list, this subheading constituting one
key difference between Roman Catholic and Protestant systematic theologies.

14 This development will be examined more fully in Ch. 3.

theology respects the fact that doctrinal exploration is an aspect of the multi-disciplinary character of the theological task. It respects, further, the way in which Christian worship and spirituality actually work.[15] It acknowledges that Christianity, like all religions, operates with a heavy use of story. It does justice also to the weight of Christian art. Despite the fact that there have been bitter disputes throughout Christian history about the legitimacy of portraying the figure of Jesus, and in using art at all to aid Christian devotion, the history of Christian art clearly contributed to substantiating the centrality of Jesus the Christ in Christian belief and practice. This is a point where theology cannot but learn from popular spirituality.

Focusing: sources and themes

The language of centrality can be problematic, as we saw in Chapter 1. It is salvageable with respect to Christology's centrality in theology, so long as margins are respected alongside centres. In terms of the subject matter of this chapter (where do you *start* in theology?), respect for Christology's centrality is required in the context of a distinction between *starting point* and *focus* in theology. Where you start may not be where you need to finish. Even though Christian theology inevitably starts with an experience of Christ, the exposition of the theological implications of that

---

15 Despite Christian recognition that prayer is offered in the name of the Trinity, or happens explicitly *in* the Spirit, *through* the Son, *to* the Father, the nature of Christian devotion in relation to the figure of Jesus/Christ is, I suggest, deeper and more complex than such a regulative account of Christian liturgy might suggest. See e.g. Hurtado's study, *Lord Jesus Christ: Devotion to Jesus in Earliest Christianity*, Grand Rapids and Cambridge: Eerdmans, 2003. Jesus/Christ has thus been central to Christian worship and spirituality from the start, but this has also created problems for monotheism. I do not wish to address here the question whether these problems are greater in the modern period (e.g. since the rise of history and the emergence of the Quest of the Historical Jesus) or simply a perennial and consistent dimension of Christian theology.

experience may begin in different places for different people, or for different traditions, e.g. with an exposition of the doctrine of the Trinity, or the Holy Spirit. But the centrality of Christ and Christology in Christian experience and thought will still be reflected in the way a theology is developed. Christ and Christology will be the *focus* of such a theological exposition. This distinction between starting point and focus must now be drawn out.

The distinction I am drawing became very clear to me as a result of teaching systematic theology.[16] The ways in which a course is structured and taught and the nature of the interaction between teacher and students all contribute to how Christian theology is presented and received. Issues of starting point and focus are crucial in such a context. Where a course starts, thematically, may imply that this is the obvious point of entry into Christian theology. Begin by studying the nature of religious language, or by looking at the context of theology within spirituality and worship, and this implies that what follows will not be comprehensible without such general considerations. Begin with the doctrine of the Church, and this can suggest that theology's primary locus is the Church. Yet where a course begins may not indicate where the emphasis should be placed. One former colleague declared that she began her own doctrine course with the Church precisely because it is *not* the most important theme; as students took a few weeks to settle into a course, it was best to begin with something less significant so that they had not missed much by the time the really important material was introduced.

The exploration and presentation of theology can thus start at many points. Add into that educational mix the various differentials introduced by a student group and the picture is more complex still. Students with Christian beliefs are likely

---

16 As I have done in three distinctly different settings: that of a theological college, and in two publicly funded higher education settings – a college and a university. In the first, all were Christian believers; in the second and third there was a mix of those of Christian faith, other faiths and no professed faith.

to draw on their own experience, and some may have strong experiential starting points (an experience 'of conversion', 'of Christ', 'of fellowship', 'of being saved', 'of the Spirit'). Others may deem that theological reflection is provoked primarily by the Church's worshipping life and so they seek a doxological approach to systematics. And others, whether inside or outside of the Christian belief system, may assume that Christian theology is inevitably shaped by doctrinal history and that everything derives from the doctrine of the Trinity, with which any self-respecting course of Christian theology should begin.

It is here where the significance of the distinction between starting point and focus becomes most apparent. The methodologically Christocentric approach I am seeking to follow throughout this book deems not that Christology is the only legitimate *point of access*, or *starting point*, to theology, but that it will inevitably prove to be Christian theology's *focal point*. It is around Christology that all Christian theology revolves (even the doctrine of the Trinity). The discipline of Christian theology exists for the purpose of clarifying a concept of God, shaped with respect to what needs to be said about Christ. This does not mean that this is the way in which *all* enquirers will enter the discipline, nor that they will begin there in presenting it to others (inside or outside the Church). But it does mean that the sub-themes of Christian theology are not all of equal weight. Even if they all certainly interrelate, they are also to be evaluated in their respective significance. Which theme or themes should control others will remain a matter of contention within Christian systematics. My own project begins from the premise that Christology is the key, and thus the focal point of all Christian thought and practice.

The renowned work of dogmatics *The Christian Faith* by Friedrich Schleiermacher, whose work will be examined more fully later, illustrates the points I am making in this chapter. We may speak of a *chronological* starting point for theology. For Schleiermacher this was the 'Christ-piety' in which he was immersed from an early age and which he spent a lifetime exploring further.[17] We may also speak of a *presentational* starting point. Schleiermacher does not begin his dogmatic work either with a section on Christology or with an exposition of what he understands Christ-piety to be. Rather, he seeks to identify features in human experience in relation to which the dogmatic exposition of Christian theology that follows will make sense.[18] This does not reduce theology to apologetics. But the author who had written *Speeches on Religion to its Cultured Despisers* just two decades earlier could do nothing but bear in mind that he needed to convince his contemporaries that Christian faith and theology were worth bothering with.

Readers of *The Christian Faith* can be left in no doubt about the focal point of the work. It is Christology. We may term this the *logical* (or even *theo-logical*) starting point of the work, for it is from here, despite the structure of its contents, that all else flows. In the same way that centres and margins interrelate, so also we see that the logical starting point and the focal point of a theology coalesce to signify the 'creative core' of an exposition of Christian theology.

---

17 Schleiermacher's piety was nurtured among Moravians and underwent severe testing and developed as a result of formal theological study. But he concluded in 1802 that he had 'become a Herrnhuter [Moravian] again, only of a higher order' (cited in B. A. Gerrish, *A Prince of the Church: Schleiermacher and the Beginnings of Modern Theology*, London: SCM Press, 1984, p. 13). On the significance for his theology of Schleiermacher's early years see M. Redeker, *Schleiermacher: Life and Thought*, Philadelphia: Fortress Press, 1973, ch. 1, and Part 1 of K. Nowak, *Schleiermacher: Leben, Werk und Wirkung*, 2nd edn, Göttingen: Vandenhoeck & Ruprecht, 2002.

18 The First Section of the First Part of Schleiermacher's *The Christian Faith* is headed 'A Description of our Religious Self-Consciousness in so far as the Relation between the World and God is expressed in it' (*The Christian Faith*, Edinburgh: T. & T. Clark, 1928 [1830–1]), pp. 142–93. The work begins with a lengthy methodological section of which, as Ch. 4 will make clear, I regard ch.1 Section IV to be especially important: 'The Relation of Dogmatics to Christian Piety' (*The Christian Faith*, pp. 76–93). Its 'centre' as far as content is concerned is, however, clearly its Christology (pp. 374–475).

Starting point and focus: a summary

Christian theologians begin their task at many different points, and place emphasis on different sources or resources. However, the inevitable centrality of Christ in Christian thought and practice means that Christology functions as the central theme in a Christian systematics. Christ is therefore also the focal point of Christian theology, in that Christian theology is engaged in the ongoing task of obtaining ever greater clarification of who God in Christ is, and what God in Christ is doing in the world today.

3

Christocentrism as Theocentrism

Centres and centrisms

Christocentrism is dangerous. The centrality of Christ in Christian thought and practice may seem obvious, but it is harder than it sounds to sustain that centrality and make it methodologically significant in all Christian thinking and acting. Christocentrism can easily be misconstrued, as this chapter will make clear. Turning the centrality of Christ into an 'ism' may itself be deemed suspicious. Many recent writers have drawn attention to the inherent dangers of a Christocentric approach to theology. For example, in an early orientation-finding chapter to his provocative systematic theology *Not Every Spirit: A Dogmatics of Christian Disbelief*, Christopher Morse builds on the insights of Ernst Troeltsch and Karl Barth in determining whether Christocentrism plays a role in Christian theology. He writes:

> The kind of christocentrism Troeltsch rejects should be rejected, for it amounts to saying that Christianity itself, or the Christian religion, is Lord and Saviour of all peoples and all other religions. But if the Jesus Christ attested in the gospel is not synonymous with any religion, including historical Christianity, but is the identification of both the oppression to be overcome and the power that overcomes it, as Barth argues, then christocentrism has a very different significance.[1]

---

1 C. Morse, *Not Every Spirit: A Dogmatics of Christian Disbelief*, Valley Forge: TPI, 1994, p. 30.

Morse indicates that Christocentrism is to be rejected *in one form*, yet needs to be held onto in another. We must, then, carry this important insight forward: we have to find *an appropriate form* of Christocentrism with which to work.

Another view of Christocentrism can be found in the work of Jean Milet. In Milet's *God or Christ? A Study in Social Psychology*, theocentrism and Christocentrism appear sharply polarized.[2] Milet contends that 'to reduce, attenuate or alter in one way or another . . . the attraction exercised by one or other of these two poles is to alter the very essence of Christianity and to rob it of its nature'.[3] Chapter 2 of his book is devoted to characterizing the two centrisms as quite distinct forms of belief. Thus he says of Christocentrism: 'If one holds that every religious truth finds its source entirely in the Christ, a historical person, who lived a specific existence in a known country and in a clearly defined period, one will naturally be led to favour the historical, the concrete, what is lived and felt, in a word the existential, to the detriment of the rational.'[4] Theocentrism, by contrast, is focused on 'the highest object of thought to which the human spirit can devote itself'.[5] Four chapters then explore the fluctuating fortunes of these two 'poles' throughout Christian history.

Milet's contribution, despite its intention, is in danger of suggesting that Christocentrism obscures theocentrism rather than helping define it. Instead of the centrality of Christ shaping and focusing a practical, working concept of God, Milet's attempt to recover a bipolarity between theocentrism and Christocentrism only leads to a suspicion that ultimately Christocentrism is more unhelpful than helpful. It is theocentrism that matters

---

2 J. Milet, *God or Christ? A Study in Social Psychology* London: SCM Press, 1981. For a discussion of Milet, see e.g. C. Henry, *The Identity of Jesus of Nazareth*, Nashville: Broadman Press, 1992, pp. 115–24.

3 Milet, *God or Christ?*, p. 2.

4 Milet, *God or Christ?*, p. 46.

5 Milet, *God or Christ?*, p. 37.

most.[6] Admittedly, he contends that Christianity is forever struggling with the creative tension between the two poles. But it could be argued that Milet offers a false dichotomy rather than a true bipolarity. Though he offers some very helpful insights about the social psychology of the two emphases in Christian belief as it stands, his position considers Christocentrism negatively.

A definition of Christocentrism can be found in *The Oxford Dictionary of the Christian Church*. Two definitions of 'Christocentric' are in fact given, and it is worth quoting them in full:

(1) A word originally used of systems of theology which maintain that God has never revealed Himself to man [*sic*] except in the Incarnate Christ. Christocentric theology bases itself on a literal interpretation of Mt. 11:27, to the exclusion of the passages in Scripture which seem to refer to or imply a revelation in nature, and thus precludes the possibility of natural theology altogether. Among its modern advocates are A. Ritschl, W. Herrmann, and K. Barth.

(2) More generally, of any set of religious beliefs which is focused primarily on the Person of Christ.[7]

This twofold definition neatly encapsulates the problem. The second definition leaves the reader wondering what all the fuss is

---

6 This is, of course, scarcely surprising in any theology. But if when Christians have to do with Christ they really do have to do with God, then we are struggling with a peculiar bipolarity. The fact that Milet uses his reading of theocentrism, especially a recovery of a notion of transcendence, in order to renew 'christocentricity' suggests where the emphasis in fact lies (*God or Christ?*, ch. 9). But would it not be possible to recover an emphasis upon transcendence (if such be deemed to be needed) in Christian thought and practice within a different, more consistently Christocentric approach? Then we are simply (!) dealing with definitions in Christology and their impact within theology. This, I suggest, is how it is best to see Christianity as a whole 'at work'.

7 F. L. Cross and E. A. Livingstone (eds.), *The Oxford Dictionary of the Christian Church*, Oxford: Oxford University Press, 1997, p. 336.

about, being so weak as to serve merely as a reminder that every form of Christian thought or practice is going *in some sense* to be 'focused primarily on the Person of Christ'. It is the first definition that helps us see what is at stake. Aside from the question of whether the three theologians cited espouse all that the definition suggests, it is not clear that a Christocentric approach to Christian thought and practice need specify that God has *only* revealed God's self in Christ.[8] To say that God is Christ-like or to say that God has paradigmatically or even uniquely revealed God's self in and through Christ constitute two ways in which the being and action of God can be explored christocentrically without also claiming that this is the *only* place where God is revealed.[9] It seems to me that neither of these statements functions as restrictively as the first definition above suggests. Nor does either statement descend to the platitude of the second definition. The creative rediscovery of what Christocentrism must mean for Christian thought and practice will therefore be found within the conceptual space left open between the first and second definitions. There is more, in short, about Christocentrism yet to be uncovered.

Leaving aside the *de facto* negativity of Milet, and the undue restrictiveness of *The Oxford Dictionary of the Christian Church*'s first definition, it is necessary to return to Christopher Morse's challenge. Is there an appropriate form of Christocentrism which is workable in Christian theology today? I shall proceed in three steps. First, I shall make use of a helpful insight from John Cobb Jr to set out a basis for proceeding. Second, I shall clarify a number of misunderstandings of Christocentrism, which must always be borne in mind as challenges and criteria for the correction of

---

8 This would, in any case, come close to being 'Christomonism', to be explored later in this chapter.

9 W. J. Wildman, *Fidelity with Plausibility: Modest Christologies in the Twentieth Century*, New York: SUNY Press, 1998, a work I came across long after my own project was well advanced, addresses these issues in a helpful and thorough way.

distortions. Third, I shall locate the project I am undertaking in relation to some different voices on the contemporary theological scene, that is, those who would claim that the rediscovery of the doctrine of the Trinity is, in fact, the better way of fashioning the Christian theological task today.

First, then, I draw on the work of John Cobb Jr. Responding to the work of the pluralist scholar of religion, John Hick, in 1988, Cobb stated:

> in strictly orthodox terms, Christocentrism is already theo-centrism. It is only because Christ is God that faith can be centred in Christ . . . By Christocentrism, I mean something like centering in grace. Grace is of God and is indeed . . . God. It is God as efficaciously present in creatures, especially human ones. If shifting from Christocentrism to theocentrism means anything here, it means shifting from God as grace to God as transcendent, from the Second or Third members of the Trinity, perhaps, to the First, or even from the Trinity as a whole to the Godhead. It is because I understand Hick's proposal of a shift from Christocentricity to theocentricity as a shift from a focus on grace as God's creative and redemptive activity in the world to a transcendental noumenal reality devoid of all attributes that I strongly oppose it. *What we need is a shift from a bad Christocentrism to a good one.*[10]

As with Morse, there is an acknowledgement here that Christo-centrism can go wrong. More than Morse, however, Cobb press-es strongly for the decisive role in Christianity to be played by Christocentrism. It is crucial, says Cobb, to get Christocentrism right: the very being of Christianity depends on it. At issue is what kind of God we are dealing with, and how that God interacts

---

10 J. Cobb Jr., 'Critique of J. Hick "An Inspiration Christology for a Religiously Plural World"' in S. T. Davis (ed.), *Encountering Jesus: A Debate on Christology*, Atlanta: John Knox Press, 1988, p. 28 (my italics).

with the world of which we are a part. Cobb gives us our first clear hint that a failure to get Christocentrism right will mean a failure to respect the concrete presence of God in the world. In offering his proposal in opposition to Hick, Cobb reminds us that to seek a 'good Christocentrism' does not inevitably also lead to the adoption of an insulting stance towards religions other than Christianity.

The way forward is clear. It became evident as a result of the first two chapters that Christ is central to Christianity, and therefore Christology is the focal point of Christian thought and practice. We can now see that maintaining the appropriate focus will be fraught with difficulty. Theologians need to operate with *the right kind of Christocentrism*. So what are the bad forms? I now turn to the task of identifying those forms.

Bad Christocentrisms: a *Via Negativa*

This section defines fourteen ways in which either an attempt to be Christocentric has lost its way or a rival alternative has intervened misleadingly and masqueraded as Christocentrism. I have grouped the fourteen distorted forms into eight theological distortions, five ethical distortions, and a fourteenth as a summary of them all. This division should not, however, be viewed too strictly, as there is naturally overlap across the lists. First, then, the theological distortions.

Jesusology

I begin with a cluster of ways in which preoccupation with the figure of Jesus obscures the christological task. These can all be grouped under the first heading: Jesusology. At its most basic, Jesusology substitutes the 'Quest of the Historical Jesus' for the task of formulating a Christology. This was often the result, if not always the intent, of so many endeavours attached to the so-called 'Old Quest' for the Historical Jesus in the late nineteenth century, and could thus be considered as a distortion caused by historical positivism.[11]

Jesusology can also take the form of a dependence upon the 'Jesus of the Gospels' or 'the Jesus of the New Testament'. Martin Kähler's appeal to the 'historical biblical Christ' nearly falls into this trap. Kähler's distinction between the so-called historical Jesus and the historical biblical Christ was profoundly influential and represented the first major critique of the first form of Jesusology identified above. However, Kähler saw the 'biblical Christ' functioning in formal terms in a similar way to the historical Jesus. A narrative (biblical) Jesus functioned for Kähler in a similar way, theologically speaking, to the Jesus constructed by the historians to which Kähler was objecting. The 'biblical Christ' could simply replace the 'historical Jesus' as the norm for Christology. The latter was, for Kähler, both unreachable and desirable. The former would keep theology on the right track.

Kähler was, of course, assuming that the 'biblical Christ' is more uniform than may actually be the case within the New Testament texts. In the end, his stress upon preaching (on the 'preached Christ') prevents his being subject to the charge of Jesusology.[12]

---

11 I make the distinction between intent and achievement simply because so much gospels material about Jesus which would later be considered as historically inauthentic was included within the Jesus-pictures produced. 'Jesus' was thus normative for theology on grounds other than those proposed: the 'Jesus' supposed to be the Jesus of history often proved to be the 'Jesus of the Gospels' or of a particular New Testament evangelist. This is the basic argument of my study of Albrecht Ritschl's Christology, *Albrecht Ritschl and the Problem of the Historical Jesus*, San Francisco: Edwin Mellen Press, 1992.

12 In other words, he in fact draws upon a much broader base of Christian tradition in order to construct his Christology (see esp. M. Kähler, *Die Wissenschaft der christlichen Lehre von dem evangelischen Grundartikel aus im Abrisse dargestellt*, Neukirchen-Vluyn: Neukirchener Verlag, 1966 [1905]; also H-G.Link, *Geschichte Jesu und Bild Christi: Die Entwicklung der Christologie Martin Kählers*, Neukirchen-Vluyn: Neukirchener Verlag, 1975).

However, the biblicism of his emphasis upon the 'Christ of the New Testament' suggests that his theology depends directly upon a biblical-narrative Jesus.

A third form of Jesusology goes in the opposite direction from the second. Rather than broaden out the Jesus of history into a narrative Jesus distilled from a gospel, the Gospels as whole, or the New Testament, the third form digs more deeply within the earthly Jesus, seeking to identify a particular aspect of his teaching or activity which then functions as the core of Christianity. This core takes the form of 'the teaching of Jesus' (e.g. as for Harnack, who emphasized the fatherhood of God and human brother-hood[13]) or 'the Kingdom of God' (e.g. for Rauschenbusch[14]). A 'canon within the canon' of Jesus tradition is thus identified and becomes a timeless truth which is Jesus-focused, but which can be detached from the concrete figure himself.

Appeal to the historical or the biblical Jesus can take any of these three forms, and can often slip between them. The Latin American liberation theologian Jon Sobrino stresses categorically the centrality of 'the concrete Jesus of history' in his *Christology at the Crossroads*. If his Christology were simply to be received on the terms in which he presents it, then it would be inadequate. But in fact Sobrino offers a much more rounded Christology than his method implies. He has offered a 'historical Christology' (his term) capable of supporting a Christocentric theology.[15] It is thus based on an *actual* method which deviates from the Jesusology he espouses. His Christology uses much more than the 'historical Jesus'.

None of these three forms of Jesusology will suffice in the task of constructing a Christology for today. They imply a past focus, a

---

13 Especially in his famous lectures, *What is Christianity?*, first delivered in Berlin in 1899, and published in 1900.

14 See below, Ch. 5.

15 His position is summarized in J. Sobrino sj, *Christology at the Crossroads*, London: SCM Press, 1978, ch. 11.

biblical-narrative base, or an appeal to a truncated form of Jesus-tradition, all of which are simply too meagre to do justice to what Christian tradition does with the figure of Jesus.

Jesusolatry

There is, however, a fourth, more subtle form of Jesusology. In some forms of Christian worship and spirituality, the name of Jesus is often used in an almost exclusive sense, replacing reference to God, Father, Christ, Lord or Spirit. 'Lord' may admittedly appear as the most ready replacement, if one is offered at all. But this form of 'Jesus-piety' is willing to see no distinction between the various names of God or (to speak in trinitarian terms) between the persons of the Godhead. Jesus is worshipped, prayed to and sung about, and use of the name 'Jesus' can be held to include all christological titles or divine names. It could, of course, be argued that it is possible for a Christian worshipper to sing, pray and worship in such a way that exclusive reference to Jesus suffices, though such a spiritual diet is unlikely to be adequate. Failure to name God, or to refer to God in terms of the Father/Mother, Son and Spirit, or to praise God as Lord, Word or Wisdom, is more likely to lead to a distorted theology and a truncated spirituality. A sub-Christian spirituality will result, where the complexity of what is entailed in the act of praying to Jesus is not respected.

Rather differently, in his contribution to the collection *Asian Faces of Jesus*, C. S. Song[16] fails to do justice to the many different levels on which his use of the name Jesus has to be received in order to make sense of his 'quest for the real Jesus'. So, from a quite different part of the Christian tradition, a similar problem appears to that created by Western charismatic worship.

16 C. S. Song, 'Oh, Jesus, Here with Us!' in R. S. Sugirtharajah (ed.), *Asian Faces of Jesus*, Maryknoll: Orbis/London: SCM Press, 1993, pp. 131–48, esp. pp. 142–8.

This fourth form of Jesusology, then, runs the risk of being Jesusolatry. Many caveats, qualifications and explanations may be offered by a Christian worshipper who uses the name 'Jesus' almost exclusively. Nonetheless, when a first-century name comes to carry all that is entailed in the worship and praise of God, then the potential to mislead is great. The danger of Christians worshipping a human figure is all too near at hand.[17]

Crucicentrism

The third distorted form of Christocentrism is crucicentrism. To speak of the cross as central to Christianity seems as self-evident as speaking of the centrality of Christ. Need it even be discussed? Art exhibitions dealing with the figure of Jesus/Christ are invariably preoccupied with crucifixions.[18] The cross, with or without the tortured figure of Jesus upon it, has been a major symbol for Christian worship if not from the start of Christianity, then at least from a relatively early phase of its history.[19] Entire movements of Christian spirituality can be said to be cross-centred.[20]

---

17 D. M. Baillie noted von Hügel's reference to 'Christism' and Weinel's charge of 'Jesuanism' in relation to many of the forms of Jesusology and Jesusolatry listed here (*God Was in Christ*, London: Faber & Faber, 1961 [1948], p. 41).

18 See e.g. the catalogue for the millennium exhibition at the National Gallery in London, G. Finaldi *et al.*, *The Image of Christ: The Catalogue of the Exhibition Seeing Salvation*, London: National Gallery, 2000.

19 The cross 'was not used in the earliest centuries, because of its shameful association with crucifixion, the death penalty for the worst malefactors' (P. and L. Murray, *The Oxford Companion to Christian Art and Architecture*, Oxford and New York: Oxford University Press, 1996, p. 123). Crucifixes appeared in Christian art after about four centuries. In the medieval period crosses and crucifixes became more commonplace in Christian art and spirituality.

20 E.g. within medieval Catholicism, in Moravian Pietism, in forms of Lutheranism, in evangelicalism and even in forms of Anglican Catholic Modernism (see e.g. A. R. Lilley's 1924 quotation, cited in G. Wakefield, *Methodist Spirituality*, Peterborough: Epworth Press, 1999, p. 64, concerning Christian teaching having 'planted the cross at the heart and centre of the prayer-life').

Writers of devotional and scholarly works regularly speak of the cross as the key to Christianity.[21] There is no doubting the proven spiritual, devotional, ethical and political power of the cross as a symbol, within Christianity and beyond.

This does not alter the fact that it is limited in scope as far as gaining a grasp of what Christianity aspires to, and can also be profoundly psychologically damaging when used as an isolated religious symbol. If Christ is not viewed as both crucified *and* risen, then the Christian story of God remains only half-told. Pre-occupation with the cross, apart from the empty tomb, visions of Jesus, the risen body, or some other way of speaking of Christ's continued life, is thus sub-Christian. Focus upon a crucified form can be inspiring and releasing.[22] But if this is seen as the whole picture of Christianity, and in fact communicates a view of a God who finds torture acceptable, or implies that suffering is in itself always a necessary or even good thing, then all suffering is held to be sanctified.

The symbol of the cross is vital for Christianity. But it is not central in the sense of serving as the only thing that Christ stands for. It is the life, death and resurrection of Jesus Christ *together* that constitute the centre of Christianity. So Christocentrism is again distorted when Christ's risen body, while always bearing the marks of suffering, is not kept in view alongside the cross.

---

21 E.g., despite much emphasis on 'the whole Christ', P. T. Forsyth speaks of 'Christ and His cross' as the answer to the meaning of history (1909: p. 228), and as the 'key' to all morality (ibid., p. 232). See also *The Cruciality of the Cross*. Talk of the centrality of the doctrine of the atonement merely spells out this same emphasis in a particular way, often specifying a particular understanding of atonement (a substitutionary theory) as necessary. Baillie, whose 1948 study explores the relationship of atonement and incarnation, offers a critique of crucicentrism (Baillie, *God Was in Christ*, pp. 190–7, esp. p. 197).

22 See, for example, the moving account of a response to the 'Christa' figure reported in S. B. Thistlethwaite, *Sex, Race and God*, New York: Crossroad, 1989, pp. 92–3, an echo of many examples of how crucifixes down the centuries have 'worked' for people.

Christomonism

Christomonism is the view that the whole of reality can be seen to be encompassed by or in Christ. There is, in fact, no reality beyond Christ. In a strict sense, as with all forms of monism, Christomonism should not be a possible position for a Christian to hold simply because Christian faith accepts a distinction between God and the created order. Monism identifies the creator and the created. Here, however, I am using the term 'Christomonism' to denote the view that access to and from God is so wholly controlled by reference to Christ, that no other form of identification of who and what God is proves possible.

Expressed in this way, this distortion of Christocentrism may be difficult to discern. The Christian claims to know who God is because of Jesus Christ. Christocentrism only becomes Christomonism, however, when all other claims to know God are then excluded. While a christological centre is, then, claimed *for Christians*, this does not amount to a claim that all that there is to know of God is known by Christians, or absorbed within a Christian understanding of reality. Even if Christians might claim that all is or will be brought together 'in Christ', this does not mean that Christians can already see the whole of God in Christ. The necessary reticence and appropriate mystery which lie at the heart of theology prevents a methodological Christocentrism claiming too much for its conclusions.

Christomonism is nevertheless a real danger. Karl Barth is acknowledged as a quintessentially Christocentric theologian, so strongly did he emphasize the christological basis of theology.[23]

---

23 He was, of course, identified as such in one of the definitions of 'Christocentric' cited earlier in this chapter (see above n. 7). Barth's Christocentrism is evident throughout all his major work, and all the more so in his earlier dogmatics lectures than the later, unfinished *Church Dogmatics*, where he had at least begun to fill out more fully the trinitarian basis of his theology, even if his pneumatology remained weak (being incomplete). Barth's Christocentrism

As a consequence of this, a lively discussion has pervaded the reception and exploration of Barth's theology with respect to what Dietrich Bonhoeffer called its 'revelatory positivism'.[24] The extent to which Barth saw all God-talk as possible only because of God's revelation in Jesus Christ leads to the possible accusation that despite his intent Barth runs the risk of collapsing all God-talk into Christology. In Barth's work, the centrality of Christ, and thus of Christology in theology, is such that when the reality of God is spoken about, we can only really speak of Christ. Gerhard Ebeling made the same critical judgement about Bonhoeffer, given the latter's tendency to address all dogmatic problems christologically.[25]

Within Christian thought, then, the all-consuming character of Christology can mean that all dogmatic issues, in being inevitably related to Christology, become distorted or short-circuited. For example, the Spirit can be understood in no other terms than as the Spirit of Christ. Christology then becomes not explanatory and illuminating, but restrictive. Similarly, the Church may be construed only in terms of Christ, and by no other means. Where

---

is affirmed by Riches and termed 'radical christo-centrism' by Mackinnon in their respective studies in S. W. Sykes and J. P. Clayton (eds.), *Christ, Faith and History: Cambridge Studies in Christology*, Cambridge: Cambridge University Press, 1972 (J. K. Riches, 'What is a '"Christocentric" Theology?'; D. MacKinnon, '"Substance" in Christology – A Cross-Bench View', p. 292). See also G. Hunsinger, *How to Read Karl Barth*, Oxford: Oxford University Press, 1991, pp. 225–33; G. Hunsinger, *Disruptive Grace: Studies in the Theology of Karl Barth*, Grand Rapids: Eerdmans, 2000, pp. 283–6; and above all B. L. McCormack, *Karl Barth's Critically Realistic Dialectical Theology: Its Genesis and Development 1909–1936*, Oxford: Clarendon Press, 1995, pp. 453–5.

24 D. Bonhoeffer, *Letters and Papers from Prison*, London: SCM Press, 1971, pp. 280 and 286. For the content of, and background to, this discussion, see e.g. J. A. Phillips, *The Form of Christ in the World: A Study of Bonhoeffer's Christology*, London: Collins, 1967, ch. 12; and S. Fisher, *Revelatory Positivism?: Barth's Earliest Theology and the Marburg School*, Oxford: Oxford University Press, 1988, esp. ch. 6.

25 G. Ebeling, cited in Phillips, *The Form of Christ*, pp. 28 and 260.

there is no space between 'Christ' and 'Church', then neither definition can inform the other.

Such an approach is problematic not only within Christian theology. In interfaith encounter, the collapse of theology into Christology can prove an obstacle to the possibility of dialogue.[26] If divine reality is so wholly consumed by Christ and Christology, there is no space – not even conceptually – for the comparative study of competing truth-claims to begin.

Barth has many defenders. The form of his Christocentrism is seen, in the work of Carl Braaten, for example, directly to require articulation in trinitarian terms.[27] Thus Barth's Christocentric approach ultimately accounts for the trinitarian renaissance which his work in part inspired. Barth's theology could, in fact, be held to be an example of the way in which Christomonism is prevented, and an appropriate Christocentrism achieved. It is not my intent to defend or critique Barth here.[28] We need only note that his theology is a major form of Christocentric theology, and, with its 'revelatory positivist' tendency, is prone to the charge of Christomonism. We can also note therefore that the same charge may well be brought against the position to which this present study will move. A way must be found to prevent a charge of Christomonism being justified.

---

26 See e.g. S. Samartha, 'The Cross and the Rainbow: Christ in a Multireligious Culture' in J. Hick and P. F. Knitter (eds.), *The Myth of Christian Uniqueness*, Maryknoll: Orbis 1987, pp. 69–88, here pp. 79–81; and also *One Christ – Many Religions: Towards a Revised Christology*, Maryknoll: Orbis, 1991, where Samartha spells out the limitations of both 'Jesusology' and 'Christomonism'.

27 C. Braaten, *No Other Gospel!: Christianity among the World Religions*, Minneapolis: Fortress Press, 1992; esp. ch. 3. Braaten is, however, critical, through appeal to the Lutheran notion of the two kingdoms, of Barth's 'christocratic approach', by which he means Barth's tendency to support the imposition of Christian categories upon public life (ibid., p. 130).

28 I do not, though, believe that a charge of Christomonism against Barth would be sustainable.

Anthropocentrism

Humankind as a whole can furtively replace Christ at the heart of Christian theology. If this occurs, then a further alternative to Christocentrism becomes evident: anthropocentrism. Barth and Bonhoeffer are two of the twentieth century's fiercest critics of such a tendency. Barth found the approach especially prevalent in nineteenth-century liberalism, in the light of what he claimed was the subjective turn in theology away from God to the human believer.[29] Bonhoeffer located anthropocentrism as a strain in 'liberal, mystic pietistic, ethical theology'.[30]

The danger inherent in this distortion of Christocentrism can also move in a different ethical direction. Preoccupation with the human can lead to a disregard for the rest of creation. Anthropocentrism thus not only obscures the centrality of Christ but also leaves no room for Christ to relate beyond the human, to the created order as a whole, within an understanding of the 'cosmic' or 'ecological Christ'.[31] At its most dangerous, this anthropocentrism can lead to the worship of humanity in place of the worship of God. Perhaps, then, this is the most dangerous distortion of all.

It comes about for two very understandable reasons. First, exploring the person and work of God in relation to a human figure invites this easy mistake. Interest in the earthly Jesus was accentuated by the 'Quest of the Historical Jesus', which took shape within the liberalism that Barth so despised. It seemed a logical result of the statement 'the Word was made flesh'. Second,

---

29 Leading to Barth's famous statement that liberal theology amounted to 'speaking of man in a loud voice'.

30 Bonhoeffer, *Letters and Papers*, p. 286.

31 Differently explored, e.g., in A. D. Galloway, *The Cosmic Christ*, London: Nisbet, 1951; R. R. Ruether, *To Change the World*, London: SCM Press, 1981; M. Fox, *The Coming of the Cosmic Christ*, San Francisco: HarperSanFrancisco, 1988; and in the work of Teilhard de Chardin.

anthropocentrism and a concern for salvation go together very easily. Those who feel themselves 'saved', in whatever sense that term is intended, are talking about themselves when talking about the dynamics of salvation. This is not in itself a bad thing. It is inevitable.[32] Where Christ is involved in salvation, then Christology is also inescapably autobiography. Despite Bonhoeffer's attack, liberals, mystic pietists and ethical theologians could be forgiven for responding: but human beings seem to be of great concern to God. Concern for the self becomes anthropocentrism, and thus problematic, where the role God plays in and through Christ in the human experience of salvation is obscured.

The scale of Barth's opposition to anthropocentrism and the reasons for it should not, therefore, be overlooked even if there is much more to be said.[33] The force of his response to the problems of the theology of his day reflects the level of danger inherent in this particular distortion. Furthermore, the fact that Bonhoeffer was able to point out how diverse theological outlooks might be equally affected by this distortion reminds us that anthropocentrism is not a problem for liberals alone.

Androcentrism

The theological distortion of anthropocentrism has ethical forms, as mentioned, and yet can also take on a more specific theological form. 'Can a male saviour save women?' is a question posed by feminist theologians; and it points out in a stark way how

---

32 As rightly recognized by Carter Heyward, *Speaking of Christ*, New York: Pilgrim Press, 1989, p. 45.

33 Barth notoriously linked his opposition to his teachers' supporting the German war effort at the start of World War I, thus concluding that their theologies must be wholly misguided. The logic is difficult to fault, but the facts are somewhat obscure, and plenty of liberals did not, of course, support the war. On this, see e.g. Matthias Wolfes, *Protestantische Theologie und moderne Welt*, Berlin: De Gruyter, 1999, pp. 17–20.

Christocentrism can become not merely a focus on the human but a focus on the male. It is not just human beings who replace Christ, but men. Men can thus become, in effect, the object of worship.[34]

The causes of such a distortion are not difficult to locate. It is Jesus who is called Christ. The maleness of Jesus of Nazareth can thus function normatively. It is held to matter theologically that Jesus was a man. Secondly, men alone have been priests, ministers and pastors for much of Christian history. Jesus the Christ's most obvious symbolic, public representatives, and the authority figures in the Church, are thus male; and through their leadership of Christianity's ritual practices they constantly reinforce the impression that Christ-centredness means male-centredness.

In response to all of this, one need only refer to the doctrine of incarnation. However much the content and meaning of incarnation must be teased out, at its heart is the conviction that God became human, not that God became a male. There can be no escaping the specificity of Jesus' maleness, just as there is no escaping his Jewishness. But, unlike the Jewishness, without which Jesus is simply not comprehensible, it is far from clear that Jesus' maleness is constitutive of the insights he conveyed, the activity he embodied, or the salvation he is said to bring.[35] On the contrary, it is unlikely that Christianity would ever have been able to develop and adapt in the way that it has, had the maleness been more than a merely culturally conditioned historical inevitability (as opposed to a theological necessity).

In relation to the second cause: most Christian denominations

---

34 An insight encapsulated in Mary Daly's memorable and oft-cited statement: 'If God is male, then the male is God' (*Beyond God the Father*, Boston: Beacon Press, 1973, p. 19).

35 There are, of course, feminists who have come to the conclusion that Christianity is, in fact, irredeemably sexist and that this relates in no small way to the maleness of Jesus; see e.g. D. Hampson, *Theology and Feminism*, Oxford: Blackwell, 1990, ch. 2, esp. pp. 75–8.

now ordain women as ministers and priests. Leadership is widely exercised by women across the churches.[36] There is, in other words, no obvious reason why Christocentrism should continue to be misconstrued in an androcentric way.

This distortion is, however, reinforced in a number of other ways, often more subtle than may first meet the eye. The historical facticity of the maleness of Jesus of Nazareth is reflected in Christian art. It could be argued that the sheer power of the visual, and the interrelationship between theology and spirituality brought about by a focus upon the crucified figure, have together reinforced the centrality of maleness in a way that no doctrinal formulation or *de facto* representative leadership ever could.

A second means of reinforcement interweaves with this point. The isolated male figure feeds, and is fed by, a tendency towards praise of the heroic individual male.[37] Despite the fact that the crucified figure subverts so many ways in which the 'heroic' is usually conceived, the isolated figure remains a male figure. Attempts by feminist artists and sculptors to portray a woman on a cross received understandable objections on historical grounds,[38] but much more than mere historical accuracy was at stake for opponents: not least a lurking cultural assumption that only males can function in such an isolated, heroic way.

If there exists, then, some kind of link between this distortion of Christocentrism and the hankering for an isolated hero, it is worth noting the consequences. An isolated hero might seem to fit in with a need for a saviour figure. But this overlooks five

---

36 Though the difficulty even now of securing a full role for women in leadership in churches, whether a denomination ordains women or not, should not be underestimated. Patriarchy has a long history, and is not easily destroyed.

37 H. Moxnes, *Putting Jesus in His Place: A Radical Vision of Household and Kingdom*, Louisville and London: Westminster John Knox Press, 2003, p. 11.

38 That is, it is not clear that women were crucified. Such artistic efforts are, however, making a profound theological point, of course, and often doing so very successfully. See again Thistlethwaite, *Sex, Race and God*, pp. 92–3.

aspects of corporateness present within the Jesus narratives: the communal dimension of the Judaism out of which Jesus sprang, Jesus of Nazareth's own practice, early Christian community-formation, the constantly communal emphases of the Church and the love-hate relationship which the Church enjoys with the Kingdom it seeks to serve. Attention to androcentrism as a distortion of Christocentrism enables us to see how swiftly the communal dimension of the reality of Christ can be overlooked. Jesus is always called Christ in the context of followers. There is even a sense in which God, in Christ, reveals a dependence upon those who follow. Avoiding the trap of androcentrism prevents us from worshipping God in the image of the independent, isolated male self.

Logocentrism, bibliocentrism or bibliolatry

'The Word became flesh' (John 1.14). In large parts of Christianity, however, the Word has become 'words'. Such 'logocentrism' can itself take on a variety of forms. It can mean, first, the priority of rationality over all other forms of human experience, as the way in and through which God in Christ becomes known. Linking the insights of postmodern philosophers[39] and charismatic theologians,[40] the critique of such logocentrism reasserts the heart, the emotions and the spirit (human and divine) as key aspects of Christology (and thus Christocentrism), opening up

---

39 Especially the work of Derrida, whose definition of (opposition to) logocentrism goes much further and deeper than the working definition used here, by rejecting all fixed meaning in favour of total flux. Though I accept we live in (postmodern) times where such fluidity and fragmentation is often presented as 'the way things are', theology will, by definition, resist a totally fluid view of reality, even while accepting the difficulty of the challenge of speaking of God at all in contemporary Western culture.

40 J-J. Suurmond, *Word and Spirit at Play*, London: SCM Press, 1994, pp. 42–51.

also recognition of the value of developing a pneumatological Christology.[41]

Second, logocentrism takes the form of an opposition to the use of the visual arts in theology. Despite the crucial role played by the arts in Christian thought and practice, it is astonishing how relatively little *theological* reflection makes explicit use of them.[42]

Third, the priority of 'words' can mean the priority of books. Not only are the visual arts devalued in Christology but also oral culture can seem less significant than the world of the educated, or at least that of 'book-users'. This has been highlighted especially in critique deriving from the Third World of so much Western theology. Liberation theologians have drawn attention in many

---

41 D. Jasper, *The Study of Literature and Religion*, Minneapolis: Fortress Press, 1989, pp. 113 and 118, picks up on this in relation to the use of literature in theology, and the consequences for the use of the Bible. On a Spirit-Christology, see e.g. R. Del Colle, *Christ and the Spirit: Spirit Christology in Trinitarian Perspective*, Oxford: Oxford University Press, 1994, and 'Schleiermacher and Spirit Christology: Unexplored Horizons of *The Christian Faith*, International Journal of Systematic Theology 1, 1999, pp. 286–307.

42 Perhaps not quite so astonishing within Protestantism, given its emphasis upon 'the Word'. For recent examples of the interaction of theology, the arts and popular spirituality and culture, see e.g. C. Marsh and G. Ortiz, *Explorations in Theology and Film*, Oxford: Blackwell, 1997; R. K. Johnston, *Reel Spirituality: Theology and Film in Dialogue*, Grand Rapids: Baker Academic, 2000; G. Lynch, *After Religion: 'Generation X' and the Search for Meaning*, London: Darton, Longman & Todd, 2002; J. Lyden, *Film as Religion: Myths, Morals and Rituals*, New York and London: New York University Press, 2003; C. Marsh, *Cinema and Sentiment: Film's Challenge to Theology*, Milton Keynes: Paternoster Press, 2004; G. Lynch, *Understanding Theology and Popular Culture*, Oxford: Blackwell, 2005. Alongside such work, the investigations into the 'material' of religion, including Protestantism, e.g. by David Morgan and Colleen McDannell, are hugely important. On the theological importance of the visual arts, see e.g. J. Begbie, *Voicing Creation's Praise: Towards a Theology of the Arts*, Edinburgh: T. & T. Clark, 1991; F. B. Brown, *Good Taste, Bad Taste and Christian Taste: Aesthetics in Religious Life*, New York: Oxford University Press, 2000; W. A. Dyrness, *Visual Faith: Art, Theology and Worship in Dialogue*, Grand Rapids: Baker Academic, 2001; and also C. Marsh, 'Religion and the Arts' in C. Partridge (ed.), *Dictionary of Contemporary Religion in the Western World*, Leicester and Downers Grove: IVP, 2002, pp. 65–8 (and the literature cited there).

ways to the importance of Christologies articulated by those either less well educated or more used to operating in an oral culture.[43]

More particularly, fourth, with Christianity being a 'religion of the book', it is necessary to note the way in which Christianity can become twisted into a 'bibliocentric' religion: a religion not just of books but of the one book, the Bible. The Bible can become so central, as has happened in some forms of Protestantism, that Christianity becomes a 'bibliolatrous' religion in which, in effect, the Bible is worshipped in place of Christ. Striking is the extent to which this overlooks Luther's criterion for adjudging the respective value of scriptural books – according to whether they 'promote Christ'.[44]

Logocentrism therefore takes at least four forms. Overcoming it requires that the Bible be used appropriately in Christian theology, lest it be required to function for purposes a book could not possibly fulfil. To interpret the Bible and Christian faith, more than mere rationality will be needed. And the movement beyond rationality alone will require that theology attend to much more than words.

---

43 E.g. E. Cardenal, *Love in Practice: The Gospel in Solentiname*, London: Search Press, 1977, though also Volker Küster's concluding insights in *The Many Faces of Jesus Christ*, London: SCM Press, 2001, ch. 13. It is striking that this theological observation meshes also with the historical conclusions often drawn by New Testament scholars about the 'orality' of the earliest Christian communities (e.g. Werner H. Kelber, 'The Quest for the Historical Jesus: From the Perspectives of Medieval, Modern, and Post-Enlightenment Readings, and in View of Ancient, Oral Aesthetics' in J. D. Crossan *et al.*, *The Jesus Controversy: Perspectives in Conflict*, Harrisburg: TPI, 1999, pp. 75–115, esp. pp. 108–112; the importance of the orality of the earliest Jesus traditions is also fundamental for J. D. G. Dunn, *Jesus Remembered*, Grand Rapids and Cambridge: Eerdmans, 2003).

44 The charge has often been made and proponents need not be catalogued here. One interesting way in which this has been picked up recently, however, is in Daniel Adams' review of William Dyrness's 1990 book *Learning about Theology from the Third World* (*Interpretation* 47, 1993, p. 104). Writing from Korea, Adams questions the way in which Dyrness has made scripture the measure of Christ and not vice versa. Even though this, as indeed is the case with Luther himself, raises the question as to how Christ is known in order to be the measure of scripture, it is an important observation.

Ecclesiocentrism

This final theological distortion of Christocentrism aims to make Christ central but in practice replaces Christ with the Church. It is built on solid foundations – above all, the Pauline notion of the Church as the body of Christ (1 Cor. 12). But the reality of Christ becomes identical with the space occupied by 'Church' and by the human relationships that constitute 'Church'. The Church's own preoccupations with who 'is church' or who is 'in church' become the key questions about who is 'in Christ', or who 'is Christ's'. In the process, the notions of God alone being able to perceive who are God's people, and of Christ being present beyond the Church as we know it, have disappeared from view. The Church's undoubtedly important roles – of making plain the way of God in the world and of being a place where the presence of God can be celebrated – turn the Church into an absolutized institution. It seems to follow logically that it is only in or through the Church that such things occur, and that Christ can be found.

Within this distortion of Christocentrism two key aspects of Christian theology's own internal, critical, self-regulating procedure are lost. First, any notion of Christ being a critic of the Church – for example via the principle that only that which 'promotes Christ' is truly Christian[45] – cannot come into play. Rather than enabling Christianity to be Christocentric, then, the distortion of ecclesiocentrism prevents the Church being Christ's witness. Second, the notion of a necessary distance between Church and Kingdom has gone missing. The Kingdom of God cannot be identified with the Church, however much – in faith and hope – the Church must believe that its self-understanding and activity

---

45 This adapts Luther's criterion for judging the adequacy of the books of the Bible. A further Reformation-inspired definition of the Church, of course, is 'where the pure Word of God is preached and the Sacraments [are] . . . duly ministered' (19th Article of the Thirty-Nine Articles of Religion of the Church of England).

overlap with the Kingdom of God. When no distinction is drawn, the Church cannot be internally critical about its own religious and ethical practice. 'We must', therefore, 'resist the temptation to reduce the universality of Christ to the universality of the visible, institutional Church.'[46]

As with Christomonism, avoiding ecclesiocentrism will be a major challenge for this present enquiry, given the prominence it will give to the notion of constructing a corporate Christology. Indeed, any understanding of Christology as concrete and communal will be prone to the danger of replacing Christ by those who it is claimed embody Christ and are devoted to Christ today.

The eight theological distortions just listed provide an indication of how easily a Christocentric approach to Christian reflection can become skewed and how serious the consequences can be. There are, however, further dangers deriving from practice and ethical outlook.

Christian imperialism

The first ethical distortion of Christocentrism is the assertion of the superiority of Christianity over other religions. It is not surprising that those actively engaged in interfaith dialogue have felt the need to argue for theocentrism over and against Christocentrism in order to prevent this distortion occurring. Christians' reference to Christ's centrality for Christian thought and practice, alongside claims for universality and uniqueness, quickly lead to a stated or implied argument that Christianity is superior. In order to resist such easy equations, and mindful of their own actual experience, interfaith practitioners have largely avoided

---

46 M. Amaladoss, 'The Pluralism of Religions and the Significance of Christ' in R. S. Sugirtharajah (ed.), *Asian Faces of Jesus*, Maryknoll: Orbis/ London; SCM Press, 1993, p. 99; Amaladoss notes ecclesiocentrism as a problem in interfaith dialogue, as a corollary of the 'inclusivist' position (p. 86).

references to Christocentrism, lest they be misunderstood in their encounters and dialogues.[47]

Christocentrism *need not* entail a claim for Christianity's superiority, however. Chastened by the experience reported by interfaith practitioners, systematic and practical Christian theologians must note that Christocentrism needs reconstructing as an internal matter for Christianity. *Christocentrism is a strategy for defining what Christianity itself is, how Christianity works and how Christians view reality.* Reluctance to assert a Christocentric focus in an interfaith context may well be understandable, but it is vital as far as the self-definition of Christianity is concerned. The trinitarian doctrine of God is often highlighted now as that which is distinctive of Christianity, and which must therefore be offered as the key contribution by Christianity to interfaith dialogue.[48] However, the Trinity itself is a conceptual framework deduced from, and necessary for the understanding of, the claim that 'God was in Christ'.[49] For this reason, Christocentrism may be being too easily dispensed with, when there is yet more to be gleaned from the fact that Christianity works primarily in a Christocentric way.[50]

---

47 Hence e.g. Knitter's and Samartha's emphasis upon a 'theocentric Christology' (P. Knitter, *No Other Name? A Critical Survey of Christian Attitudes Toward the World Religions*, London: SCM Press, 1985, ch. 9; S. J. Samartha, 'The Cross and the Rainbow', p. 81) or Hick's 'Copernican revolution' from a 'Christianity-centred or Jesus-centred to a God-centred Model of the Universe of Faiths' (cited in Knitter, p. 147).

48 See e.g. G. D'Costa (ed.), *Christian Uniqueness Reconsidered: The Myth of a Pluralistic Theology of Religions*, Maryknoll: Orbis, 1990, Part I.

49 As will be considered later in this chapter.

50 One of the most striking, and surprising, sources of critique of such an assertion of Christian superiority (imperialism) is to be found in the later work of Karl Barth: *Church Dogmatics* IV/3, p. 91 (cited in Braaten, *No Other Gospel!*, p. 57); see also p. 97 – where Barth is found opposing all forms of 'self-glorification of the Christian', which therefore entails refusing to absolutize 'our own Christian subjectivity or that of the Church and its tradition'.

Christofascism

Christofascism is a corollary of the crucicentric distortion of Christocentrism. Concentration upon the suffering of Jesus the Christ is too easily twisted into a justification for suffering – including the bringing about of the suffering of others. Here, what is undertaken 'in the name of Christ' – internally within Christianity, or by Christians to others – becomes the centre of Christianity. Christ is identified in and by the actions of Christ's followers. Therefore whatever Christians may do, in being seen as the action of Christ, becomes the way in which Christ 'works' today.

This argument only works well when the actions of Christ's followers are deemed to be good or just. The popular complaint against Christianity is precisely that it has undertaken some shocking atrocities throughout history 'in the name of Christ'.[51] When taken to its negative extreme, therefore, Christofascism becomes, in effect, the vengeful actions of Christians in response to the murder of their innocent founder.

To such critique of Christianity should be added the voices of those who rightly note Christianity's anti-Semitism or contribution to the earth's exploitation, or its racism, sexism or heterosexism (within and beyond the Church).[52] Dorothee Soelle is credited with first using the term 'Christofascism' in relation to all forms of Christian fundamentalism.[53] The term can also be used more broadly, to encompass all oppressive uses of Christianity in

---

51 See e.g. L. Kennedy, *All in the Mind: A Farewell to God*, London: Hodder & Stoughton, 1999.

52 One particular form of this – the damaging aspects of the alliance between Christian thought and practice and the promotion of the patriarchal family – will surface in the discussion of Rita Nakashima Brock's work in Chapter 6.

53 See Fox, *The Coming of the Cosmic Christ*, p. 175; it is adopted in Braaten, *No Other Gospel!*, p. 52 , where the work of Driver, Ruether and Soelle receives mention.

the name of Christ, or all forms of claiming to be 'in Christ' while behaving in an oppressive way. To those unsympathetic to Christ-ianity's purpose or achievements, Christianity as a whole will seem Christofascist. To those within Christianity who work for its constant reformation, this will be an important distortion to be aware of, for history shows that Christianity needs constantly to discover and correct its own Christofascism.[54]

Christofascism goes hand in hand with Christian masochism, especially – but not only – for women.[55] For every case of oppression happening in the name of Christ, there is also an oppressed. All too often, the oppressed feels compelled, in the name of Christ, not to name the oppression for what it is, and to endure it. The ease with which the attempt to be Christ-centred can become tragically skewed on two fronts within this sphere of ethical practice thus becomes very apparent. A correction of this particular distortion of Christocentrism can only be based on an appropriate and effective understanding of Christ as a liberator who truly liberates, and is not simply called such. Christ, we might say, is only as good as the way Christ is presented by, and embodied in, followers, disciples and friends.

Nationalism or ethnocentrism

One of the most public and catastrophic distortions of Christo-centrism has been when a particular people has so identified itself with Christ that its own activities and beliefs become normative in Christology and the many ways in which Christ needs to be understood and expressed become stifled. Perhaps the clearest example of this in the history of Christianity is the dominance of the 'White' Christ throughout the world, and the Europeanism that

---

54 On the way in which Christian ethics develops, see esp. T. Driver, *Christ in a Changing World*, London: SCM Press, 1981, p. 54.

55 On 'Christian masochism' see D. Soelle, *Suffering*, London: Darton, Longman & Todd, 1975, ch. 1.

accompanied this emphasis.[56] Only relatively recently in the West has the shift begun 'from a Europe-centered world to a human-kind-centered world'.[57] The length of time this has taken and the fact that so much of the world is affected as a result of European expansionism are signs of how deeply the forms of this 'White Christ' have influenced the shaping not just of Christianity but of many of the world's social, political and economic structures.

Correction of such dominance cannot, of course, lead to a culture-less Christ, as all Christologies emerge from and expound a particular culture in seeking to speak of God in Christ. But examination of the White Christ has led to the recognition that Christology and cultural critique go hand in hand. We cannot exempt our images of Christ from such critique. Scrutiny of Christologies is part of cultural critique, enabling us to see the deep, resonant metaphors which affect not simply our theology but the very foundations of our culture, even for those who may deem themselves to have no theology.

The 'White Christ' is one but certainly not the only example of how racial imperialism or ethnocentrism may take the place of Christocentrism. Indeed, because the movement to correct forms of the White Christ has entailed the self-assertion of other racial groups, the danger is always present that one example of this distortion of Christocentrism may simply be replaced by another. Hence the 'Black Christ' can be both the necessary discovery and appropriate assertion of an authentic Black theology and spirituality and a claim of racial or cultural superiority that would distort Christ just as White Christians have done for so

---

56 The 'White Christ' can itself be subdivided into particular forms of White ideology (see, for instance, A. Davies, *Infected Christianity: A Study of Modern Racism*, Kingston and Montreal: McGill-Queen's University Press, 1988, chs. 2–5, where 'The Germanic Christ', 'The Latin Christ', 'The Anglo-Saxon Christ' and 'The Afrikaner Christ' are studied and critiqued).

57 The phrase is from David Bosch, *Transforming Mission*, Maryknoll: Orbis, 1991, p. 451.

long.[58] The difficulty of noting this possibility is naturally that Black Christology so richly opens up much more than merely the racial and cultural elements in Christology: for example, dimensions of Christ's suffering, Christology and solidarity between people, Christology as lived experience.[59] And it does so not despite attention to Black experience, but precisely because of it. However, the possibility of this same distortion occurring within any racially and culturally aware Christology must be acknowledged.

Egocentrism

Egocentrism takes the theological distortion of anthropocentrism to a logical conclusion. Concentration on the individual male figure in Christology can lead to the practice of a highly individualistic spirituality, what we may call the 'Jesus and me' syndrome. This is often implied in critiques of anthropocentrism.[60] To cite one example, though perhaps he was not fully familiar with the extent to which the text has proved influential within world Methodism, it is hard not to suspect that Bonhoeffer might have balked at John Wesley's account of his 'heart-warming' encounter, given the intense nature of the experience to him as an individual.[61]

---

58 On this, see e.g. Davies, *Infected Christianity*, pp. 105–16; P. Pope-Levison and J. Levison, *Jesus in Global Contexts*, Louisville: Westminster/John Knox Press, 1992, pp. 153–6, esp. re the critical reception of Cleage's *The Black Messiah* within Black theology itself; also K. B. Douglas, *The Black Christ*, Maryknoll: Orbis, 1994; esp. chs. 4–5.

59 C. Marsh, 'Black Christs in White Christian Perspective: Some Critical Reflections', *Black Theology* 2.1, 2004, pp. 45–56.

60 It is no accident that Bonhoeffer's critique is against movements in theology and spirituality which display individualistic tendencies.

61 'In the evening I went very unwillingly to a society in Aldersgate Street ... I felt my heart strangely warmed. I felt I did trust in Christ, Christ alone, for salvation; and an assurance was given me, that He had taken away my sins, even mine, and saved me from the law of sin and death.' Wesley's Journal entry for 24 May 1738, cited in B. Tabraham, *The Making of Methodism*, Peterborough: Epworth Press, 1995, p. 28.

At this point we encounter again one of the difficult implications of a salvation-oriented faith such as Christianity. If Christianity fails to affect people individually in a deep, life-shaping way, then its purpose is questionable. However, personal faith need not be individualistic faith, even while we appropriate and live a life of faith both individually, as well as communally. Some Christian movements do indeed seem preoccupied with 'personal salvation' or with 'personal authenticity' or 'personal transformation'. As a result, interpersonal aspects of faith can become obscured. This may in turn mean that egocentrism prevents the possibility of Christocentrism operating.

An appropriate Christocentrism in Christianity will, then, always require that Christ is understood and received in a communal context. Jesus is seen to be Christ in the context of his followers and is proclaimed Lord by believers (past and present), always with reference to other believers. Once more, an indication is given of how to re-focus Christocentrism: via a communal emphasis in Christology.

Activism

The 1960s proved to be a striking chapter in the recent history of Western Christian theology. The decade is, in turn, vilified and praised. It is vilified as the time in which Christianity lost its way in the West, when the crisis caused by modernity reached its peak and secularity took hold, even with the blessing of some Christians. It is praised as a time when hope was raised of Christianity genuinely coping with the challenge of modernity, and evolving appropriately.[62] Uses of the figure of Jesus within some of the versions of Christianity proposed during that time

---

62 For an account of the sense of disappointment of those who had such high hopes of the theological reflection undertaken in the 1960s, see e.g. J. Bowden, *Voices in the Wilderness*, London: SCM Press, 1977.

are especially noteworthy. Bonhoeffer's work was appropriated by 'death of God' theologians, who had time for Jesus but felt the need to dispense with God.[63] Bonhoeffer's Christology had also been used in J. A. T. Robinson's *Honest to God*, whose central chapter, 'A Man for Others', proved to be a linchpin in the presentation of Robinson's case.[64]

Such theological movements provided a basis for a swathe of Christian activism. The combination of a resistance to metaphysical speculation and attention to the politically charged actions of Jesus of Nazareth proved a heady mix. Those who write books can scarcely be accused of being 'unreflective', but the two examples just cited can serve as published representatives of an undoubted 'activist' streak in modern Christology. When such a strain of ethical spirituality takes shape within Christian life, it can sometimes be less reflective than would be desirable. 'What Jesus stood for', 'what Jesus would do in this situation', 'the values of Jesus', 'Kingdom values', 'the biblical mandate' or 'the will of God' seem so plainly evident as to need little pause for thought. Seen in this light, the possibility of Christocentrism becoming skewed into an *unreflective* activism, which replaces Christ with ethical practice, can be shown to be a problem not only for so-called, would-be or actual radicals. Many forms of 'Liberal Protestantism' are an easy target here.[65] Driver's search for an 'ethical Christology' derives from a similar background, being more consciously

---

63 See e.g. T. J. J. Altizer and W. Hamilton, *Radical Theology and the Death of God*, Harmondsworth: Penguin, 1968, esp. pp. 36–62, 118–23.

64 J. A. T. Robinson, *Honest to God*, London: SCM Press, 1963, pp. 64–83, accepting that Robinson recognized regularly after publication that he had not constructed his book to stand the close scrutiny it later received!

65 See e.g. the comment of Phillips: 'The Christian life in the world was defined in terms of "vocation" and an ethical activism which sought the realization of Christian "ideals". At its best, Liberal Christianity took these ideals from those "ethical teachings" of Christ which were capable of realization in earthly society, fighting courageously against the brutality, greed and inhumanity of late nineteenth-century industrialism and nationalism with the religious principles to which the name "social gospel" was affixed.

undertaken in a multi-faith context than was the case either for nineteenth-century Liberal Protestantism or even for 1960s theologians. His work raises the inevitable question whether, within such an enterprise, Christology is reduced to ethical conduct without remainder.[66]

There are other examples of activism within Christianity which need not be related to Liberal Protestantism. The tendency towards hyperactivity in Methodism, for example, correlates a reluctance to articulate a clear theology with an at times feverish desire to foster a distinctive ecclesial practice. The Christ-centred rationale to make God available to those often socially excluded from the riches of Christianity is often emphasized within this activity, serving as a reminder that Christocentrism is not to be seen as a merely theoretical matter. But without the 'thought', the 'practice' too easily becomes an unreflective activism. Ethics forms a crucial part of Christianity, but when Christocentrism has become an unreflective activism, a socially committed Christianity has lost its way and the question arises whether the ethical conduct undertaken is any longer Christian.

Christolatry

The final distortion to be identified can be regarded as a summary category for those already discussed, but it also enables us to consider one further dimension in the possible distortion of Christocentrism. 'Christolatry' is the term given to Christology

---

At its worst, the dialectical nature of Christian existence in the world was lost sight of, and adherents of a tamed "Liberalism" emptied it of its traditional Christian content and simply added a dash of piety to what had become essentially a capitulation to the economic, political, and social order in which they lived' (J. A. Phillips, *The Form of Christ in the World*, p. 223).

66 Though the counter-question should readily be posed: is any ethical conduct reduced to conduct without remainder? All actions have a theory of some kind behind them, even if rarely or never articulated. If Driver's ethics are christological, then it is not possible for them to be reduced to conduct without remainder: the Christology is part of the ethics.

by feminist theologian Mary Daly.[67] Two of the three critiques of Christology Daly offers in her work have been covered in this discussion under different headings: Jesusology and androcentrism.[68] It is doubtful whether the strategy I am adopting here – of arguing that what Daly identifies as problems with Christology are, in fact, distortions of what Christology is supposed to do – would be acceptable to Daly.[69] Nevertheless there is value in adopting Daly's critical term 'Christolatry' in a slightly different way.

Christocentrism becomes Christolatry when any attempt to fashion an understanding of Christ becomes an absolute task. Christian theology becomes absorbed in the christological task to such a degree that concern for a doctrine of God disappears. In contemporary Christian discussion this must inevitably mean: Christocentrism becomes Christolatry whenever it fails to be a trinitarian Christocentrism. In my view, however, it is preferable to talk in terms of a Christocentrism in service of, and supported by, an adequate doctrine of God, rather than to speak only of the Trinity, however important and useful that doctrine is to Christian reflection. In this way, the necessary dialectic is respected between Christology and the doctrine of God within systematic theology.

'Christolatry' can also mean that a particular Christology becomes an absolute, and no other Christology is considered. Again, this understanding can be seen to overlap with other distortions (e.g. ethnocentrism, anthropocentrism, androcentrism) which merely show that some other reality has replaced Christ and become an idol. Christolatry results when one's own, particular

---

67 M. Daly, *Beyond God the Father*, Boston: Beacon Press, 1973, cited in Pope-Levison and Levison, *Jesus in Global Contexts*, p. 152.

68 This deals with Daly's objections to dependence upon a past, limited historical figure and focus upon the maleness of Jesus. Whether recognition of androcentrism also adequately addresses Daly's critique of the way that Christology turns Jesus into a 'father figure' remains to be seen, especially as a consequence of the later discussion of Brock's work.

69 Especially given the post-Christian position to which Daly has clearly moved, in the content of later writings.

Christology is asserted as if nothing is to be discovered or learned about Christ from any other source.

We see, then, that those who argue for theocentrism in Christian thought and practice are correct up to a point. An error intervenes in the assumption that in order to be theocentric, one must cease to be Christocentric. In Christianity, rather, one *must* be Christocentric *in order to be* theocentric. One will only err if one absolutizes one's understanding of the way to God in and through Christ, or if any of the distortions addressed in this chapter comes into play.

Putting the doctrine of the Trinity in its place

Radical, methodological Christocentrism is admittedly unfashionable. In the contemporary climate of theology in the West, the doctrine of the Trinity is much more prominent as the starting point, centre, focus and goal of Christian theology. Some account of how this present proposal fits into current trends is therefore called for.

The vast number of studies that have appeared on the doctrine of the Trinity in recent years, not to mention the systematic theologies or other theological studies that are shaped around or work towards the doctrine, is probably surpassed only by the number of books to have appeared on Jesus of Nazareth.[70] Whatever

---

70 E.g. D. Brown, *The Divine Trinity*, London: Duckworth, 1985; J. Moltmann, *The Trinity and the Kingdom of God*, London: SCM Press, 1981; the British Council of Churches Working Party reports and study guide, *The Forgotten Trinity*, London: BCC, 1989–91; C. Gunton, *The Promise of Trinitarian Theology*, Edinburgh: T. & T. Clark, 1991; C. M. LaCugna, *God for Us*, Edinburgh: T. & T. Clark, 1991; but also W. Pannenberg, *Systematic Theology Vol.1*, Edinburgh: T. & T. Clark, 1992 (in systematic theology); the British Methodist Church's report, *Called to Love and Praise*, Peterborough: Methodist Publishing House, 1999 (in ecclesiology); R. Greenwood, *Transforming Priesthood: A New Theology of Mission and Ministry*, London: SPCK, 1994 (in ministry).

the reasons for this,[71] it can hardly be deemed an inappropriate development in Christianity. Christian faith is, after all, a trinitarian faith: in Christian belief and understanding, God is not an internally static God. Christians support a 'differentiated' and not an 'undifferentiated' theism. In Christian eyes, this enables God's dynamism to be better grasped and provides a framework for what Christians want to say about Christ. Seen from this perspective, there should not be a problem. Trinitarian Christocentrism should be the inevitable outcome. To oppose Christocentrism with Trinity-centredness would ultimately entail setting up a false dichotomy.

However, the form and nature of some of the contemporary discussion about the Trinity deserve to be unpicked a little. Some features of the rediscovery of the doctrine in the West seem more continuous with the reasons why the doctrine fell into neglect in the first place than its current proponents are willing to admit.[72] An abstractness is present, which serves as a reminder of why the doctrine of the Trinity has so readily been overlooked in Christian practice. In the need to correct Christocentrism via the location of Christology within a trinitarian hermeneutic, 'the approachability of God', evident in the ways that Christians have done their God-talk when talking about Jesus/Christ, becomes lost.

---

71 The search for the 'distinctively Christian' in the context of interfaith dialogue, the impact of Eastern upon Western Christianity, the contributions (in both Protestant and Roman Catholic traditions) of particular theologians – Barth and Rahner especially, the desire to find resources for a relational understanding of God, the reaction against Jesucentric liberalism, the desire to respect the worshipping community more in Christian thought, can all be cited as possible reasons.

72 In particular, the view that the doctrine of the Trinity was not, in fact, closely connected with Christian practice, and was caught in a particular philosophical framework which modern Christianity could not easily appropriate. The notion that 'Jesus', by contrast, seemed to make God very accessible, though fraught with its own difficulties (as this book makes clear), was at least understandable.

Schwöbel's chapter on the current 'crisis' in Christology[73] is a good example of a meticulous and lucid exposition of some contemporary problems in Christology, together with some suggested remedies. He notes the urgency of the call for a Christocentric approach to Christian theology. In going on to map the nature of Christology's current crisis, he is critical of the simple dualisms and false tracks adopted in the modern period. Identifying the need for a trinitarian hermeneutic is, in his view, no simple return to the past. The use of resources from trinitarian reflection enables Christology, he claims, to overcome its modern/ist crisis: the tendency to propose a Christology in effect on binitarian lines, focused too statically on the two natures of the Son, with a weak sense of the contemporary presence of the Spirit.[74]

There is little doubt that in this present study I reach a point that may prove appealing to Schwöbel. However, I reach it via a very different route. If I do so with an implicit trinitarian hermeneutic, then so be it. But my reservation about following Schwöbel's own, rather involved, trinitarian path relates to the 'Brief Unscientific Postscript' with which he concludes his chapter. Schwöbel writes:

In view of the seriousness of the modern christological crisis, and faced with the fragmentary and limited character of theological reflection attempting to overcome it, the prospects of a full recovery would seem decidedly gloomy, if the healing process had to come exclusively from theological thought. Perhaps it is a necessary reminder for theologians that the true resources for overcoming the crisis of Christology are to be found in the scriptural witness and the worship of the Christian community of faith whose life is a far more promising sign of hope than theological thought could ever be.[75]

---

73 C. Schwöbel, 'Christology and Trinitarian Thought' in C. Schwöbel (ed.), *Trinitarian Theology Today*, Edinburgh: T. & T. Clark, 1995, pp. 113–46.

74 Schwöbel, 'Christology and Trinitarian Thought', p. 125.

75 Schwöbel, 'Christology and Trinitarian Thought', pp. 145–6.

This is a sober statement, a reminder that Christian thought is not everything, and that theologians have their limits. Yet I find myself less able than Schwöbel to be so unqualifiedly positive about the 'worship of the Christian community of faith'. This is not because of the God who is worshipped, but because so much Christian worship, and so many manifestations of Christian community, seem to impoverish the God who is worshipped. Many of my concerns throughout this book, and the way I address them, no doubt fall into the 'modern' concerns which Schwöbel finds so distracting. But the ways I work towards solutions are, in my view, ultimately more practical, more accessible and more connected with the way that Christology *actually works* in Christian communities than the suggestions with which Schwöbel proceeds so hopefully.

The trinitarian hermeneutic which lies behind what I conclude perhaps needs spelling out by others, or at another time. For the moment I am happy simply to accept that the doctrine of the Trinity is doing its work in Christianity, not as the last word about God but as a key way in which Christians have always sought to make sense of what God has done and is doing 'in Christ'. It is, however, very evident that a great many Christians do not gain their primary access to God *consciously* through trinitarian reflection, even if they may well encounter the God to whom the doctrine of the Trinity points.

Summary

Christocentrism, then, is prone to easy and dangerous distortions. This chapter has mapped the main problems that Christocentrism must face. I suggest that it is nevertheless essential for Christian thought and practice to follow a Christocentric path, and to a radical degree. For only in this way can the understanding of God which has come in and through the experience of Jesus the Christ be appropriately maintained.

Although such an approach may appear at times to prevent the focus on the Trinity that so much contemporary theology calls for, I believe this not to be the case. It simply puts the doctrine of the Trinity in its appropriate place. It is also my contention that the doctrine of God, which the idea of the Trinity seeks to grasp, is in danger of not being Christocentric enough if the doctrine of the Trinity too easily becomes the starting point and focus of Christian faith. The full significance of this claim is what the rest of this book, and its companion volume, seek to explain.

Part Two

Towards a Corporate Christology

4

Friedrich Schleiermacher:
Christ-Piety

A discussion of contemporary theology's handling of the figure of Jesus Christ does well to begin with the so-called 'father of modern theology', Friedrich Schleiermacher.[1] Schleiermacher's thought has set the agenda for much theological reflection, especially in northern hemisphere Protestantism, over the past two centuries. Even where his procedure may have been roundly criticized or

---

1 For excellent studies of Schleiermacher, see M. Redeker, *Schleiermacher: Life and Thought*, Philadelphia: Fortress Press, 1973; K. Nowak, *Schleiermacher: Leben, Werk und Wirkung*, Göttingen: Vandenhoeck & Ruprecht, 2002; and many works by B. A. Gerrish: 'Friedrich Schleiermacher' in N. Smart *et al.* (eds.), *Nineteenth Century Religious Thought in the West Vol. 1*, Cambridge: Cambridge University Press, 1985, pp. 123–56; *A Prince of the Church: Schleiermacher and the Beginnings of Modern Theology*, London: SCM Press, 1984; and selected essays in *The Old Protestantism and the New: Essays on the Reformation Heritage*, Edinburgh: T. & T. Clark, 1982 (chs. 11–12); and *Continuing the Reformation: Essays on Modern Religious Thought*, London and Chicago: The University of Chicago Press, 1993 (chs. 7–9 and 12). J. Macquarrie, *Jesus Christ in Modern Thought*, London: SCM Press, 1990 (ch. 9), deals directly with Schleiermacher's Christology, as does R. R. Niebuhr, *Schleiermacher on Christ and Religion*, London: SCM Press, 1965. The following general discussions of Schleiermacher are also helpful: C. Welch, *Protestant Thought in the Nineteenth Century: Vol. 1 (1799–1870)*, New Haven and London: Yale University Press, 1972, ch. 3; H. Berkhof, *Two Hundred Years of Theology*, Grand Rapids: Eerdmans, 1989, ch. 3; and R. R. Niebuhr, 'Friedrich Schleiermacher' in M. E. Marty and D. G. Peerman (eds.), *A Handbook of Christian Theologians*, Cambridge: Lutterworth, 1984 (=1965), pp. 17–35.

rejected, as in the work of Karl Barth, Schleiermacher was still the sounding board or benchmark.[2] That he can be readily identified as a Christocentric theologian is itself significant.

I have opted to examine Schleirmacher's Christology, and the place of Christology within his theology as a whole, under the heading of 'Christ-piety'. This is a risky move. It perhaps implies at the outset that Schleiermacher's theology is reducible to what believers believe, rather than an exploration of who God is. Not surprisingly I reject such a charge. But I do want to acknowledge that the value of Schleiermacher's approach for this investigation lies in the way in which and extent to which his thought constantly takes into account Christ (as objective reality), the Christian believer, the relation between Christ and the believer, and the actual practice of Christian living.[3]

Schleiermacher's theological method

Schleiermacher is often regarded as the 'theologian of experience' par excellence, but such a description is misleading if this also implies a method of proceeding: *from* (general human) experience

---

2 For Barth's critique, see e.g. K. Barth, *Die protestantische Theologie im 19. Jahrhundert: Ihre Vorgeschichte und ihre Geschichte*, Zürich: Theologischer Verlag, 1981, pp. 379–424 (ET *Protestant Theology in the Nineteenth Century: Its Background and History*, Grand Rapids: Eerdmans/London: SCM Press, 2002). Barth was, of course, deeply respectful of Schleiermacher's endeavour (see esp. K. Barth, *The Theology of Schleiermacher*, Grand Rapids: Eerdmans 1982), and that he was in some respects not as distant from Schleiermacher on some matters as Barth may like to have supposed is evidenced by the juxtaposition of their respective 'types' of theology in Hans Frei's account (*Types of Christian Theology*, New Haven and London: Yale University Press, 1992, pp. 34–46).

3 On the significance of the term 'piety' for an understanding of Schleiermacher's dogmatic work, see the translators' introduction (by James Duke and Francis Fiorenza) to F. D. E. Schleiermacher, *On The Glaubenslehre: Two Letters to Dr. Lücke*, Chico: Scholars Press, 1981, pp. 11–12.

to Christian theology. Experience is certainly a vital factor in Schleiermacher's theology. It is also true that the manner in which he expounds his dogmatic system suggests, on a casual glance, that he moves from a general human experience to Christian content.[4] However, to draw such a conclusion ignores what Schleiermacher says of his own method, and what he actually achieves.

Schleiermacher is explicit about the ordering of the parts of his main work of dogmatics, *The Christian Faith*. In his 'Second Letter to Dr Lücke' (1829), he mentions that he thought of reversing the first and second parts of the work, when preparing a second edition.[5] That he did not do so, Schleiermacher accepts, still leaves him open to the misunderstandings of his approach that followed the work's initial appearance: namely, that he is a speculative theologian spinning out ideas from a general account of human experience; or that he is a pantheist.[6] He notes that reversing the order would have reassured his Christian readers, and made his account of the religious self-consciousness much more acceptable, merely through its coming after the section on Christology. He chose not to make this change, and therefore misunderstandings do still occur.

Schleiermacher had already written the *Speeches on Religion* for the 'cultured despisers' of his day (1799).[7] When going on to construct a Christian dogmatics, he could not neglect 'the present

---

4 In *The Christian Faith* (Edinburgh: T. & T. Clark 1928 [1830–1]) the exposition of the 'religious self-consciousness' (§§32–49) precedes the expositions of the attributes of God and the world (these sections constituting Part One of the work). Part Two comprises sections on sin and grace, the latter multiply subdivided into Christ, redemption, election, church, sacraments, eschatology. A notorious 'Conclusion' (on the Trinity) rounds off the work.

5 Schleiermacher, *On the Glaubenslehre*, pp. 55–60.

6 This point is examined by B. A. Gerrish in his Foreword to the first paperback edition of *The Christian Faith*, Edinburgh: T. & T. Clark, 1999, pp. vii–ix.

7 The most recent edition in English is Richard Crouter's translation of the first edition (*On Religion: Speeches to Its Cultured Despisers*, Cambridge: Cambridge University Press, 1988).

needs of our church', not only internally but also with respect to Christians' interactions with non-members.[8] The procedure of *The Christian Faith* could thus be said to be informed by an apologetic purpose similar to that at work in the *Speeches*. While its layout does not reflect directly Schleiermacher's actual theological method, an apologetic purpose is implicit. Schleiermacher is 'upfront' – quite literally – about the role of experience in religion. He believes he can only understand the religious self-consciousness because of his own experience of Christ. Furthermore, he holds to the view that 'religion' only exists in the form of particular (historical[9]) religions, and not in any general form. He therefore accepts that his understanding of the 'religious self-consciousness' will be a particular account of religious experience, deriving from intense exploration of the believer's consciousness, and thus inevitably relating to his own Christian faith. But his exposition of Christian consciousness out of the context of the particularity of Christianity is offered in a way which he hopes may be accessible to those who do not profess Christian faith.

Schleiermacher thus articulates a position from firmly *within* Christianity. He presents an exposition of the Christian faith in the form of an appeal to readers to relate their experience to what he describes. His work has an apologetic purpose without simply being a work of apologetics. His strategy is to enable people (even the cultured despisers) to build on their limited grasp of Christian faith, on their longing for religion as contained in their aesthetic sensibilities, or on an emerging existential self-

---

8 Schleiermacher, *On the Glaubenslehre*, p. 60. Schleiermacher was always concerned with the 'eternal covenant' between philosophy and theology, culture and theology, a scientific worldview and theology, i.e. between the explicitly theological, and non-theological accounts of reality (on which, see esp. G. Spiegler, *The Eternal Covenant: Schleiermacher's Experiment in Cultural Theology*, New York, Evanston and London: Harper & Row, 1967).

9 The term 'positive' was also often used by Schleiermacher and other nineteenth-century theologians when denoting the historicity of religions.

understanding,[10] so that they might find a point of contact with Christianity. He is not offering a generalized account of human experience that is equally accessible to all people and is uninformed by reference to Christian experience and practice, to the Christ experienced, or to the God upon whom all creation depends.

Schleiermacher's method is to understand and expound Christian doctrines as 'accounts of the Christian religious affections set forth in speech'.[11] He grasps the theological task in terms of the explication of Christian experience. It is specifically an experience of God in Christ that he seeks to describe. In Schleiermacher's view, such an experience characterizes the whole Christian life. Interpreting the 'Christ-piety' which Schleiermacher identifies as the heart of Christian belief, then, entails exploring Christocentrism in a form in which spirituality and dogmatics meet and inform each other.

Schleiermacher's Christocentrism

Summarizing Schleiermacher's position succinctly, Martin Redeker writes: 'The center of his theology is Christology. Schleiermacher thinks *christocentrically*, but not *christomonistically*.'[12] The statement could have been written with this present book in mind. Accepting that distortions of Christocentrism are possible, and that Schleiermacher was himself accused of misinterpreting Christianity, Redeker defends Schleiermacher against one major

---

10 The 'feeling of absolute dependence', around which the theological anthropology of *The Christian Faith* revolves, is misunderstood when seen only in psychological terms (see e.g. Redeker, *Schleiermacher*, pp. 113–19, Duke and Fiorenza in Schleiermacher, *On the Glaubenslehre*, pp. 12–21, Macquarrie, *Jesus Christ*, ch. 9, esp. pp. 193–5).

11 Schleiermacher, *The Christian Faith*, p. 76.

12 Redeker, *Schleiermacher*, p. 149; Redeker's emphasis.

such charge and reasserts the validity and success of his achievement: his theology was indeed Christocentric. What does this
amount to? In its most general form, Schleiermacher himself
describes it as follows: 'Christianity is a monotheistic faith, belong-
ing to the teleological type of religion, and is essentially distinguished from other such faiths by the fact that in it everything is
related to the redemption accomplished by Jesus of Nazareth.'[13]
Christology is undoubtedly the *doctrinal* focus of Schleiermacher's system.[14] But it would be wrong to see Schleiermacher's
Christocentrism as pertaining merely to the task of expounding
a Christian dogmatics. This is clear even from the words already
cited. *Everything* is related to the redemption accomplished by
Jesus of Nazareth – all ethics, worship and spirituality, as well as all
themes of Christian doctrine. This coheres with Schleiermacher's
approach to Christianity as a whole. To use Redeker's words once
more:

> Doctrine and reflection . . . are not themselves the foundation
> but that which has been founded. The certainty of salvation
> and of faith rests on the existential experience of revelation
> and not on correct theological understanding and formula-
> tion. Christian faith is therefore never faith in correct doctrine
> and the dead letter but in the living relation between God and
> humankind.[15]

Christocentrism for Schleiermacher is therefore both doctrinal

13 Schleiermacher, *The Christian Faith*, p. 52. This statement is the
heading for §11. In all I have counted 37 such clear statements of the nature of
Schleiermacher's Christocentrism in *The Christian Faith* alone. This particular
version of his Christocentrism is, admittedly, guilty of 'Jesusology' in its form.
But redemption is, of course, the focus.

14 More particularly, Redeker, *Schleiermacher*, p. 131, comments: 'The
section on the divine status of the Redeemer in *The Christian Faith* is no doubt
the heart of Schleiermacher's dogmatics.' He is referring to §§92–105.

15 Redeker, *Schleiermacher*, p. 40 (adjusting the exclusive language of the
translation).

and *experiential.* 'Living fellowship with Christ' (the Redeemer) reveals itself as the hallmark of Schleiermacher's Christocentrism. Although Christocentrism is expressed in terms of the centrality of Christology in dogmatics, this is only because of the actual centrality of Christ within the Christian life. In this sense, given that doctrines are 'religious affections set forth in speech', 'living fellowship with Christ' has clear priority. This is the heart of what I am calling Schleiermacher's 'Christ-piety'. No doctrine would have been either required or possible without such fellowship with Christ. So how is this 'living fellowship' to be understood, and what form does it take?

First, living fellowship with Christ is the form in which a Christian becomes conscious of God.[16] As such, it is an essential feature of Christian life. Failure to relate a sense of God to Christ makes a claim to be God-conscious sub-Christian.[17] Second, it is not merely an individual experience. Although there is certainly a personal element, an individual Christian always stands in relation to other Christians. Living fellowship is thus necessarily corporately grounded and corporately celebrated.[18] Third, living fellowship with Christ celebrates the receipt of grace: it is a redemptive experience. As such, this 'total effective influence of Christ' continues 'the creative divine activity out of which the Person of Christ arose'.[19] Fourth, with respect to the ongoing Christian life, living fellowship with Christ entails, in broadest terms, 'regeneration and sanctification'.[20] Fifth, living fellowship with Christ, though the hallmark of a Christian and thus the key feature of Christian unity, is experienced in different forms.

---

16 *The Christian Faith*, pp. 371–3 (§91).

17 *The Christian Faith*, p. 371.

18 *The Christian Faith*, pp. 358, 106. Re corporate celebration, see e.g. §141 on the Lord's Supper.

19 *The Christian Faith*, p. 427.

20 *The Christian Faith*, pp. 476–510; which Schleiermacher expounds in terms of conversion, justification and the sins and good works of the regenerate believer.

There is therefore scope, in Schleiermacher's understanding, for diversity in experience of Christ.[21]

This condensed description of Schleiermacher's version of Christocentrism does not do him full justice. Yet even in such compressed form it confirms the way in which corporate experience of Christ lies at the centre of his entire construal of Christianity. Other facets of Christian practice and belief come into play, and he draws on aspects of doctrine beyond Christology. But it is through the category of experience of Christ/the Redeemer, and through Christology, that Schleiermacher claims to grasp and expound the heart of Christianity. He may even be regarded as something of a 'Christ-mystic'.[22] Indeed, the nature of his devotion to the figure of Jesus Christ suggests that, in a clear sense, he never ceased to belong to the Moravians, among whom he received his education during his late teens. If this characterization of Schleiermacher's spirituality and theology is correct, then we can say that the Moravian, which Schleiermacher was prepared to grant that he remained,[23] sought to develop a corporate, mystical understanding of Christ that was firmly linked to and expressed through the particular forms of the Christian religion.[24] If he ended up too ecclesiastical for many Pietist Protestants, he did not lose the intense, personal power of the religious experience that he saw at the heart of Christian faith, grounded in the believer's living fellowship with Christ. So what understanding of Jesus Christ supported this notion of 'living fellowship with Christ'?

---

21 *The Christian Faith*, p. 372.

22 Cf. Redeker, *Schleiermacher*, p. 138; for a brief discussion, see also Macquarrie, *Jesus Christ*, pp. 197–8, 210.

23 See Ch. 2 n. 17 above.

24 Though I do not believe his understanding of Christ was ever wholly ecclesiastical, as his recognition of the importance of friendship, family life, music and political structures confirms.

Schleiermacher's understanding of Jesus Christ

Schleiermacher is thought to have been the first scholar to offer public lectures on the life of Jesus. He gave the first of his five series of lectures (all delivered in Berlin) in 1819. The fifth series (1832) provided the basis of the published text, which finally appeared in English in 1975.[25] The decisive work on the Synoptic Gospels (by Weisse and Wilke), which would begin to question the argument for Matthean priority, and Strauss's *Life of Jesus Critically Examined* would not appear until the 1830s. It is clear, then, that Schleiermacher was ahead of his time. He was already undertaking critical work on the Gospels with a view to expounding what Jesus was actually like as a historical figure. It is therefore to be expected that his *Life of Jesus* lectures would prove important for his Christology, especially as much gospel criticism undertaken throughout the nineteenth century would interweave with the Quest of the Historical Jesus.

The Life of Jesus lectures are crucial for an understanding of Schleiermacher's Christology, though not in the way that one might expect. The extent to which they depend upon the Gospel of John must be noted. In the light of later study of the Gospels and of historical Jesus research throughout the nineteenth and twentieth centuries, the manner of Schleiermacher's theological use of data from the historical study of the life of Jesus in his Christology now seems questionable. After the various Quests of the Historical Jesus it is no longer possible to appeal easily to the Fourth Gospel as a source of data about the historical Jesus.[26] Even so, it should

---

25 F. D. E. Schleiermacher, *The Life of Jesus*, Philadelphia: Fortress Press, 1975 (edited and introduced by Jack Verheyden). The original German text of 1864 comprised a combination of Schleiermacher's brief notes, and the notes of five students who heard the 1832 series.

26 This remains true despite attempts throughout the twentieth century (e.g. P. Gardner-Smith, C. H. Dodd, J. A. T. Robinson) to point to the presence of historically reliable material within the Fourth Gospel.

come as no surprise that material from Schleiermacher's lectures built into his Christology is unlikely to be a series of historical statements, quarried in positivistic fashion through supposedly objective research. Schleiermacher's whole approach to theology, and to the place of Christ within it, certainly does not begin there, and uses historical material only with great circumspection.

Early on in the lectures themselves, Schleiermacher is unequivocal about the limits of what it is possible to achieve through historical enquiry into the Gospels: 'it is undeniable that we cannot achieve a connected presentation of the life of Jesus'.[27] His *Life of Jesus* lectures will not, then, deliver a 'Life of Jesus'. Nevertheless, they supply useful material for his Christology, even if the terms on which Schleiermacher used this material must be subjected to critical scrutiny.[28] We must, however, be careful not to judge Schleiermacher too harshly. He was undertaking his own critical readings of the Gospels.[29] He had few textbooks at his disposal and deserves credit for being among the first to explore the complex interplay of three factors: a critical reading of the Gospels, the gathering of historical data about Jesus and the theological use of the Gospels. He addressed these factors in relation to a practically oriented, experientially rooted, theologically grounded and doctrinally sensitive Christology. This was no mean achievement.

If there are historical data built into Schleiermacher's Christology, it is certainly not with such data that he begins.

---

27 Schleiermacher, *Life of Jesus*, p. 43.

28 Indeed, it is not surprising that critics are suspicious that he finds the Gospel of John so historically conducive to the building of his Christology. Strauss's ruthless criticism of Schleiermacher is also no surprise (D. F. Strauss, *The Christ of Faith and the Jesus of History: A Critique of Schleiermacher's 'The Life of Jesus'*, Philadelphia: Fortress Press, 1977; German original 1865).

29 He was willing to make judgements which would still today raise eyebrows in churches, even if not in universities or seminaries: e.g. where Jesus was born is of no consequence; birth narratives are unnecessary; the virgin birth sends us on the wrong track.

His Christology begins from the experience of Christ within the believing community. A summary by Redeker is again helpful:

> Schleiermacher's Christology ... is not based on a historicized causal relationship moving from the historical effect back to its cause, but upon the immediate existential experience of the revelation in Christ. The questions of historical criticism about the reports of the Gospels are no longer fundamental. What is central is the actual present life-relation to the present and living Christ. It is for the sake of Christ that Schleiermacher believes in the biblical reports.[30]

What is being said about Christ on the basis of this 'immediate existential experience of the revelation in Christ'?[31] Three main features of Schleiermacher's Christology must be highlighted. First, Jesus/Christ is, for Schleiermacher, the one who embodied perfect God-consciousness.[32] It is not altogether clear whether Schleiermacher thinks that this perfect embodiment of God-consciousness by Christ entails his being different in kind, or merely in degree, from his followers.[33] But Christ is certainly

---

30 Redeker, *Schleiermacher*, p. 132.

31 And leaving aside for the moment the fraught, but important, question as to how one guarantees that it is Christ with whom one has to do when an 'immediate existential experience' is being interpreted.

32 From here on in my discussion of Schleiermacher I shall usually speak of 'Christ', as this is Schleiermacher's usual reference to Jesus/Christ in *The Christian Faith*, even though he is at times quite clearly referring to Jesus of Nazareth. 'God-consciousness' – a central concept throughout *The Christian Faith* – is a basic human awareness, as a creature, of one's dependence upon the creator, and is also termed a 'feeling of absolute dependence' (*The Christian Faith*, p. 17). God-consciousness and self-consciousness cannot, in Schleiermacher's view, be separated, and understanding and articulating each is possible only through a particular ('positive') religious tradition – hence the exposition of Part I of *The Christian Faith* only being possible because of knowledge of Part II.

33 A crucial section is *The Christian Faith*, §92, though see also §94. Redeker argues for a qualitative uniqueness of the God-consciousness of Jesus and thus of the one possessing that consciousness (*Schleiermacher,*

archetypal (*urbildlich*) in so far as his God-consciousness is the empowering source for all ensuing possession of such God-consciousness.[34] Such consciousness of God was not part of human experience before Christ. After him, it is not possessed merely through copying his behaviour. For Christ to be an exemplar (*Vorbild*) would not be enough. Christ empowers.[35] For Christian believers, possession of God-consciousness is thus participation in the same consciousness of God enjoyed by Christ and results from living relationship with him. To this extent, within that living relationship, they are dependent upon Christ's archetypal consciousness of God.

Christ is, second, the Redeemer. Consciousness of God comes through participation in the community of the redeemed. This means that God-consciousness is not merely a private matter. It comes as an inevitable result of participation in a community of believers who know what it is to be forgiven and to forgive, and who are therefore already experiencing in part the blessedness (*Seligkeit*) which membership of the redeemed community brings with it. Schleiermacher explores the basis of Christ's redemptive work in terms of the 'threefold office' of Christ (as prophet, priest and king),[36] and within this exploration he includes his discussions of many topics that would traditionally have come under the heading of the 'work of Christ'.[37] In these discussions Schleiermacher presents Christ as our 'satisfying representative' (*genugtuender Stellvertreter*). By this he means that Christ reveals

---

pp. 134–6). Macquarrie (*Jesus Christ*, pp. 203, 206–7) stresses more the extent to which Schleiermacher interprets the incarnation as a 'natural fact' (and entitles his chapter on Schleiermacher, somewhat misleadingly, 'Humanistic Christology'), though highlights the anomaly of the special implanting of God-consciousness, a point I shall consider further below.

34 *The Christian Faith*, §93.

35 *The Christian Faith*, §100.

36 *The Christian Faith*, §§102–5.

37 Including, therefore, Christ's teaching, miracles and the meaning of atonement.

what it is possible for a human being to be.[38] It is through Christ's suffering and death that we are enabled to see the awfulness of (our own) human sinfulness. We become aware through Christ's intense identification with human sinfulness why his death functions redemptively and why it has been interpreted by means of theories of vicarious satisfaction. The suffering of Christ, Schleiermacher suggests, *is* vicarious in so far as Christ identifies with those who are not even aware of their own sin. Further, 'Christ certainly made *satisfaction* for us by becoming, through his total action, not only the beginning of redemption in time, but also the eternally inexhaustible source, adequate for every further development, of a spiritual and blessed life.'[39] But participation in the redemptive activity of God in Christ does not remove from us 'the necessity of pursuing this spiritual life by our own endeavour in fellowship with him'.[40] In this sense, the 'satisfaction' by which Christ has begun and resources the redeemed life is *not* vicarious. The focus for Schleiermacher is, however, clearly upon the God-consciousness that is brought to the believer through Christ's activity: the Redeemer's assumption of believers into the power of his God-consciousness *is* his redemptive activity.[41]

This redemptive activity of Christ is, however, thirdly, community-creating. Only in this way is Christ, acting on God's behalf, also in the business of 'person-forming'.[42] Individuals are shaped in their individuality not independently of others, but in interdependence upon others. Human beings therefore can only aspire to being fully human through experiencing such interdependence 'in Christ', in living fellowship with Christ. The absolute dependence upon God is reflected in interdependence upon other believers. There is thus a direct link between the empowering

---

38 *The Christian Faith*, p. 461.
39 *The Christian Faith*, p. 461.
40 *The Christian Faith*, p. 461.
41 *The Christian Faith*, p. 425.
42 The term is Redeker's (*Schleiermacher*, p. 137).

of God-consciousness, redemptive activity and community-formation. Christ brings all of these dimensions into being for the believer, and theology (and Christology specifically) begins only because people have communal and individual experience of all three facets of Christ's being and activity (person and work).

In Christian understanding, community-creation entails 'church'. But it was much less clear for Schleiermacher than it would later prove for Dietrich Bonhoeffer that the concrete bodies of believers, to which all Christians must inevitably belong, can be said to 'be' Christ.[43] Certainly Schleiermacher worked tirelessly himself in and for the institutional (Reformed and then United) church of his day. He clearly worked with a christologically and pneumatologically defined notion of the Church, which enabled him to cross over from invisible to visible definitions (and vice versa). However, while 'living fellowship with Christ' would always be communal, and while religion must always take a concrete form, Christ remains, for Schleiermacher, distinct from any particular human institution. We shall, though, need to press the question of the institutional form of 'being in Christ' in due course.

As Redeker rightly states: 'In Schleiermacher's Christology everything is concentrated on the present living relationship with Christ.'[44]

> The foundation and point of departure for his dogmatic investigations [in Halle] is the reality of the living community of Christians. The basis of this reality is found in Christ – not in the historical Jesus, but in the Christ whose image is efficacious in the community . . . simultaneously as 'corporate act' and as 'corporate possession'.[45]

Decades before the blossoming of the Quest of the Historical

---

43 E.g. through an equation of 'Christ' and 'Church' via the concept of the 'Body of Christ'. More will be said on this in *Christ in Practice*.

44 Redeker, *Schleiermacher*, p. 143.

45 Redeker, *Schleiermacher*, p. 84.

Jesus, then, and a century earlier than the Liberal Protestant dog-matician Ernst Troeltsch (1865–1923), Schleiermacher worked consciously with the theological traditions which flowed out of the Protestant Reformation yet was aware of the impact of critical study of the Bible and the Christian past upon theology. At the same time, he was mindful of the fact that theology must deal with Christianity as living religion. Out of respect for the living quality of Christianity, and without neglecting the need to point to the continuity between the past of Jesus and the presence and presentness of Christ, Schleiermacher focused upon the Christian sense of living in fellowship with Christ. His entire theology was based upon it, and the God-consciousness, redemptive activity and community-forming significance of the present, living Christ succinctly express Schleiermacher's understanding of the focal point of Christian spirituality and theology.

Schleiermacher's approach: four critical questions

God-consciousness and the isolation of the historical Jesus

How is Schleiermacher's approach to be assessed? A first critical question relates to the interplay between his exploration of the life of the earthly Jesus, as it takes shape within his Christology, and the emphasis he places both historically and theologically on the power of Jesus' God-consciousness.[46] Schleiermacher's Christology does not *depend* on his being able to locate and estab-lish 'beyond reasonable (historical) doubt' the type and degree of God-consciousness on the part of Jesus of Nazareth accord-ing to historical data which his study of the Gospels enables him to conclude. That Schleiermacher believes he can, in fact, draw

---

46 In many ways, Schleiermacher's work signals in advance what will prove to be a major feature of the 'Jesus of history/Christ of faith' debate a century and more later.

such conclusions (with reference largely to the Gospel of John) is simply a bonus to him. But he has not set up his theological method, and construed the relationship between historical and theological enquiry in Christology, in such a way that he must defend his theological claims point-for-point in a positivistic, historical fashion.[47] The way he has set up the interplay is nevertheless instructive for our enquiry.

Schleiermacher primarily explores the person and work of Christ in relation to the lived experience of Christ in the living fellowship with Christ enjoyed by members of a believing community of Christians.[48] Alongside this christological exploration, Schleiermacher remains keenly interested in what we may call the 'formation' of a Christian, in terms of the dynamic between a person's individuality[49] and their formation as a person through fellowship with God and other people. His attention to 'God-consciousness', then, within the process of a person's spiritual formation, interweaves with the development of his Christology. God-consciousness, as a person-forming factor in a Christian's life, is dependent upon the God-consciousness of Christ.

In exploring the God-consciousness of Jesus, then, historical enquiry, theological exploration and spirituality are brought together. The corporate dimension of the experience of God-consciousness is prominent in Schleiermacher's understanding of spiritual formation. However, when the relationship of history to theology is examined, the corporate emphasis largely disappears. Why should this be? Why should the God-consciousness, which

---

47 Unlike a later, critical sympathizer, Albrecht Ritschl, who felt the need to do so (even if Ritschl's own approach did not carry it through; on which, see C. Marsh, *Albrecht Ritschl and the Problem of the Historical Jesus*, San Francisco: Edwin Mellen Press, 1992, esp. pp. 53–5, 158–74).

48 An approach which leaves Schleiermacher open to the charge of turning Christology into pneumatology or, worse, of replacing the one believed in with the believer.

49 A concern especially, though by no means exclusively, in his *Soliloquies* (ET Chicago: Open Court, 1926, of German original *Monologen* of 1800).

Schleiermacher believes always to be fundamentally communal for Christ's followers, not have been equally communal for Jesus himself? In Schleiermacher's reading, Jesus' God-consciousness would appear to have been much more an individual affair, a Father and Son matter, emerging as a God-consciousness of such a kind, quality and power that it would prove sufficiently generative for all Christians thereafter. True, there are some traces in Schleiermacher's work of a recognition of the significance of Jesus' interaction with others.[50] But these do not seem to be constitutive of the God-consciousness which Jesus enjoyed. Others may be offering him interpretations of who he is, but Jesus does not really seem to need them. His task is self-expression on the basis of the special God-consciousness implanted in him. He may only gradually have discovered who he was, but even as a child he was a dominant partner in relationships. If there was reciprocity in his human relationships, the reciprocity was, in Schleiermacher's view, not equal.[51]

Nor could there be such an equality. Christ could not, for Schleiermacher, in any sense be dependent on others (God apart) for the discovery and content of his God-consciousness. And thereafter Christ, as God acting, could only ever be the giver, the imparter of God-consciousness to others (who would then discover God-consciouness in Christ, among a concrete body of other believers). Perhaps we must say that Christ, for Schleiermacher, really must have been a different kind of human being, despite all Schleiermacher's attempts to argue for the (relatively) normal development of Jesus.[52]

---

50 E.g. Schleiermacher, *Life of Jesus*, pp. 123–9 (Lecture 19). Reference could also be made to the sense that, in developing in a normal human way, Jesus was dependent on knowing his own people's tradition and history and finding his place within it (p. 104).

51 Schleiermacher, *Life of Jesus*, p. 129.

52 Accepting that Christ remained without sin, a theological judgement which Schleiermacher is happy to qualify to the extent that this does include his being free from intellectual error (see Schleiermacher, *Life of Jesus*, p. 108).

The end result is a view of the singularity of Jesus in terms not merely of his uniqueness or exclusive dignity but also of his solitariness – a conclusion that goes against the grain of much of Schleiermacher's understanding of spiritual formation. One may have expected from Schleiermacher's emphasis upon living fellowship with Christ that incarnation must mean interdependence.[53] One might have hoped to find such interdependence reflected in Schleiermacher's reading of the Gospels, and of the historical life of Jesus. But this would be to expect too much. Schleiermacher could scarcely have come to such a conclusion in his own time. Perhaps, now, we must.

Problems with the humanity of Jesus the Christ

A second critical question to be posed of Schleiermacher's Christology pertains to his talk of the 'implanting' of God-consciousness in Jesus.[54] In his attempt to articulate an understanding of Christ whose humanity is as close as possible to our own, Schleiermacher has to account for Christ's God-consciousness being of such a consistent degree and quality that it empowers our own. His conclusion is that Jesus received a 'special implanting' of God-consciousness, in a way that marks him out as distinctive from the rest of humanity. Macquarrie comments:

> What is this implanting? The expression is obviously a metaphor, but I think it is not a good metaphor. It pictures the God-consciousness as some distinct 'thing' that gets inserted into the person of soul. If this happened 'in the beginning' of Jesus' life, does this mean that we go back to the mythological idea that

---

53 Leaving aside the question whether incarnation pertains to Jesus/Christ alone or to the nature of God's presence in the world more broadly, and also the question whether incarnation and attention to 'living fellowship with Christ' are in practice identical.

54 I owe this critique to Macquarrie, *Jesus Christ*, pp. 207–8.

even in the womb Jesus was conscious of being the Son of God? Schleiermacher did not believe that . . . there is a logical defect in Schleiermacher's christology. He has promised to expound the incarnation as a natural fact, but has introduced a 'new implanting' of the God-consciousness which appears to be no less supernatural than a virgin birth.[55]

Macquarrie is surely right in his critique. Schleiermacher has not remained true to the basic intent of his Christology at this point. Though conscious of always walking a tightrope between Docetism and Ebionism, he errs here towards the former.

A challenge to any contemporary Christology is how to make sense of the humanity of Christ – so that Christ's solidarity with the rest of humanity is both plausible and salvific – without engagement with the divinity of Christ (and thus with God in and through the humanity of Christ) disappearing altogether.[56] For his part, Schleiermacher could not find a way for the generative God-consciousness, which he deemed Christ to possess, to emerge as a 'natural fact'. Had he realized, and corrected, the extent to which his position so depended upon the singularity and solitude of Jesus, he may have found a way forward.

By respecting the way in which Schleiermacher emphasizes the corporate reception of Christ, however, it is possible to see how this weakness in his Christology can be addressed. In the same way that Christ is now experienced corporately so also the source of the generative God-consciousness to be found in Jesus should be identified in a communal context. As noted above, the

---

55 Macquarrie, *Jesus Christ*, pp. 207–8. The criticism is echoed in H. Schwarz, *Christology*, Grand Rapids and Cambridge: Eerdmans 1998, p. 220.

56 This remains Macquarrie's own interest, in seeking to develop, at the end of the twentieth century, a 'Christology from below', while retaining a clear sense that such a Christology cannot be merely functional; it must be a form of ontological Christology. Again, I agree. But more of a 'relational ontology' seems necessary than Macquarrie's view implies.

God-consciousness enjoyed by Jesus must be recognized to have emerged and developed not only individually but also as a result of Jesus' interactions with others. Schleiermacher's appeal to a special implanting of God-consciousness in Jesus is thus a further example of Schleiermacher's continuing tendency to isolate Jesus. He has not, in other words, carried back his insights about the contemporary experience of Christ into his interpretation of Jesus as the Christ. Schleiermacher's appeal to a special implanting of God-consciousness in Jesus overlooks what happens *between* people. By a more consistent shift of focus to a corporate Christology than Schleiermacher has achieved, it is possible to note how humanity can be transformed by the presence and action of God in the 'in-between' spaces.[57] To be human means to be in relationship, and to stand in relation to an 'other'. The humanity of Jesus the Christ is impaired not merely, then, by talk of a special implanting of God-consciousness, but by the fact that Schleiermacher has isolated Jesus and been unable to see his especially powerful, generative God-consciousness emerging in appropriately human ways.

Schleiermacher's appeal to a special implanting of God-consciousness thus undoubtedly impairs his Christology's attempt to acknowledge the full humanity of Jesus the Redeemer. Macquarrie is right. Whether it is then wise to seek to reappropriate the Chalcedonian definition of the person of Jesus Christ through identifying and supporting its 'governing intention', as Macquarrie tries to do, is another matter.[58] While it may be true that any orthodox Christology will need to show that it upholds Chalcedon's 'governing intention', the insight which emerges

---

57 Important links are forged here, of course, with the discussion about margins in Ch. 1. What happens at the margins, between people and between groups, proves revelatory. God's Otherness can be encountered as 'Other' when human beings encounter each other as 'other' and resolve neither to be in conflict nor to overlook difference.

58 Macquarrie, *Jesus Christ*, pp. 383–6.

here is that full support for the humanity of Christ may be better obtained through respect for Jesus the Christ's interaction with others than through scrutiny of his psychological make-up.

Is sin actually dealt with?

There is, however, a third aspect of Schleiermacher's Christology to be critically examined, for he is often charged with having a weak doctrine of sin.[59] There is not space for a full discussion of his understanding of sin or his conclusions concerning the doctrine of atonement. Suffice it to say that he rejects the substitutionary atonement theory of Jesus' death, according to which Jesus' death was somehow *required* by God for the forgiveness of human sin. At the same time, he wrestles with the range of traditions that sought to explicate the meaning of Jesus' death, convinced that some value will be found within them. He is fully aware that he must offer some account and interpretation of the suffering and death of Jesus within a contemporary Christology constructed to serve Christian living.

Schleiermacher identifies a vicarious dimension in the activity of Jesus Christ. This occurs, however, in his suffering and not through any theory of vicarious satisfaction which may be attached to Jesus' death. As noted earlier, Schleiermacher accepts that in his suffering Jesus Christ identified even with those not conscious of their sin. This experience of suffering beyond what he in any sense 'deserved' ('one in whom there is no moral evil ought not to suffer'[60]) is vicarious in a 'general sense'. The generous self-giving of God is thus strikingly apparent when, in the person of Jesus Christ, God continues to be revealed as the one available to redeem and to reconcile in Christ even those who are not yet conscious of their sin. Schleiermacher is clear that we could not

---

59 Even Redeker admits that this charge may carry weight (*Schleiermacher*, p. 130).

60 *The Christian Faith*, p. 461.

have redeemed ourselves, could not have created the redeemed community, and could not have discovered God-consciousness by our own efforts. And it is through participation in Christ that the God-consciousness which accompanies redemption and the blessedness of reconciliation are enjoyed.

Less clear is how the sin, with which theories of vicarious atonement seem to deal, is handled in Schleiermacher's theology. What Christ achieves is 'sympathy with misery'.[61] Identification, not satisfaction, is the form of Christ's sin-bearing. But what happens to Christ's redeeming function? Is participation in God-consciousness, even when empowered by Christ, enough to save? Schleiermacher's critics think not: a weak doctrine of sin and a weak doctrine of redemption go together.[62]

Schleiermacher's stress upon 'fellowship' does give him some ground on which to respond to his critics, however. Redemption occurs via incorporation into Christ. God-consciousness is not the sole component of redemption, for redemption results in the blessedness of fellowship, a 'reconciling activity'.[63] Paragraph 101 of *The Christian Faith* is a powerful exposition of the present enjoyment of the blessedness of fellowship: pain and suffering remain part of human experience, but the consequences of sin are overcome for the person who is 'in Christ'. Participation in 'vital fellowship with Christ' negates the impact of one's inevitable, continuing participation in the corporate life of sin.

Schleiermacher's theology is admittedly undeveloped in its clarification of the institutional contexts within which such blessed fellowship is enjoyed. It is too simple to equate such fellowship with 'church' alone, and Schleiermacher would not want to, however important he recognizes the Church to be. Christocentrism at its best, as Schleiermacher himself recognizes,

---

61 *The Christian Faith*, p. 436.
62 Barth, *The Theology of Schleiermacher*, pp. 195–7.
63 *The Christian Faith*, §101.

de-centres 'church'. Schleiermacher's theoretical and practical concern for home, society, education and nation demonstrates that he was not obsessed by 'church' as a social reality. But how he would have seen the reconciling activity of Christ actually taking effect in these and other social and political contexts is not wholly clear.[64] Despite his awareness of a the range of kinds of experience of Christ, of the existence of many religions and of the need for interaction between those of faith and those without faith, he operated in a context where Christianity remained culturally dominant. He did not, therefore, have to face the full potential radicalism of Christocentrism in terms of how the quest to participate in the new humanity in Christ would take institutional shape. The reception and development of his thinking in contemporary theology invites reflection on how 'living fellowship with Christ' is to be understood in a more complex culture than Schleiermacher experienced.

Schleiermacher's weakness with regard to the doctrine of sin is not, then, to do with whether or not he adopts an adequate theory of atonement. His weakness is, rather, that he leaves ill-explored both the social contexts in which, and the means by which, 'the disappearing corporate life of sinfulness' is brought about by the presence of 'Christ in us'.[65] Exploration of the conquering of sin could benefit from being more closely allied to the corporate understanding of sin and redemption present in Schleiermacher's thought. Given that it is within concrete settings

---

64 On Schleiermacher's contributions to politics, see e.g. Redeker, *Schleiermacher*, pp. 87–100; Nowak, *Schleiermacher*, Part 3, esp. chs. 1, 5 and 13; and now, comprehensively, M. Wolfes, *Öffentlichkeit und Bürgergesellschaft Friedrich Schleiermachers Politische Wirksamkeit*, Berlin: De Gruyter, 2004. See also the significant study by P. E. Guenther-Gleason, *On Schleiermacher and Gender Politics*, Harrisburg: TPI, 1997, the conclusions of which are highly pertinent for where I shall end up at the end of *Christ in Practice*.

65 *The Christian Faith*, pp. 437–8; cf. A. Ritschl, *A Critical History of the Doctrine of Justification and Reconciliation*, Edinburgh: T. & T. Clark, 1872, §64.

of human relationships that the costly complexity of sin and redemption have to be worked out, Schleiermacher's attention to the corporate nature of redemption, and the direct link with his Christology, merit further scrutiny.[66] Correction of the residual individualism in his Christology would help: that is, his under-standing of Jesus the Christ is simply not relational enough, either in terms of his understanding of Jesus as Redeemer, or in terms of the reception of redemption within the living fellowship of Christ. If 'Christ in us' is not merely the relation of teacher to pupil, and Christ is not simply a model to be imitated,[67] then how Christ 'is' in 'us' deserves closer articulation, with respect both to the indi-vidual and to the communal forms in which Christ's person takes shape.[68]

The form of Christ

Finally, Schleiermacher can be asked: what form, then, does the present Christ take? If Christ is to be understood in such a close relationship to the believing community, is Christ to be *identified with* that community? Or is Christ somehow independent of it? But, if so, what exactly *is* Christ? For readers already attuned to forms of christological enquiry informed by the probings of Bonhoeffer, such questions will be familiar. The questions of

---

66 By which I mean: how do, e.g., sin, relationship and lack of relationship, and redemption/salvation take shape in, e.g., family, church, friendships, work-teams, without simply being understood as 'applied ethics' in such contexts? I shall take up this question in *Christ in Practice*.

67 *The Christian Faith*, p. 438.

68 This third discussion point does, of course, overlap with the question of Schleiermacher's pneumatology, given that 'in the public teaching of the Church regeneration is usually ascribed to the Divine Spirit' (*The Christian Faith*, p. 490). Schleiermacher is reluctant to accept this oversimplified doctrinal division, choosing to explore regeneration in christological terms. However, this inevitably leaves him open to the standard charge against so many Western Protestants, of having a weak pneumatology.

the form of Christ, and whether Christ, for Schleiermacher, may be said to be 'Christ existing as community' are so close to the nature and structure of Bonhoeffer's approach that we must be careful not to distort and mishear Schleiermacher's own contribution. Bonhoeffer rules out the question of *what* Christ is as inappropriate, for it would miss the personal dimension to the key question of Christology (which can alone be *who* is Christ?). But to pose the 'what?' question of Schleiermacher reminds us that later debates come to mind in the process of critically receiving Schleiermacher's theology. Does the corporate emphasis upon Christ in Schleiermacher's thought lead to the identification of 'church' and 'Christ'?

As suggested earlier, at first this seems unlikely, for Christ clearly comes to the believer *in* and *through* 'church' for Schleiermacher. The Redeemer is not collapsed into the redemptive community, however crucial the community proves for the Redeemer to be identified. The question of 'what' the Redeemer then achieves, however, discloses something of a gap in Schleiermacher's thought. A number of answers seem possible. The Redeemer is (or was) certainly a past historical figure. Schleiermacher's keenness to stress the continuity between the Jesus of history and the present Christ is confirmed through his lectures on the life of Jesus. But the physical body of Jesus of Nazareth is, of course, no more. The emphasis therefore upon the 'presentness' and presence (and upon the risen body) of Christ switches attention to a spiritual, incorporeal reality.[69] Whatever Schleiermacher's conclusion about the relationship between Christ and the Spirit, his stress upon the

---

69 At this point, a full discussion would be needed to establish whether Schleiermacher sees any effective difference between Christ and the Holy Spirit, or whether the Spirit is no more than the continued impact of Christ in the present (be that in church or in the Kingdom of God). *The Christian Faith*, §§108, 121–2 are especially important here. In my view, a simple identification is not made, though Schleiermacher is simply Pauline in the extent to which he reveals how thorny an issue this is for any Christian theologian.

historicity of forms of the believing community suggests a very concrete answer to the question of what Christ is today. Christ as the Church would seem Schleiermacher's closest possible answer to the question.

At the same time, the defintion of 'church', in typical Protestant fashion, as the truly regenerate, prevents any lazy identification of the institutional church as the sole locus of God's redeeming activity. Nevertheless Christ 'is' present in a concrete body, even if not identified with that body (i.e. a body of believers). If Schleiermacher has not quite dotted and crossed all his letters in spelling this out, there is nevertheless sufficient in his work to suggest that, whatever the fundamental differences between them, Schleiermacher is an early precursor of Bonhoeffer in the degree to which 'Christ' and 'community' are brought into the closest proximity. Taken alongside an insight reached in the previous section, however – that Schleiermacher leaves undeveloped the institutional contexts in which 'blessed fellowship' is enjoyed – it becomes evident that the corporate forms of Christ in the world today continue to need clearer articulation.

Schleiermacher's Christocentrism reconsidered

Where are we left with regard to Schleiermacher's understanding of Christocentrism? What are we to make of the centrality of his experiential and theological exploration of 'living fellowship with Christ'? I noted at the start of this chapter the appropriateness of beginning my doctrinal conversations with modern theologians with a dialogue with Schleiermacher. We can now see that, in setting the agenda for much of the theology of the last 200 years, he presented a clear challenge. Christian theology's task is to interpret the relationship between *the corporate reception of Christ* on the part of contemporary believers and *the being and presence of Christ* as the being and presence of God both in the person of Jesus and in believers who follow him, as individuals and as a community.

Later theological discussion discloses the complexity of that challenge. Schleiermacher was quite clear that an interpreter of Christ needs experiential involvement in order to offer an accurate interpretation. He was equally clear that safeguards had to be built into the process of interpretation, lest the interpretation offered be not of Christ but merely of human subjectivity. Corporateness and the mutual critique which occurs within the diversity of the forms and contexts of the reception of Christ provide at least some protection against wild enthusiasms. At the same time Schleiermacher was very clear that it is *Christ* that is being interpreted. A real 'otherness' of Christ is respected in Schleiermacher's Christology, even if the being and presence of Christ are radically redefined in corporate terms.

The value of Schleiermacher's contribution for setting out the modern doctrinal framework of our enquiry into Christocentrism can be summed up as follows. First, despite addressing the historical Jesus/Christ of faith question and pressing for a firm, historically demonstrable link between Jesus of Nazareth and the Christ of Christian faith, his version of Christocentrism proposes that the starting point and focus of Christian thought and practice should be the present corporate experience of Christ among contemporary believers. Second, without downplaying the life and death of Jesus in his Christology, he steers us towards the living Christ. His reading of Christ is ultimately resurrection-driven through its emphasis upon the contemporary life of Christ. Third, the corporateness at the heart of his Christology implies a critique of individualism in theology, whether that be in the form of overemphasis on individual theologians or the experience of individual believers (a methodological individualism), or of individualism even in respect of Christ. This critique of individualism is admittedly undeveloped in Schleiermacher's thought. Furthermore, with the hindsight of the history of the

Quest of the Historical Jesus, we can see how easily the positive and important insights which Schleiermacher's Christology and Christocentrism provide can be submerged within a quest for the solitary unhistorical Jesus. For Schleiermacher, Christocentrism must always mean the centrality of the Redeemer as evidenced in the existence of a redeemed people. This does leave him open to the charge of effecting a shift in theology towards anthropocentrism. The turn is not, however, towards individualism. He recognizes the importance of a redeemed people and wants to use and work from their experience. This corporateness in his Christology is why his approach remains fruitful. Neither his Christology nor his Christocentrism are, however, reducible to anthropology or ecclesiology, despite his recognition of the importance *for Christology* of recognizing what it means to be *in Christ*. Christ is not reducible to the sum of believers' experience of Christ, even while their capacity to speak of Christ at all is bound up with participation in Christ's presence.

In simplest, summary form, then, Schleiermacher's legacy to Christian thought and practice is his recognition of the importance of 'Christ-piety'. In developing his Christology, Schleiermacher took the risk of keeping his interpretation of Christ closely connected with the context, form and content of the reception of Christ by believers. The charge of anthropocentrism levelled against him could not, however, be further from the truth. To explore Christ-piety as Schleiermacher understands it entails wrestling directly with Schleiermacher's Christology. Christ-piety denotes the form in which redemption offered by God is received. This piety is communally based, being itself corporate, yet is also enjoyed experientially within the life of the individual believer. Christ-piety is thus always both personal/individual and communal. If either pole is missing, then either Christ is not taken to heart in the life of the believer, or Christ is in danger of being understood to be in the individual believer's control (and even made in their own image). The communal dimension of this

Christ-piety thus reminds the believer of the objectivity of God's action in Christ, as received beyond the individual but nevertheless within the concreteness of human experience.

Later theology has made much of Schleiermacher's method and approach but has perhaps underplayed the Christ-piety which lies at the heart of his thought.[70] It has been uncomfortable with the Romanticism and the Moravian roots of his theology, aspects not conducive to more exclusively rational receptions of his work. It may now be time to reassess these features of Schleiermacher's approach more extensively both for a better understanding of Schleiermacher himself and for more creative interaction with his work.

---

70 Except, perhaps, in the work of Schleiermacher scholars themselves. Gerrish's work is especially valuable here.

5

Walter Rauschenbusch: Christ-Society

Walter Rauschenbusch (1861–1918) is a logical conversation partner if you are seeking to engage with an account of Christian thought and practice which takes Christianity's social dimension seriously. As the primary exponent of the 'social gospel', Rauschenbusch offers much material for any investigation into Christology and Christocentrism which:

- takes the figure of Jesus seriously in both Christian thought *and* practice;
- is informed through biblical study and historical-critical enquiry into the figure of Jesus;
- endeavours to resist the tide of individualism in theology;
- respects the contemporary socio-political context within which theology is done.

Rauschenbusch was a Christocentric thinker and practitioner, for most of his theological work revolves around a detailed exploration of the figure of Jesus. He was a pastor first and a church historian second, in terms both of the chronology of his life's work and of the relative priorities given to each aspect of his vocation. However, a glance at his main published works reveals how crucial the investigation and exposition of Jesus/Christ were for him.[1] Rauschenbusch investigated not only the teaching of Jesus but also the 'life' of Jesus/Christ,[2] and sought to identify the 'mind' (or 'thought' or 'purpose') of Jesus/Christ[3] and to explore 'the personality' of Jesus/Christ.[4] He was especially keen to note how such explorations would lead to clarification of Jesus' 'social aims' or 'social principles'.[5] Our task, according to Rauschenbusch, is to locate 'the soul of Jesus' as 'the luminous centre of our moral and spiritual world'.[6]

The structure of his works reveals the form of his Christo-centrism. In his first main published work, *Christianity and the Social Crisis* (1907), Rauschenbusch reviews pre-Christian Jewish history and Christianity's own history in relation to the social awareness of the two religions. 'The Social Aims of Jesus' is the second of four historical chapters. It summarizes the fruits

---

1 In this chapter, and at many points later in this book, I shall often refer to 'Jesus/Christ'. In this chapter, this reflects the lack of precision as to whether Rauschenbusch is referring to Jesus, the historical figure from Nazareth, or Jesus Christ, the object of Christian faith. Later in the book, I use the form to indicate that Christology is quite clearly doing more than interpret Jesus the historical figure, but that 'Christ' is certainly interpretative, and that Christian Christology always refers to Jesus.

2 E.g. W. Rauschenbusch, *A Theology for the Social Gospel*, New York: Macmillan, 1917, p. 14; *The Righteousness of the Kingdom*, Nashville: Abingdon Press, 1968, pp. 129–30, 150.

3 E.g. W. Rauschenbusch, *Christianity and the Social Crisis*, Louisville: Westminster/John Knox Press, 1907 (reprinted 1991), pp. 340, 361, 362, 416; Rauschenbusch, *Theology*, pp. 217, 235, 273.

4 E.g. Rauschenbusch, *Christianity*, p. 179; *The Social Principles of Jesus*, New York: Grosset & Dunlap, 1916, pp. 43, 194; *Theology*, pp. 54, 151, 154, 162; *Righteousness*, pp. 122, 127–8, 131. On the importance of the concept of 'personality' not merely in Rauschenbusch but throughout twentieth-century American social thought, see now E. McCarraher, *Christian Critics: Religion and the Impasse in Modern American Social Thought*, Ithaca and London: Cornell University Press, 2000; also C. H. Evans, *The Kingdom Is Always But Coming: A Life of Walter Rauschenbusch*, Grand Rapids and Cambridge: Eerdmans, 2004, e.g. pp. 157, 293.

5 Rauschenbusch, *Christianity*, ch. II; *Social Principles, passim*.

6 Rauschenbusch, *Christianity*, p. 93.

of Rauschenbusch's historical-critical reading of the Bible, with the aid of a range of examples drawn from the scholarship available in his day. The clear, intended end of such enquiry is the identification of an authoritative, norm-creating interpretation of the figure of Jesus, in relation to which all ensuing forms of Christianity must then be adjudged.[7]

The form of this 1907 text anticipated that of Rauschenbusch's 1912 work, *Christianizing the Social Order*. A chapter of the later work entitled 'The Social Christianity of Jesus' is Rauschenbusch's answer to the question of where a faith might be found to overcome the churches' ecclesiastical and social conservatism and their reluctance to address the pressing social, political and economic issues of the day.[8] Again, an exploration and exposition of the figure of Jesus shape the ensuing enquiry.

A 1916 text, *The Social Principles of Jesus*, provides an example of Rauschenbusch as practical, Christian educator. Though not a scholarly work – it was written for practical use by the YMCA – it reveals admirably the way that Rauschenbusch's thinking works. In the first part the 'social convictions of Jesus' are explicitly stated to be 'axiomatic'. Rauschenbusch then invites the reader on a daily basis to work through some carefully selected passages from the Bible (mostly from the Gospels), offering reflections within a chosen theme on each text. The reader is encouraged to agree that the Gospels inevitably lead to a clear conclusion as to Jesus' philosophy and practice: serving others,[9] valuing every human person,[10] experiencing and fostering fellowship,[11] and standing

---

7 E.g. as in the use of 'the mind of Jesus Christ' as the criterion for Christian ethics (*Theology*, p. 217).

8 Rauschenbusch, *Theology*, p. 12; *Righteousness*, p. 117.

9 Including via healing (which itself has social consequences), Rauschenbusch, *Social Principles*, p. 3.

10 *Social Principles*, p. 17.

11 *Social Principles*, pp. 21–5.

alongside ordinary people.[12] In these and similar principles and practices, the tone for Christianity is set by Jesus.

According to *The Social Principles of Jesus*, the 'axiomatic social convictions of Jesus' can also be expressed as 'the social ideal of Jesus'. This latter forms the second part of a 1891 manuscript, published posthumously, the content of which is none other than an exploration of the Kingdom of God. The Kingdom of God has been, from the first, what made Christianity 'revolutionary'.[13] And though not strictly speaking a conceptual invention of Jesus, after Jesus it could not but be defined in relation to him.[14] The Kingdom of God thus proves to be a distinct emphasis in Rauschenbusch's thought, uniting key features of his interpretation of early Christianity.

Jesus/Christ can thus be for Rauschenbusch the 'initiatory power of the Kingdom of God'.[15] Expressing the relationship between Jesus/Christ and the Kingdom yet more starkly, Rauschenbusch declares:

> If the Kingdom of God was the guiding idea and chief end of Jesus – as we now know it was – we may be sure that every step in his life, including his death, was related to that aim and its realization, and when the idea of the Kingdom of God takes its due place in theology, the work of Christ will have to be interpreted afresh.[16]

---

12 *Social Principles*, pp. 34, 43; also Rauschenbusch, *Theology*, p. 84 and *Righteousness*, p. 120; on early Christian communities and ordinary people, see e.g. *Theology*, pp. 120, 159.

13 Rauschenbusch, *Righteousness*, pp. 79–116.

14 *Righteousness*, pp. 118–32.

15 *Righteousness*, p. 118; also Rauschenbusch, *Theology*, p. 54, 'He was not merely an initiator, but a consummator.'

16 Rauschenbusch, *Theology*, p. 144; cf. *Christianity*, pp. 54–5. The full significance of the words 'when the idea of the Kingdom of God takes its due place in theology, the work of Christ will have to be interpreted afresh' will need further consideration in due course.

Rauschenbusch's Christocentrism thus takes the form of the centrality of the Kingdom of God. The Kingdom of God is not to be reduced to a mere set of ideas deriving from, or relating to, Jesus. The concrete embodiment of the Kingdom of God is to be understood as integrally linked to him, though we must yet explore in precise terms what this means. Rauschenbusch requires his readers not to sidestep the challenge of this important social concept. If Jesus/Christ is central to Christianity, and if the social concept of the Kingdom of God was central to Jesus' whole existence, then Christianity is unreservedly a social religion. And to interpret it as anything less will be to misconstrue both its and Jesus' purpose.

Rauschenbusch's theological method

Rauschenbusch's theological method can be characterized as a *biblical theology*, which is constantly being redefined on the basis of *pastoral practice*, *pastoral solidarity* and undertaken with fullest sensitivity to *church history*.[17] It would be wrong to ascribe to Rauschenbusch a fully worked out, experiential methodology

---

17 In reaching judgements about Rauschenbusch's work, I have depended heavily upon the work of W. Hudson's introduction to *Walter Rauschenbusch: Selected Writings*, New York, Mahwah: Paulist Press, 1984, pp. 1–41; P. M. Minus, *Walter Rauschenbusch: American Reformer*, New York: Macmillan, 1988; R. T. Handy (ed.), *The Social Gospel in America 1870–1920*, New York: Oxford University Press, 1966; G. J. Dorrien, *Reconstructing the Common Good: Theology and the Social Order*, Maryknoll: Orbis, 1990, ch. 2; and M. Stackhouse 'The Continuing Importance of Walter Rauschenbusch' in Rauschenbusch, *Righteousness*, pp. 13–59; but on this point especially, D. A. Peitz, *Solidarity as Hermeneutic: A Revisionist Reading of the Theology of Walter Rauschenbusch*, New York: Peter Lang, 1992. The invaluable study by Evans, *The Kingdom*, appeared too late for me to take full account of, though I have sought to draw attention to where his discussions link with my own, and its contents cohere with my reading of Rauschenbusch. Indeed, this chapter responds to his appeal for Rauschenbsuch's *theology* to be taken more seriously.

for theology. Welcome though such a discovery might be for the purpose of demonstrating the relevance of his thought and practice today, it is unlikely to be historically accurate. He was clear in some aspects of his procedure, but less clear (and certainly less specific) in others, and he nowhere fully articulated in theoretical terms the method by which he worked. Given the theological climate of his time, the situation then of the Baptist movement (English- and German-speaking branches), and the institutional settings within which he worked, he was often required to fight on a number of fronts.[18] This complicates the task of gaining clarity about the logic of his procedure at all points.

The structure of the works already mentioned does indicate that Rauschenbusch perceived the task of Christian theology as largely comprising the exposition of biblical material, and this suggests the extent to which he construed theology in the form of *biblical theology*. To take *Christianity and the Social Crisis* as the clearest example: the chapter from that work already referred to ('The Social Aims of Jesus') is evidence for Rauschenbusch's version of Christocentrism. Rauschenbusch seeks a Christocentric reading of the Bible. The first three chapters find him handling the neces-sary materials: prophets, Gospels, Acts and the New Testament letters. These are the key texts for developing the theology Rauschenbusch deems necessary for the Church and society of his day. If it may be argued that the biblical exposition is biased, being controlled by a particular angle of reading, then so be it.[19] Rauschenbusch merely reveals by the manner of his exposition that he believes he must

---

18 On which see esp. Minus, *Rauschenbusch*, chs. 7–9.

19 This is an aspect which I do not think Rauschenbusch himself would dispute. He is, after all, wanting to offer, and promote, a social reading of the scriptures. In this he sounds very contemporary, even if he pre-dates the theoretical sophistication brought by awareness of the necessity (indeed, inevitability) of 'interested', perspectival readings of the Bible. Given the background from which he came, and the contexts within which he worked, Rauschenbusch would, however, doubtless also wish to claim that the Bible 'really is' about the things he highlights within, from and on the basis of it.

start with the Bible, engage directly with its contents, and be seen to build on its material as a foundation.

His theology is not, however, simply biblical exposition. He builds into his theology throughout a keen dialogue with the demands and questions that *pastoral practice* brings to his belief and thought. More precisely: though there are consistent emphases of belief and thought throughout his life, the new insights and challenges brought by life-experiences continually press upon the neatness and coherence of those beliefs and ideas. Furthermore, the insights and challenges are not secondhand. They derive from his own experience, especially (as all the textbooks that mention Rauschenbusch recognize) from his time as a pastor in central New York City.[20] The social reading of the Bible, the social recasting of the themes of Christian theology, the urgency of addressing the economic, social and political questions of the day and the critique of contemporary Christianity and church life are all interwoven into Rauschenbusch's theology from the 1890s onwards. They can all be related to his actual pastoral experience. The goal of all his endeavours, indeed, is practical. 'The social gospel is above all things practical. It needs religious ideas which will release energy for heroic opposition against organized evil and for the building of a righteous social life.'[21] A clearer statement of Rauschenbusch's lack of interest in an uninvolved theology would be hard to find.

A third dimension of Rauschenbusch's method takes him beyond the realm of those who simply 'link experience and practice'. Unlike many theologian-pastors in the history of Christian theology, Rauschenbusch is linking experience and practice in his theological reflection, on the basis of *pastoral solidarity* with people unlike himself, people in dire social and economic situations. His work is thus a testimony to the struggle of working

---

20 As pastor of the Second German Baptist Church in the city's West Side, where Rauschenbusch arrived in 1886 (Minus, *Rauschenbusch*, ch. 4; Evans, *The Kingdom*, ch. 3).

21 Rauschenbusch, *Theology*, p. 42.

through the implications of such solidarity. Peitz's work on Rauschenbusch, which notes this element of solidarity throughout Rauschenbusch's life and thought, is particularly important here.[22] 'Solidarity' is a concept often featuring in his writings.[23] It results from, and relates to, both Rauschenbusch's understanding of what it means to be human, and the actual discoveries he made as he was compelled, through his pastorate in New York, to rethink all that Christianity meant, and all the theology that he had been taught.

A fourth dimension of Rauschenbusch's method in theology relates to what he spent much of his later working life engaged in: the teaching of *church history*. Rauschenbusch's is not a 'historical theology' in the sense of revisiting particular thinkers from the Christian past or particular phases in the life of the Church in order to see what can be deduced from them for today. Nor is he concerned to present a comprehensive 'history of theology'. Rather, as he develops his socially aware biblical theology, he keeps the backdrop of Christianity's history in mind. He therefore draws on examples from Christian history in order to unfold particular theological points he wishes to make.[24] If the impression is given that Rauschenbusch quarries Christian history for illustrations to make a point, then he may not dispute this. He is, however, using church history in theology in order to be mindful of the strengths and weaknesses of the Christian past.

Two further aspects of Rauschenbusch's method cut across the four dimensions just examined. First, he is concerned throughout to keep alive a *dialogue with other disciplines*, beyond theology and

22 See e.g. Peitz, *Solidarity*, pp. 38–41, 53, 68, 138, though note also her comment: 'Rauschenbusch never systematically outlined his understanding of human solidarity' (p. 76).

23 E.g. Rauschenbusch, *Christianity*, pp. 84, 141; *Social Principles*, pp. 21, 24, 196; *Theology*, pp. 9, 27, 81, 94, 102, 108–9, 148, 174–5, 202, 230, 244.

24 See e.g. *Theology*, ch. IV; *Christianizing the Social Order*, New York: Macmillan, 1912, pp. 69–122.

history, with sociology, economics and psychology in particular.[25] Rauschenbusch could undoubtedly have drawn more from these disciplines than he actually did. Even so, the significance of his step towards an interdisciplinary approach to theological reasoning should not be downplayed. Second, note should be taken of the way in which – over time – the *Kingdom of God* became not just the substantive heart of Rauschenbusch's theology but also a methodological linchpin. If Rauschenbusch's Christocentrism can in large part be characterized in terms of the centrality of the Kingdom of God, then it is not surprising that the centrality of that doctrine should in turn influence the way in which he expounds and develops all features of his theology. In bringing the Kingdom of God to the forefront of Christian thought and practice, the social gospel is concerned with 'a progressive social incarnation of God'[26] and with 'the creation and progress of social redemption'.[27] This concern also influences 'the approach to the theological problems of the person and work of Christ'.[28] In a very striking passage, Rauschenbusch notes what such an emphasis will entail for the task of formulating an adequate concept of God:

> The Kingdom of God is the necessary background for the Christian idea of God. The social movement is one of the chief ways in which God is revealing that he lives and rules as a God that loves righteousness and hates iniquity. A theological God who has no interest in the conquest of justice and fraternity is not a Christian. It is not enough for theology to eliminate this or that autocratic trait. Its God must join the social movement.[29]

25 Rauschenbusch, *Christianity*, p. 150; *Social Principles*, pp. 23, 196; *Theology*, p. 5. This strategy relates also to his desire to see the Church as an institution collaborate with other organizations (*Social Principles*, p. 164).

26 Rauschenbusch, *Theology*, p. 148.

27 Rauschenbusch, *Theology*, p. 146.

28 Rauschenbusch, *Theology*, p. 146.

29 Rauschenbusch, *Theology*, p. 178.

Rauschenbusch's biblical theology, then, is undertaken on the basis of pastoral practice and solidarity, has a pre-eminently practical purpose and is worked out against a backcloth of the history of the Church. It draws on disciplines beyond theology and has the Kingdom of God as its methodological focal point.

Rauschenbusch's Christology

How does Rauschenbusch's understanding of Jesus/Christ fit into his method? The first, most straightforward way of grasping Rauschenbusch's Christology is to pay attention to the way he presents the historical figure of Jesus of Nazareth. Though at times he switches rather incautiously between 'Jesus' and 'Christ', it is clear that a great many such references are to the first-century Palestinian figure, whose 'life', 'teaching', 'mind', 'purpose' and 'personality' prove decisive for the development of Christianity as a religious movement capable of transforming human society.

Jesus was certainly a teacher. Given Rauschenbusch's claim that a 'church based absolutely on the teachings of Jesus would be the most revolutionary society on earth',[30] it is not surprising that he is keen to clarify the content of that teaching. But what did this 'young man from Nazareth' achieve? For Rauschenbusch, Jesus 'gave the final and satisfactory expression to many of the darkest truths of human life'.[31] Though continuing in the Jewish prophetic tradition,[32] he was a critic of some of the popular hopes of his day, developing Jewish nationalism into a universal hope.[33] He taught much about his own identity, calling himself Son of man and Son of God.[34] Above all, he taught about the Kingdom of

30 Rauschenbusch, *Righteousness*, p. 122.
31 Rauschenbusch, *Righteousness*, pp. 121–2.
32 Rauschenbusch, *Christianity*, pp. 64–5.
33 Rauschenbusch, *Christianity*, pp. 57, 61.
34 Rauschenbusch, *Righteousness*, pp. 122–3.

God, which constituted the very centre of his thinking, teaching and acting.[35] The Kingdom of God was 'the hope of social perfection'.[36] It is 'a collective conception, involving the whole social life of man. It is not a matter of saving human atoms, but of saving the social organism.'[37] It is, however, God who creates the Kingdom of God.[38] Even if an evolutionary dimension may be stressed by Rauschenbusch,[39] it is not 'man-made evolution' that brings the Kingdom about.[40]

In a striking, if incautious, early phrase, Rauschenbusch refers to the 'Christianity of Jesus'.[41] It is clear from the context that he means the Christianity that flowed from Jesus, and continues to exist under the inspiration of the Spirit of God as found in Jesus. However, it is also necessary to specify the ways in which Rauschenbusch qualifies and extends his understanding of Jesus beyond that of 'Jesus the teacher', lest his use of the word 'teacher' imply that Rauschenbusch was finally interested only in Jesus' moral usefulness. However much Rauschenbusch wanted to clarify Jesus' teaching, and to use it in relation to the pressing moral and socio-political questions of his day, he knew that more was needed.[42] He also knew that even an understanding of

---

35 Rauschenbusch, *Christianity*, pp. 54, 67, 340; *Theology*, p. 141.

36 Rauschenbusch, *Christianity*, p. 111.

37 Rauschenbusch, *Christianity*, p. 65.

38 Rauschenbusch, *Christianity*, p. 63.

39 Rauschenbusch, *Christianity*, p. 59; *Social Principles*, pp. 76, 88. It is also true to say that Rauschenbusch ultimately speaks in terms of 'revolution' more than evolution, despite his recognition of organic development (e.g. *Righteousness*, pp. 118, 122, 128–9, 146, 151, 176, 262; *Christianity*, pp. 81, 179; *Social Principles*, p. 185). It can, however, be argued that his references to 'revolution', because they are scaled down in his later work, do give way to the recognition of the Kingdom's organic, evolutionary coming.

40 Rauschenbusch, *Christianity*, p. 63.

41 Rauschenbusch, *Righteousness*, p. 144.

42 'We need a combination between the faith of Jesus in the need and the possibility of the kingdom of God, and the modern comprehension of the organic development of human society' (*Christianity*, p. 91).

Jesus which left him as a teacher of moral truths, presenting to the reader of the Gospels a neatly packaged ethical system, was misguided.

> The teaching of Jesus was always fragmentary. He spoke as the needs of his hearers prompted. There is none of the rounded symmetry of an elaborate system, going back to the beginnings and working everything out to the details . . . In systematizing the ethical principles of Jesus, we must not forget . . . that he presupposes the plain moral convictions of humanity.[43]

Not only was Jesus' teaching fragmentary, but also he plugged into existing ethical thought. We should not, then, look for any distinctiveness, or sense of uniqueness, of Jesus in his ethical teachings alone.

Jesus was more than an ethical teacher.[44] If he may function as an ethical model, then we must be aware that his life, and not just his teachings, proves instructive for his followers.[45] We must, says Rauschenbusch, go beyond Jesus' teachings to see how important his own religion is for him.

> No comprehension of Jesus is even approximately true which fails to understand that the heart of his heart was religion. No man is a follower of Jesus in the full sense who has not through him entered into the same life with God. But on the other hand no man shares his life with God whose religion does not flow out, naturally and without effort, into all relations of his life and reconstructs everything that it touches. Whoever uncouples the religious and the social life has not understood Jesus.[46]

---

43 Rauschenbusch, *Righteousness*, pp. 64–5.

44 Rauschenbusch, *Righteousness*, p. 63; *Christianity*, p. 49.

45 E.g. Rauschenbusch, *Righteousness*, pp. 237, 257, though the examples used here of Jesus siding 'with feminine feeling against masculine hard-headedness' (p. 257) will need to inform our reception of Rauschenbusch in due course!

46 Rauschenbusch, *Christianity*, p. 48.

Appreciating Jesus' grasp of the relationship between religion and life is thus crucial for understanding both Jesus himself and how religion is to work today. And within the task of understanding Jesus, we must observe the centrality of the relationship he enjoyed with God his Father.[47]

Jesus did more than teach the Kingdom: he embodied it.[48] He established a group of people to continue his work ('Jesus sought to duplicate himself in his disciples'[49]). Though Jesus/Christ can be said to have 'founded' the community which became the Church,[50] it is clear that the relationship between Jesus/Christ and the community that followed him (beginning with the group of disciples) is rather more complex than mere historical continuity. This is the case even though Rauschenbusch emphasizes historical progression. 'Christ was formed in them . . . They lived over again the life of Christ.'[51] Despite what may be felt to be the limitations of the framework within which he is working,[52] Rauschenbusch is also keen to work with an understanding of Jesus/Christ which respects the doctrine of the spirit (this being the spirit which was in Jesus, the spirit of Christ).[53] This understanding in turn relates directly to his social sense of Christianity, resulting from exploration of the community that derives its origin from Jesus and Jesus' attention to the Kingdom of God.[54]

---

47 Rauschenbusch, *Christianity,* p. 48; *Righteousness,* p. 123.

48 Rauschenbusch, *Righteousness,* p. 126: 'Jesus bore the Kingship of God within him' (p. 130). This is an early clue to the way Rauschenbusch wrestled with the tension between the Kingdom as an inner experience and as a social phenomenon.

49 Rauschenbusch, *Righteousness,* p. 149.

50 Rauschenbusch, *Righteousness,* p. 151.

51 Rauschenbusch, *Righteousness,* p. 150.

52 Historicality of religion, social realities of religion, impact of the Jesus of history, concreteness of Christian communities past and present.

53 E.g. Rauschenbusch, *Christianity*, pp. 142, 308–9, 348; *Social Principles*, p. 43; *Righteousness*, pp. 148, 176.

54 E.g. Rauschenbusch, *Christianity*, p. 287; *Righteousness*, pp. 85–6, 144–6, 155.

It is at this point that Rauschenbusch's handling of the 'personality of Jesus' is best explored. 'Personality' is clearly a key word for Rauschenbusch.[55] It is part of his own version of the results of the 'Quest of the Historical Jesus'. Rauschenbusch really does think he gets inside Jesus' mind to some degree.[56] But it is more than this. The 'personality' of Jesus is clearly, for Rauschenbusch, a major way in which the continuing impact of Jesus, beyond the life of the historical Jesus of Nazareth, can be grasped. There are occasions in Rauschenbusch's writings when we seem to be dealing with the historical effects of Jesus of Nazareth's life.[57] At the very least, then, his personality represented 'a new type in humanity'.[58] But, beyond this, Rauschenbusch evidently uses the concept of personality as nearly a synonym for the post-resurrection spirit of Jesus/Christ.[59] Thus, while for much of his work Rauschenbusch seems to be focusing exclusively upon Jesus of Nazareth, it is clear that he is nevertheless wrestling with the continuing impact of Jesus/Christ in more than the simple terms of historical cause and effect.

---

55 Note the continual emphasis upon the importance of this concept in W. P. Weaver's examination of studies of the historical Jesus from 1900 to 1950 (*The Historical Jesus in the Twentieth Century: 1900–1950*, Harrisburg: TPI, 1999). See also secondary literature cited above, n. 4.

56 See esp. Rauschenbusch, *Theology*, pp. 151–5.

57 Rauschenbusch, *Social Principles*, p. 194; *Righteousness*, p. 127.

58 Rauschenbusch, *Theology*, p. 151.

59 Rauschenbusch, *Righteousness*, pp. 128–9 implies more than mere historical effects. But see esp. *Christianity*, p. 179 and *Theology*, p. 100, in relation to *Christianity*, pp. 308–9, 348–9, *Social Principles*, p. 139 and *Righteousness*, p. 146 (and p. 148, where Rauschenbusch notes: 'the idea of the glorified Christ and that of the Holy Spirit were for all practical purposes nearly identical to the early Christians'). In *Social Principles*, p. 43, Rauschenbusch appears to use both personality and spirit to mean the same thing. In *Righteousness*, p. 176, there appears to be clearer demarcation ('The historical Christ, the invisible Spirit, the visible church – these are the forces of God in human history. And they are revolutionary forces.'). Perhaps this merely indicates that in the 1890s the consistency of Rauschenbusch's thought needed further polishing.

Whatever the terms of this extension of the personality of Jesus into ensuing history, it is clear that for Rauschenbusch the greatness of Jesus' religious personality should be stressed. His superiority as a religious figure is regularly mentioned.[60] As a result, he is the founder of the highest religion,[61] which in turn means that Christianity is the highest religion.[62]

Jesus/Christ is as central to the Church's grasp of the Kingdom of God[63] as the Kingdom of God is central to the whole mission (teaching, activity and being) of the historical figure, Jesus of Nazareth. But the task of following the figure of Jesus, though it should consume the lifestyles of his followers, is not reducible either to following Jesus' teachings or to copying his ethical example. Following is more about allowing one's personality to be shaped by the figure of Jesus/Christ and being part of the social movement that he began. And being within the movement entails being continually inspired by Jesus/Christ, not merely through a backward glance at the history of Jesus of Nazareth but through some sense of the ongoing presence of that personality within the resulting community of which one is a member.

Jesus/Christ in Rauschenbusch's theology: a critique

Exploring how Rauschenbusch uses the historical figure of Jesus of Nazareth in his theology is the most straightforward way of grasping his Christology. There is no doubt that more comes into play than mere exposition of 'the life of Jesus' in a historical-critical sense. Though Rauschenbusch intends to locate an interpretation

---

60 Rauschenbusch, *Christianity*, pp. 59, 139, 'the purest religious spirit known to us'; *Theology*, pp. 14, 154, 'a perfect religious personality'.

61 Rauschenbusch, *Social Principles*, p. 139.

62 Rauschenbusch, *Righteousness*, p. 127, though other passages imply this same point (e.g. *Christianity*, p. 115).

63 Rauschenbusch, *Theology*, p. 141.

of a 'historical Jesus' which can then critique and, as necessary, subvert many 'orthodox' readings of Jesus/Christ, the 'Jesus' with which he works includes some sense of *continued presence*, beyond the fact of continuing historical influence. Despite all his radicalism, then, there is in Rauschenbusch's work a basic orthodoxy: he works with an orthodox understanding of Spirit and Church. Rauschenbusch thus respected the demands of working within the Christian doctrinal tradition (broadly understood) and the realities of pastoral practice (in and outside the identifiable Church). That said, his socio-political commitments required him radically to rethink the whole of theology. As a result of this, his Christology delivers fruitful insights for the task of developing a contemporary theology.

Rauschenbusch clearly expected too much of the results of a historical-critical approach to the canonical Gospels, and is thus open to the charge of a form of 'Jesusology'.[64] But because of his social emphasis, he adds a new dimension to the way in which the historically discovered Jesus is received and used by theologians within Christian thought and practice. I shall now state strengths and weaknesses of his approach, before going on to a more focused critique of four particular aspects of his use of the figure of Jesus.

Rauschenbusch was in many ways simply locating himself within an identifiable tradition of historical-critical research. Since Reimarus (1694–1768), theologians who sought also to be historians had been reading the Gospels critically in search of 'the real, historical Jesus'. The discovered figure could then be used to confirm, oppose or adjust an orthodox Christology, depending on the outlook and intention of the theologian concerned. It would be tempting to locate Rauschenbusch merely within the final phase of nineteenth-century attempts to construct such a Jesus, so positioning his interpretation of Jesus among the

---

64 See above, Ch. 3, pp. 44–7.

'liberal lives'.[65] True though it is, to some degree, that Rauschenbsuch fits into that tradition, it is also much too simple a view.
Rauschenbusch was certainly keen to ensure that his Christology
took the Jesus of history seriously. His was, for sure, a 'Christology from below', in that it did not begin from the statements of
Christian orthodoxy about the two natures of Jesus/Christ but
pressed the question of continuity between Jesus of Nazareth and
the Jesus/Christ of Christian theology. However, he also contributed directly to the rediscovery of the theme of the Kingdom of
God, which had begun in philosophy with Kant, reached theology
in Schleiermacher, took a fresh turn with Ritschl, and then was
redirected by Weiss and Schweitzer.[66]

Rauschenbusch's own version of the Kingdom of God in the
teaching (and actions) of Jesus can be seen to be swallowed up in
the turn towards eschatology which consumed the liberal lives as
a whole. Nevertheless, that the rehabilitation of Ritschl's approach
is possible in a way which benefits the reception of Rauschenbusch's work is confirmed by Bruce Chilton's telling, and surely
correct, comment:

> We need to bear in mind that the kingdom, not the messiah, was
> the burden of Jesus' preaching and (first of all) that of disciples.
> Radical immanence, side by side with radical transcendence,
> appears to be basic to the kingdom of God, and not a subsidiary
> development of Jesus' messianic self-consciousness (whatever
> that may have been). The eschatological consensus requires
> further qualification in order to do justice to this observation
> . . . time will tell whether a fresh consensus will emerge. If it
> does, that would be the culmination of the movement Ritschl

---

65 Ch. 14 of Schweitzer's *The Quest of the Historical Jesus* (London:
SCM Press, 2000 [1906] is entitled 'The "Liberal" Lives of Jesus' and traces
developments in historical Jesus research from 1864 to 1888.

66 See e.g. chs. 6 and 7 (by Morgan and Chapman) in R. S. Barbour (ed.),
The Kingdom of God and Human Society, Edinburgh: T. & T. Clark, 1993, and
the introduction to B. D. Chilton (ed.), *The Kingdom of God*, London: SPCK/
Philadelphia: Fortress Press, 1984.

began: we will be better placed to perceive the vision of Jesus in the terms in which he framed it, rather than in those into which subsequent interpreters have sought to transfer it.[67]

Schweitzer *et al.* do not, in other words, have the last word on Jesus' understanding of the Kingdom of God.

Rauschenbusch was not an original contributor to the biblical-historical task of clarifying the meaning of the Kingdom of God. However, his appropriation of the work undertaken by late nineteenth-century historical-critics does reveal the potential of that work for understanding both Jesus and his impact upon ensuing Christian theology. Rauschenbusch's strengths are that he recognized Jesus' message as a social message and that he wrestled with the social implications of that message beyond the historical life of Jesus of Nazareth. These strengths affect his reading of the Kingdom. They also invite interpreters today to look more closely at how Rauschenbusch wove a historical-critical reading of Jesus and the Kingdom into an avowedly social theology. Rauschenbusch's own form of a 'Christology from below' is not, then, reducible to a reference back to a Jesus from the past. Christology is a social discipline in three senses. It must recognize the social context of Jesus' life and work. It must develop a social *content* in so far as it must expound the social form of living which Jesus sought to embody and proclaim (the Kingdom of God). And it must be worked out in concrete, social contexts in which the life and work of Jesus is re-envisioned and re-embodied in the present. Rauschenbusch presses interpreters of Jesus Christ, then, to develop a range of present social contexts for the active reception of Jesus' social message.

Such a procedure provides the basis for a critique of all forms

---

67 Chilton, *Kingdom of God*, p. 26. '[T]he movement Ritschl began' acknowledges that, however much his reading might have been supplanted by that of J. Weiss, Schweitzer *et al.*, it had been Ritschl who directed discussion of the meaning of the Kingdom of God within Christian theology towards close study of Jesus and the Gospels.

of religious individualism. In indicating that Jesus' social message needs to be received in and by a group and needs to be focused on the well-being and flourishing of more than the group itself, Rauschenbusch is highlighting the importance of such critique.[68] To 'understand' the Kingdom of God as preached and enacted by Jesus it is necessary to receive it socially, within a group of people who are working towards it. And given its meaning, the Kingdom of God cannot merely inspire the group that receives it, or only groups that are similar. The universalizing of the Jewish national hope, which Rauschenbusch perceived in the mutation of Judaism brought about by Jesus of Nazareth, entails working for the good of all.[69]

Second, it is clear that Rauschenbusch's campaign against individualistic theology, and against individualistic versions of Christian faith and practice, relates directly both to what he derives from Jesus of Nazareth and to what he deems churches of his day need to hear. This is the case despite the rare occasions when Rauschenbusch himself speaks of the Kingdom as an 'inner' phenomenon, or when he appears to highlight the priority of the 'inward' aspects of religion.[70] He appropriates the social message of Jesus without losing sight of Jesus' religiosity. He respects the importance of an 'inner life' while highlighting the interpersonal aspects of the Kingdom of God and resulting religious and ethical practice.

There is a positive platform on which to build here. But there are four clear areas of weakness: Rauschenbusch's handling of

---

68 The significance of an emphasis upon practice is that the consequences of one's beliefs and opinions must become visible. There is, of course, a clear parallel here with liberation theologians' emphasis upon orthopraxis, not orthodoxy.

69 At which point the question would inevitably arise as to which available political options should be followed to enable this to happen. Rauschenbusch himself favoured socialism, and was deeply critical of the capitalism then known to him.

70 Rauschenbusch, *Righteousness*, pp. 85–6, though *Theology*, p. 166.

Judaism; his use of the term 'personality'; his focus upon Jesus as a religious individual; and his sense of Jesus' and Christianity's superiority over other religious leaders or founders and religious traditions.

Jesus and Judaism

As readers of Rauschenbusch now, we have the benefit of the hindsight gained from a century's further study of the Gospels. It is therefore somewhat unfair to draw critical attention to Rauschenbusch's rather narrow and stilted approach to the Judaism of Jesus' day; he was, after all, merely reflecting what New Testament scholars and historians were telling him. Thus, statements which seem to suggest a simple contrast between Jesus and Judaism, noting how Jesus modifies and universalizes 'Judaism's extreme nationalism',[71] are unsurprising. Nevertheless, they are problematic if we are seeking to draw something positive for today from Rauschenbusch's insights. For what if the social construal of the Kingdom with which Rauschenbusch works is so bound up with a negative reading of Judaism that his reading of either Church or Kingdom as 'new' or 'real' Israel presupposes a continuing, wholesale devaluing of Judaism?[72] Rauschenbusch's approach certainly does not leave much room for respect for Judaism as a living religion. The Hebrew prophets are essential for understanding Jesus; the Jewish national hope is a vital foil for Jesus to demonstrate what a truly universalistic hope entails; the biblical figures and scriptures from Judaism's past are necessary for Christianity to take up and rework. But it is only as a past that Judaism is essential.

Having said this, much of what Rauschenbusch derives from Judaism is constitutive for his reading of Jesus and Christianity.

---

71 Rauschenbusch, *Righteousness*, p. 83.

72 The most negative passage I have located is *Christianity*, p. 113. When being most positive about the Jewish tradition, Rauschenbusch is referring to 'Jewish Christian' communities (*Christianity*, pp. 100–1).

Even if he downplays the universalizing tendencies in Judaism itself, he has nevertheless discovered them in their Christianized form. Furthermore, his reading of Jesus could not have occurred without the prophetic tradition. However crucial Jesus himself is for the social understanding of the Kingdom, that understanding is more than merely prepared for by the insights supplied by classical Hebrew prophecy. If Rauschenbusch fails to engage in critical interaction with Judaism as a living religion in his own time in a Jewish and Christian quest for an adequate understanding of 'Israel', his conclusions do not prevent his work being received in the light of such a conversation. He is still worth reading even after the work of the likes of Geza Vermes and E. P. Sanders have encouraged us radically to rethink Jesus' relationship to Judaism.

The concept of personality

What, though, is to be made of Rauschenbusch's understanding of 'personality'? It is certainly a multi-functional term. At times it means what 'made Jesus tick', or Jesus' 'character'. At other times it becomes greater in scope. Critical examination of Rauschenbusch's meaning must, however, focus less on whether Jesus' 'personality' is discoverable in any historical sense and more on the question of how the term signifies evident continuity between the 'personality of Jesus' (the Jesus of history) and his continuing effectiveness among his followers.

To begin with, in Rauschenbusch's work the continuing significance of Jesus seems to signify no more than a historical reference back to the Jesus of the past. It means the lingering impact of the past figure. Thus, in being critical of the way that orthodox Christology had usually handled the figure of Jesus, Rauschenbusch remarks: 'Even the personality of Jesus, which is the unceasing source of revolutionary moral power in Christianity, was almost completely obscured by the dogmatic Christ of the Church.'[73]

---

73 Rauschenbusch, *Christianity*, p. 179.

The personality of Jesus thus continues to inspire (as 'the unceasing source'). But it does so through being remembered.[74] Failure to recollect has been to Christianity's cost.[75] The power of Jesus Christ may lie in his personality, not in his words or teachings alone.[76] There is, then, for Rauschenbusch clearly a sense in which the power of Jesus' personality depends upon recollection of his words and deeds.

Other passages are, however, more ambiguous. In speaking of 'religious personality' in a contemporary form, Rauschenbusch states: 'The more Jesus Christ becomes dominant in us, the more does the light of God shine steadily in us, and create a religious personality which we did not have.'[77] Here, although the reference to personality is not directly to that of Jesus, the reader is forced to ask how this figure 'Jesus Christ' is to become 'dominant in us'. This is especially the case given the attention Rauschenbusch pays to exploring the personality of Jesus, and how that personality and the development of our own religious personalities are connected.

A further passage offers help here. When referring to the relationship between Jesus and 'the common people' in *The Social Principles of Jesus*, Rauschenbusch notes: 'His personality and spirit has remained an impelling and directing force in the minds of many individuals who have "gone to the people" because they know Jesus is with them.'[78] There is here the assumption of a continued presence (of Jesus' personality and spirit), which drives people towards solidarity with the 'common people'.

A further feature of Rauschenbusch's use of the term 'personality'

---

74 'We are dependent on the verbal memory of his disciples' (*Social Principles*, p. 194).

75 See also, e.g., Rauschenbusch, *Righteousness*, pp. 122, 126; *Social Principles*, p. 194; *Theology*, p. 162.

76 Rauschenbusch, *Righteousness*, p. 122.

77 Rauschenbusch, *Theology*, p. 100.

78 Rauschenbusch, *Social Principles*, p. 43.

builds on his own experience of pastoral solidarity with 'the common people'. In making a link between that experience and his understanding of Jesus, Rauschenbusch uses the term 'composite personality'.[79] Within a chapter entitled 'The Super-Personal Forces of Evil' in *A Theology for the Social Gospel*, Rauschenbusch writes:

> The social gospel realizes the importance and power of the super-personal forces in the community . . . A realization of the spiritual power and value of these composite personalities must get into theology, otherwise theology will not deal adequately with the problem of sin and of redemption, and will be unrelated to some of the most important work of salvation which the coming generations will have to do.[80]

The social emphasis which Rauschenbusch believes theology must possess will need to address good and evil not only in personal moral terms. The religious personality – to be shaped through the personality of Jesus becoming more dominant in the redeemed – must not be understood individualistically. Evil is passed from generation to generation through evil structures. Redemption must likewise be interpreted in corporate terms lest super-personal, institutional sin fail to be addressed and overcome. People are redeemed within communities and are redeemed through participation in the personality of Jesus. Rauschenbusch thus provides a means for understanding Jesus/Christ as a present, corporate personality, even if he has not himself drawn out the fullest implications of his own thinking in precise terms. Indeed,

---

79 In Old Testament studies this would be termed 'corporate personality'. For a critical examination of its use, see e.g. J. Rogerson, 'The Hebrew Conception of Corporate Personality: A Re-examination' in B. Lang (ed.), *Anthropological Approaches to the Old Testament*, London: SPCK/Philadelphia: Fortress Press, 1985, pp. 43–59 (= *JTS* 21, 1970, pp. 1–16).

80 Rauschenbusch, *Theology*, pp. 75–6.

Rauschenbusch could not draw out such an implication for one simple reason: despite his insight into 'composite personalities', he remains bound to thinking of Jesus as an individual religious hero. This is the third of the four weaknesses to be considered in Rauschenbusch's Christology.

Jesus the solitary hero

Rauschenbusch's may be a Christocentric social Christianity, but there is an unresolved tension at the heart of his Christology, and thus at the heart of his theology as a whole. Rauschenbusch's theology rotates around the individual, even solitary, figure of Jesus of Nazareth. The extent to which the individuality of the religious personality of Jesus comes to the fore in Rauschenbusch's theology means that the social emphasis is in danger of being radically qualified. It is, then, the 'young man of Nazareth'[81] who brought about the great mutation of Judaism into the form of religion which became Christianity.

When Rauschenbusch refers to 'Jesus Christ' as 'the prime force in the Christian revolution',[82] he is referring primarily to Jesus of Nazareth, no matter how much the requirements of his practical theology pull him beyond that simple identification. Rauschenbusch speaks with a rhetorical flourish of 'the equipoise of the life of Jesus'.[83] This is clearly meant to carry devotional power, and function as a spiritual example. But it is the individual Jesus who fulfils this function. When Rauschenbusch appeals to Jesus as religious hero, he suddenly disregards Jesus' social context and impact. References to the Kingdom of God are swallowed up in their relation to a single person's inner life and personal power. Even Jesus' practice of linking people together is derived from his

---

81 Rauschenbusch, *Righteousness*, p. 121.
82 Rauschenbusch, *Righteousness*, p. 118.
83 Rauschenbusch, *Righteousness*, pp. 129–30.

individual prowess as the archetypal 'religious genius' identified by the post-Enlightenment Quest, and expounded in the 'lives of Jesus' so beloved of nineteenth-century liberals.[84] Examples of such attention to Jesus' religious individuality and distinctiveness (Jesus thought, taught and undertook things like no other) are frequent in Rauschenbusch's writings.[85]

One particular form of this individuality is worth highlighting, given how often this motif has appeared in Christian writing:[86] I refer to the 'femininity of Jesus'. Rauschenbusch writes: 'Jesus sided with feminine feeling against masculine hard-headedness.'[87] This observation is made in the light of an earlier one that 'Jesus advocated and represented a higher standard of purity than his times, yet he was freer with women than the customs of his times sanctioned.'[88] It is instructive in so far as it teases out features of the Gospels' presentation of Jesus which are clearly to do with the socially revolutionary aspects of Jesus and his movement.[89] Rauschenbusch recognizes the crucial importance of this aspect of the gospel tradition. However, he can only receive that tradition within a context which enabled him to notice the originality

---

84 'Jesus not only bound men [*sic*] to himself, he bound them to one another. He founded a community, created a corporate feeling which differentiated them from the mass of men [*sic*], gave them laws of their own, and established the rudiments of an internal organization. He prayed for their unity. He expected them to continue in this society after his own departure' (Rauschenbusch, *Righteousness*, p. 151).

85 E.g. Rauschenbusch, *Christianity*, pp. 54, 59, 64–5; *Social Principles*, pp. 72, 139; *Theology*, pp. 26, 154, 166, 174–5.

86 And it is worth noting in advance how it will connect with other features of this present enquiry: the relationship between corporateness, mutuality and feminism in Christology.

87 Rauschenbusch, *Righteousness*, p. 257.

88 Rauschenbusch, *Righteousness*, p. 237.

89 Regardless of whether any particular case of these features is historically accurate about Jesus of Nazareth, even if it is highly likely that the Evangelists are building upon traditions which record examples of Jesus' practice (i.e., these kind of tales – about a 'loose man' – are not the ones you would invent for the sake of it!).

of the individual male. More tellingly still, he can only make the observation from within an ideological framework which has predefined masculinity to exclude the possibility of spontaneity, beauty or the expression of emotion.

Rauschenbusch is correct to note the way in which such concrete aspects of the Jesus tradition are preserved in the gospel texts and directly influence Christian practice. He is also right to pay attention to the communities from which the Gospels came and to which they relate. But his theological approach invites us to explore further what these aspects entail in practice for the reception and use of the Gospels. Such exploration requires moving beyond seeing Jesus merely as an individual male figure who transcended the cultural expectations of his own time.

Rauschenbusch declared boldly that 'Christ has not been exhausted'.[90] This may best be understood to mean Christ's not being fully grasped. Such an interpretation undoubtedly moves beyond Rauschenbusch's primary meaning. For him, the statement means that the teachings and activity of Jesus of Nazareth have yet to be fully tapped. Christology and Christocentrism in the present will not be able to allow the meaning of Christ to be collapsed into the religious activity of the solitary male figure, even if that life functions as a heroic (and salvific) example for all who follow. At this point, Rauschenbusch fails to carry through his social agenda in theology: he is more individualistic in his Christology than he would wish.

The superiority of Christianity

Fourth, and finally, in this critique of Rauschenbusch's Christology, mention must be made of the implications of this motif of Jesus' individual uniqueness as 'religious hero' for the way in which Rauschenbusch views the superiority of both Jesus and

---

90 Rauschenbusch, *Righteousness*, p. 122.

Christianity. In many ways, Rauschenbusch's Jesus fits firmly within the wake of the Enlightenment 'shift in the terms of heroism', towards praising spiritual giants rather than generals.[91] There is little doubt that Rauschenbusch is content to list comparatives and superlatives about Jesus ('higher spiritual insight', 'the purest religious spirit', 'highest perfection [of religion and ethics] in the life and mind of Jesus', 'perfect religious personality', '[w]e have not passed beyond his words, either in form or substance') in a way which places Jesus well ahead of the field, but leaves the reader asking on what basis the comparison has been made. To us today, Rauschenbusch's conclusion looks weak precisely because a comparative study is simply not undertaken.

Rauschenbusch, however, is willing to make similarly superior claims for Christianity:

'The Word made flesh' is the necessary condition of a truly universal religion, for no other expression of truth can serve for all classes, all nations, all times, and all grades of spiritual development. In Jesus we find all these requirements.[92]

The superiority of Christianity – as the only truly universal religion – is thus assured, and is grounded in the self-understanding, personality and activity of Jesus. The juxtaposition is even more starkly expressed elsewhere: 'Jesus Christ was the founder of the highest religion; he himself was the purest religious spirit known to us.'[93]

Such a causal link, and ideological leap, can now be seen to be unjustified and misplaced. The evident spiritual power and impact of the figure of Jesus as a historical figure merely places him within a range of 'founders' of religions, or of 'spiritual

---

91 R. Folkenflik, 'biography' in J. W. Yolton *et al.* (eds.), *The Blackwell Companion to the Enlightenment*, Oxford: Blackwell, 1991, p. 63.

92 Rauschenbusch, *Righteousness*, p. 127.

93 Rauschenbusch, *Social Principles*, p. 139.

giants' throughout human history. A desire to locate 'spiritual giants' or heroic 'founders' may not, of course, be the best way to handle religion, let alone to tackle the particular question of the role of Jesus the Christ in Christianity. That issue aside, the ease with which Rauschenbusch moves from the respect shown by an insider to a judgement which, he implies, could be made by an outsider must now be recognized as suspect.

Rauschenbusch's Christocentrism: an assessment

Rauschenbusch provides several different pointers for Christocentrism today. Though major flaws may be detectable in his Christology, the nature of his attention to the figure of Jesus within the task of constructing *a social theology* is worth revisiting. His work highlights the way in which any version of Christian thought and practice operates within a basic set of assumptions and contains a controlling interest. In Rauschenbusch's case, the basic framework is provided by the concept of the Kingdom of God, and the controlling interest is how the personality of Jesus can become the driving force not only of the Church but also of society. Because of these two emphases, 'what (and who) is theology for?' becomes a major concern of Rauschenbusch's theological activity. In this final section, I shall explore the significance of this social theological location of Rauschenbusch's approach to Christology for Christocentrism today.

We have noted a number of ways in which the social intent of the theology of Rauschenbusch manifests itself: through attention to the Kingdom of God (in Jesus' preaching and activity, and in contemporary theology); through respect for the place of the 'composite personality' in understanding the human being as a social being; through attention to the Church as a social, concrete form which approximates, but is not identical with, the Kingdom of God; through respect for the inevitable link between theology

and sociology, politics and economics. Rauschenbusch's christological concerns relate to all of these. His Christocentrism can thus
be summarized as the concretization of the centrality of the Kingdom of God in Christian thought and practice, through attention to the present experience of the embodied spirit of Christ
as a 'composite personality', evident in a variety of social forms.
Rauschenbusch is keen to stress the ongoing impact of Jesus of
Nazareth. He does so not simply through the cause-and-effect
flow of human history, but also through entertaining a sense of
the ongoing presence of Jesus/Christ. Given his social emphasis,
this can only lead to a corporate understanding of Christ in the
present. His own Christology remains flawed through its lingering
desire to highlight Jesus the religious hero, but he has established
the need for a social Christology to sustain the social theology for
which he strives.

For Rauschenbusch, Christ will be where the Kingdom of
God is (and vice versa). And this will constitute the very heart of
Christianity itself (even, we might say, the 'Christianity of Jesus').
Contrary to the easy criticism often made of Rauschenbusch, the
Kingdom of God will not simply mean an ethical programme;
ethics does not exhaust attention to the presence of Christ. It is
equally wrong to claim that Rauschenbusch, despite ultimately
proving to be quite orthodox, so domesticates the Kingdom that
it is little more than 'church' by another name. His theology opens
up a very proper modern concern for a critique of the Church.
The question 'where is the Kingdom to be found?' works with that
strand of the gospel tradition which finds Jesus portrayed at the
edges of respectable society. The refusal to interpret that tradition
merely individualistically is what drove Rauschenbusch to answer
the question 'where is the Kingdom to be found?' with his own
version of 'among the poor'. If theology and practice in Christianity did not relate to, make sense of and help transform the lot
of people he encountered in the 'Hell's Kitchen' district of New
York where he served as a pastor, then they were not Christian.

Rauschenbusch's Christocentrism was for the poor of turn-of-the-twentieth-century America, and would be critical of an individualistic theology prone to spiritualize Jesus/Christ so that the materiality of the preaching and activity of Jesus of Nazareth would be lost.

'Christ', then, must be seen as a corporate reality. Jesus/Christ is spiritually (and as such very concretely) present among groups of people embodying the same social spirit as Jesus of Nazareth. Such groups must be interpreted as manifestations of the Kingdom of God lest they be solely ethical programmes which fail to make clear their rationale or how they would command a following. It is thus the Church's job to seek to be such a group itself, and also to interpret and facilitate the existence of other such groups in the light of the Kingdom of God.

If Schleiermacher's Christocentrism takes the form of a Christ-piety centred on living fellowship with Christ, then Rauschenbusch's Christocentrism strives towards a 'Christ-society'. The goal of Rauschenbusch's thought and practice in Christology is the theological transformation of human society. In his own context he spoke of 'Christianizing' the social order, a term which now proves too closely allied to claims for Christian superiority.[94] Christocentrism can, however, focus upon relationships befitting the Kingdom of God and embodying the personality of Jesus/Christ. In this way, Rauschenbusch's approach breaks out of its limited framework. The goal of Christocentrism is revealed to be far more than the influencing of the Church alone.

Rauschenbusch's is, however, scarcely a 'theology of liberation' in the sense that it is wholly *from* the poor. He remains a paternalistic interpreter of the poor, even if his interpretation is based on real solidarity with them.[95] Furthermore, in speaking of

---

94 Evans, *The Kingdom*, pp. 55–6, 143, 232, though also p. 293; also above Ch. 3, pp. 61–2.

95 Evans, *The Kingdom*, notes Rauschenbusch's paternalistic stance or tone at a number of points through his study; e.g. pp. xx, 165, 252.

the crucial importance of the family within his understanding of social transformation, it seems certain that he had a particular bourgeois, patriarchal image of the family in mind.[96] A more detailed study of Rauschenbusch at this point would need to show how his construal of Christocentrism would be likely to subvert some of the social forms he took for granted.[97]

Rauschenbusch does, however, move further than Schleierm-acher *beyond the Church* in his development of a social Christo-logy. He therefore invites interpreters of Jesus/Christ in the present to think creatively and positively in concrete terms as to where, and with whom, Christ is present. We are also left asking who, then, and what is Christ today? And what do Christocentric thought and practice entail today?

---

96 J. F. Fishburn, *The Fatherhood of God and the Victorian Family: The Social Gospel in America*, Philadelphia: Fortress Press, 1981, esp. pp. 111–27; also 'Walter Rauschenbusch and "The Woman Movement": A Gender Analysis' in W. J. Deichmann Edwards and C. De Swarte Gifford (eds.), *Gender and the Social Gospel*, Urbana and Chicago: University of Illinois Press, 2003, pp. 71–86.

97 C. H. Evans reaches a similar conclusion in making probably the best defence of Rauschenbusch on this matter (while recognizing that not all his views are worth defending), in his study of Rauschenbusch's relationship with his daughter Winifred, 'Gender and the Kingdom of God: The Family Values of Walter Rauschenbusch' in C. H. Evans (ed.), *The Social Gospel Today*, Louisville, London and Leiden: Westminister John Knox Press, 2001, pp. 53–66: 'Rauschenbusch . . . never recognized how the conservative cultural suppositions of his day undermined the transformative social imperatives that he espoused in his public theology' (p. 65).

6

Rita Nakashima Brock: Christa/Community

Rita Nakashima Brock's *Journeys by Heart* is a study in Christology. Subtitled 'A Christology of Erotic Power', it is a critique of dominant modes of understanding the doctrine of atonement. It therefore accepts that there is an inextricable link between Christology and soteriology. It does three things of relevance to this study. It offers a radical rereading of the Gospels (the Gospel of Mark in particular). It takes orthodox trinitarianism to task for the way it has purveyed a distorted understanding of power relations. It invites readers to reconceive the task of Christology as less to do directly with Jesus as an individual figure from history and more to do with the concrete relations between the people who can be deemed to be 'in Christ'. The book's author is a contemporary theologian working out of North America, and a member of the Christian Church (Disciples of Christ). She describes her own background:

> I am a Japanese-Puerto Rican immigrant American. I was raised in a Japanese Buddhist family until, at age six, I was brought to the United States by my Japanese mother and white, Christian stepfather, making my cultural roots Asian and American.[1]

---

1 R. N. Brock, *Journeys by Heart: A Christology of Erotic Power*, New York: Crossroad, 1988, p. xvi. See also Brock, 'On Mirrors, Mists and Murmurs: Toward an Asian American Thealogy' in J. Plaskow and C. P. Christ (eds.),

Despite the vast difference between Brock's background and experience and my own, her insights and areas of exploration have proved telling for the lines of enquiry followed in this present book.

My reasons for using her work in this study are fivefold. First, Brock writes as a feminist. It should not be possible to write on Christology today without engaging with feminist theology. Second, Brock offers a communal Christology. Drawing on interpersonal understandings of the human self from both West and East, Brock's notion of Christ as 'Christa/Community' challenges contemporary Christologies which conceive their task individualistically, in relation either to the solitary figure of Jesus or to the lonely contemporary believer. Third, Brock builds into her work a recognition of the value of the historical quests of Jesus, while also offering a sharp critique of their relevance to the task of Christology. Fourth, despite the evident recasting of the entire focus and content of Christology, Brock's theology remains Christocentric. Fifth, Brock's is a liberation theology which draws upon the experience of marginalized communities, that is, of those socially, politically and economically ostracized in northern hemisphere societies.

In this study, therefore, Brock functions representatively (of liberation and feminist theologies) as well as making her own distinct contribution. Her work develops and critiques that of the two thinkers discussed so far and will, in turn, be critiqued by them. Alongside Brock's work, as I write, I am listening to the voices of many other feminists (Ruether, Fiorenza and Heyward in

Weaving the Visions: New Patterns in Feminist Spirituality, San Francisco: Harper & Row, 1989, pp. 235–43: 'I come from Japan, one of the cultures influenced by the Confucianism and Buddhism of China and India, but a culture also distinctly its own. I am also biracial, Japanese on my mother's side, in country of origin and mother tongue, and Puerto Rican on my genetic father's side. My mother married a white American soldier, like tens of thousands of Japanese women under the U.S. occupation, and we emigrated from Okinawa when I was six' (p. 237).

particular[2]) who have challenged and informed my thinking and beliefs about Jesus, early Christianity and Christology. I also hear the voices of many other liberation theologians whose experience and reflection have informed and shaped my own (Cone, Bonino, Sobrino, L. Boff[3]). That they are not also discussed here is merely a matter of space, time and the specificity of the immediate subject matter.

---

2 E.g. R. R. Ruether, *To Change the World*, London: SCM Press, 1981; *Feminism and God-Talk: Towards a Feminist Theology*, Boston: Beacon Press/ London: SCM Press, 1983; E. S. Fiorenza, *In Memory of Her*, London: SCM Press, 1983; *Jesus: Miriam's Child, Sophia's Prophet*, London: SCM Press, 1995; 'To Follow the Vision: The Jesus Movement as Basileia Movement' in M. A. Farley and S. A. Jones (eds.), *Liberating Eschatology: Essays in Honour of Letty M. Russell*, Louisville: Westminster/John Knox Press, 1999, pp. 123–43; C. Heyward, 'Doing Feminist Liberation Christology: Moving Beyond "Jesus of History" and "Christ of Faith": A Methodological Inquiry' in *Speaking of Christ: A Lesbian Feminist Voice*, Cleveland: Pilgrim Press, 1989, pp. 13–22; 'Jesus of Nazareth/Christ of Faith: Foundations of a Reactive Christology' in S. B. Thistlethwaite and M. P. Engel (eds.), *Lift Every Voice: Constructing Christian Theologies from the Underside*, Maryknoll: Orbis, 1998, pp. 197–206; *Saving Jesus from Those Who Are Right: Rethinking What It Means to Be Christian*, Minneapolis: Fortress Press, 1999; also J. Grant, *White Women's Christ and Black Women's Jesus*, Atlanta: Scholars Press, 1989; P. Wilson-Kastner, *Faith, Feminism and the Christ*, Philadelphia: Fortress Press, 1983; S. D. Ringe, *Jesus, Liberation and the Biblical Jubilee*, Philadelphia: Fortress Press, 1985; *Wisdom's Friends: Community and Christology in the Fourth Gospel*, Louisville: Westminister John Knox Press, 1999; E. A. Johnson, 'Redeeming the Name of Christ: Christology' in C. M. LaCugna (ed.), *Freeing Theology: The Essentials of Theology in Feminist Theological Discourse*, Edinburgh: T. & T. Clark, 1993; J. Schaberg, 'A Feminist Experience of Historical Jesus Scholarship' in *Continuum* 3, 1994, pp. 266–85 (reprinted in W. E. Arnal and M. Desjardins (eds.), *Whose Historical Jesus?*, Waterloo, Ontario: Wilfrid Laurier University Press, 1997, pp. 146–60); and D. Hampson, *Theology and Feminism*, Oxford: Blackwell, 1990.

3 E.g. J. Cone, *The Spirituals and the Blues*, New York: Seabury Press, 1972; *God of the Oppressed*, San Francisco: HarperSanFrancisco, 1975; *My Soul Looks Back*, Maryknoll: Orbis, 1986; J. M. Bonino, *Faces of Jesus: Latin American Christologies*, Maryknoll: Orbis, 1984; J. Sobrino, *Christology at the Crossroads*, London: SCM Press, 1978; *Jesus in Latin America*, Maryknoll: Orbis, 1987; L. Boff, *Jesus Christ Liberator*, London: SPCK, 1980; *Trinity and Society*, Maryknoll: Orbis/London: Burns & Oates, 1988.

Brock on the centrality of Jesus/Christ

Brock is not a systematic theologian. She has not, to date at least, constructed a system of Christian theology addressing all standard themes of theology. That is not how she approaches her task. This does not mean that her theological reflection lacks either coherence or systematic awareness; far from it. The fact that in her work she explores the links and tensions between some of theology's themes indicates the extent to which she draws on theology's systematic character.[4] But Brock has not presented a straightforward theoretical case for where Christian theology should begin, or on what it should focus. A practice-oriented theologian who pays close attention to the specificity of her context is not likely to do so. Yet it is clear from her writings that Brock adopts a Christocentric approach to Christian theology: she is aware that to re-examine critically what Christians have made and do make of the figure/term 'Christ' is to strike at the heart of Christian belief, thought and practice. Christianity's 'understanding of divine love and redemption in doctrines about Christ'[5] or 'the logical explanation of Christian faith claims about divine presence and salvific activity in human life'[6] is, says Brock, 'the heart of Christianity'.[7] More precisely, Christology is the centre of Christianity because 'Christ' is 'the center of Christianity'.[8]

Brock later remarks that feminist approaches to theology have necessitated a move 'toward a different center for Christian faith'.

---

4 E.g. Brock, *Journeys*, explores the links and tensions between doctrines of Christ, salvation and the human person (esp. re sin); Brock, 'Shape-Shifting Disturbances as Divine Presence' in M. Chapman (ed.), *The Future of Liberal Theology*, Aldershot and Burlington: Ashgate, 2002, pp. 170–90 considers sin in relation to aspects of the human and of pneumatology.

5 Brock, *Journeys*, p. xii.

6 Brock, *Journeys*, p. 51.

7 Brock, *Journeys*, pp. xii, xiii.

8 Brock, *Journeys*, p. 52.

Nevertheless, a key question deriving from conversation with Brock is whether the centre of Christianity with which she works has really become different, or whether it has merely been rediscovered.

Brock makes it quite clear what Christocentrism is *not*. 'In moving beyond a unilateral understanding of power, I will be developing a christology not centred in Jesus.'[9] She is therefore not open to a charge of 'Jesusology', and is seeking to respect the fact that Christology is much more than the interpretation – historical, theological or otherwise – of a single, historical figure. Her quest for a 'christology not centred in Jesus' will take her beyond any 'individualizing of Christ':

> I believe the individualizing of Christ misplaces the locus of incarnation and redemption. We must find the revelatory and saving events of Christianity in a larger reality than Jesus and his relationship to God/dess or any subsequent individual Christ . . . Both the old and new quests of the historical Jesus presuppose the primary importance of the individual. However, individuals only make sense in the larger context of events embedded in particular historical structures.[10]

At the heart of Brock's Christocentric theology, then, we should expect to find an interpretation of Christ which moves beyond the task of interpreting the historical figure of Jesus. We should also expect to find resistance, on good theological grounds, to the notion of Christ being identified wholly with a single figure. This is indeed the case.

---

9 Brock, *Journeys*, p. 52.
10 Brock, *Journeys*, p. 68.

Brock's theological method

Before presenting Brock's exposition of Christ as 'Christa/
Community', it is worth noting her theological method. Her
approach offers a liberation perspective on Christian theology,
and both her location and her procedure reflect this. It is an
unashamedly engaged and experiential method of doing theology. Though not spun out of, or derived from, experience in any
simple way, Brock's theology is nevertheless the result of what is
necessarily called forth from a variety of theological traditions by
the demands of experience.

Such 'experience' is not mere autobiography.[11] Brock writes
consciously out of the context of being an Asian-American (as
an 'Issei and Happa, a Japanese-born U.S. citizen who is half non-
Japanese'[12]). That is, she writes as part of a group for whom she
believes she has no right to speak representatively, yet among
whom she gladly sees herself and whose experience she thus
shares. She writes as a woman, and draws deeply upon her and
other women's experience, especially working with experiences
of abused women and always mindful of the damaging effects
of patriarchal culture in so many dimensions of human life (e.g.
professional and family life). She attends to and critiques especially the structures of North American family life as experienced
through the lives of children. She notes the many and diverse ways
in which children experience abuse within the family. But despite
these rich and challenging contexts, her theology is far from mere
narration of experience. Her theology is the result of the interplay between wrestling with Christian themes and insights and
the narration of her experience. Her contexts and experience are
more than mere 'background'.

---

11 And even leaving aside the very important observation that personal
experience and autobiography are far from identical; i.e., as individuals we are
not simply the stories we tell of ourselves.

12 Brock, *On Mirrors*, p. 237.

Two further experimental aspects of Brock's theology are significant. First, it is clear that Brock is actively involved in striving for the full, equal participation in public life of both women and those from ethnic minority groups. This is evidenced directly in her academic commitments, which have included participation in institutions and groups working for the development of the work of others.[13] The second important observation is the number of collaborative projects in which Brock has been engaged. From the number of co-written works she has been involved in it is clear that theology is, for Brock, not a discipline for an isolated scholar.[14] Brock's endeavours are an example of the way in which feminists highlight the extent to which all scholarship is in fact collaborative.

As a result of these diverse experiential starting points, many themes preoccupy Brock. The main ones are liberation, redemption and reconciliation; sin, failure, brokenness; community and relationality; power, powerlessness and empowerment; witness and testimony. Though some of these concerns may be considered directly theological (e.g. 'redemption' and 'sin' have entries in theological textbooks), many are not couched in customary theological terminology. This is significant. Brock does not want the traditional themes of theology so to control human experience that they ultimately devalue and stifle its force. This would be to disempower the narrator of such experience. For Brock, theology is implicit within, and relates to, praxis, and merits articulation and clarification. But how and where God is present often needs to be disclosed through analysis and reflection, and cannot

---

13 E.g. as Director of the Bunting Institute (now the Radcliffe Institute for Advanced Study, Harvard University) from 1997 to 2001 and through considerable activity in the structures of the American Academy of Religion. The Bunting Institute/Radcliffe Fellowship Program exists to promote artistic and creative work by women in a multi-disciplinary context.

14 With Naomi Southard (1987), with Susan Brooks Thistlethwaite (1996) and with Rebecca Parker (2001, and with a further study promised).

be confined always to what Christian theology has, in the past, deemed to be the case.

For Brock's experiential theology, then, reflective praxis is the context and stimulus for the critique of Christian tradition. We shall yet need to examine on what basis, and in accordance with what norms, such a praxis-oriented critique is possible. For the moment, we need simply note that when Brock addresses traditional themes of Christian theology such as Christology, atonement, the doctrine of God, sin, human being, the Church, and the Spirit, she does so on the basis of her own articulated testimony and that of many others. Such testimony calls forth from Christian tradition materials with which to work. Only when such articulation on the basis of testimony has occurred is it possible to ask – in the middle of wrestling with the respective demands of present living and the traditions of Christianity – 'what in the world is God doing?'

Brock's understanding of Jesus/Christ

Christ, for Brock, is 'Christa/Community'. To examine what this means, we must first clarify the 'erotic power' which Brock believes is located at the heart of all creative, energizing, reconciling (and thus God-inspired) communal activity in the world. 'Erotic power is the power of our primal interrelatedness. Erotic power, as it creates and connects hearts, involves the whole person in relationships of self-awareness, vulnerability, openness, and caring.'[15]

Brock is seeking to identify what it is that addresses the whole person and truly liberates. Rather than begin with an abstract definition of God she sets off from the awareness that any social or political (or theological or ecclesiastical) structures based on inequality or submission/domination are open to question and

---

15 Brock, *Journeys*, p. 26.

that positive, creative relationship is what God brings about. She must find a basis upon which it is possible to formulate an adequate doctrine of God commensurate with this insight, in critical conversation with the many materials that Christian tradition presents to her. Brock is able to locate 'original grace' within the primacy of interrelatedness. '[O]ntological relational existence, the heart of our being, is our life source, our original grace.'[16] The acceptance of the availability of 'erotic power' is thus at the same time the means of accepting the 'original grace' located at the heart of creation. The power of connectedness, of positive, creative relationship, is what restores human beings from the damage caused by the separation of people from each other. Beneath and beyond all that happens to people to cause the damage of separation, Brock believes, lies the 'erotic power' which can only be identified as the healing, community-creating presence of God. It is the human task to recover that sense of connectedness, difficult though this may be:

> While confirmation from or with the world no longer becomes necessary for a centred self to survive, the restoration of original grace is difficult because we can only come into flower with connections to other self-accepting selves. This relationality is the terrifying and redemptive grace of the character of being human.[17]

If the human task is then in any sense to 'find God', in Brock's terms it means to tap into this 'erotic power' located at creation's heart.[18] If we are to interpret Jesus/Christ in the light of this insight, then the extent to which Jesus/Christ participates in this erotic power must be the focus of any christological investigation.

---

16 Brock, *Journeys*, p. 7.

17 Brock, *Journeys*, p. 24.

18 'Heart' in two senses: centre, and as the locus of the deepest aspects of emotional life.

Brock redefines Christology on the basis of her exploration of the place of relationality in Christian thought and practice. If 'erotic power' is central to human experience of the presence of God, then Christ must in turn be understood in the light of this all-encompassing, relational insight. 'Christ' cannot be confined to Jesus; nor, indeed, can the identification of who/where this 'Christ' is be confined solely to the task of interpreting the figure of Jesus. Taking her lead from the New Testament Gospels,[19] Brock develops a corporate understanding of 'Christ'. From the start, as the Gospels themselves show, 'Christ' has always been understood in relational terms. Connecting with the historical work of Elisabeth Schüssler Fiorenza,[20] Brock notes that Jesus of Nazareth must himself be understood in the context of his own relationships with others. This is not merely a statement of the historical truism that every person has to be understood in their own context.[21] It is saying more that, if Christology focuses upon Jesus the individual in isolation, then it theologically misconstrues him. Against this background, Brock's opposition to 'the individualizing of Christ'[22] becomes clear. 'Christ' must comprise Jesus *plus* those around him who are the first into the Kingdom of God.

Yet even this does not suffice for Brock, and in two distinct ways. First, even when noting that 'Christ' is bigger than Jesus, Brock challenges the notion of 'unilateral power' that could still be implicit within the observation that Jesus and his followers *together* constitute 'the Christ'. For it would still be possible to see the sharing in 'erotic power' in terms of the followers receiving from Jesus, as the sole source of this power. But what

19 The Gospel of Mark is especially prominent (as in 'The Gospel of Mark: Erotic Power at Work' and 'The Gospel of Mark: Erotic Power in the Shadows', chs. 4 and 5 of Brock, *Journeys*).

20 Fiorenza, *In Memory of Her*.

21 Or if it is, we must accept that the truism presents a radical critique of the way that so much Christology has been undertaken, as far as the historical component within it is concerned!

22 Brock, *Journeys*, p. 68.

if Jesus received something *from* his followers, so that 'Christ' is genuinely the result of mutually shared power? What if Christ is co-constituted by Jesus *and* his followers? It is this insight which Brock draws from Mark's stories of the haemorrhaging woman (Mark 5.21–34) and the Syro-Phoenician woman (Mark 7.24–30). In relation to Mark 5 (esp. v. 27), Brock states:

> I want to suggest that the woman . . . takes away his [i.e., Jesus'] patriarchal power as a man. She breaks through the barrier of male privilege and status that separated them. Again, an old hierarchical power in Mark is replaced with a new vision, this time by the woman's action. *Her* action reveals the '*kenosis* of patriarchy.' She acts to reveal the brokenheartedness of patriarchy and cocreates Christa/Community.[23]

Drawing an observation from both texts, Brock concludes:

> The point is not Jesus' sole possession of power, but the revelation of a new understanding of power that connects members of the community. The power reversal comes from those perceived as weak who reveal the divine way of power, erotic power.[24]

Whether or not these are strictly exegetical observations is not the main point here.[25] In theological conversation with these texts, Brock has opened up an important avenue of exploration for the meaning of 'Christ' for today: Christ is more than Jesus; Christ denotes a communal relationship of embodied beings; Christ is co-constituted by all those within such a community who participate in the erotic power of God.

A second way in which we must move beyond a simple

---

23 Brock, *Journeys*, p. 84.
24 Brock, *Journeys*, p. 87.
25 Exegetical in the sense that they are the interpretations which Mark intended (in so far as one can know).

identification of 'Christ' with Jesus and those around him (in first-century terms) must also be noted. The relational, community-creating presence of God (understood as 'erotic power') cannot be confined to the first century AD. 'Christ' is co-constituted among any liberating community in which life-giving erotic power is evident. The link with the past (the past of Jesus and his immediate followers) is thus at least one of analogy. It will be more when it is claimed that it is the same divine power in which all such liberative communities participate. Erotic power is not brought about by faith in a past salvation, but in the healing deeds of the Church as the community of heart, of courage and of hope.[26]

How this analogical process operates must yet be explored in the critique of Brock's work below. For it is not immediately obvious how the stories about Jesus, the 'Christ' pointed to within the Gospels and contemporary 'Christs' all interlock. But one final piece of exposition is required first. Why call Christ 'Christa/Community'?

Building on the ways in which the figure of Jesus/Christ has sometimes been portrayed by women artists and sculptors as a woman figure, Brock is wanting to affirm, but also critique, this identification. She writes:

> In using Christa instead of Christ, I am using a term that points away from a sole identification of Christ with Jesus. In combining it with community, I want to shift the focus of salvation away from heroic individuals, male or female.[27]

It would have been understandable had Brock drawn on her feminist sympathies and simply affirmed the intent of women sculptors and painters who portray Jesus/Christ as a woman figure in order to draw attention to the way in which women have

---

26 Brock, *Journeys*, p. 103. 'Church' is here the term used for the liberating community, though it must be noted that as the community of 'Spirit-Sophia', for Brock, we should not quickly identify the Church with 'the Church as we know it'.

27 Brock, *Journeys*, p. 113 n. 2.

so often suffered, especially at the hands of men. Such portrayals relate to the way that suffering women can directly empathize with the suffering of a crucified Jesus, and feel that a crucified Jesus in turn identifies with them.[28] This would, however, be unhelpful for Brock on two grounds. For one thing, it would continue to offer to women a model of Christology and Christian practice which affirms self-sacrifice as always appropriate and laudable. Brock's work, like that of many feminists, resists this dangerous tendency. Second, to replace a male Jesus/Christ with a female figure merely perpetuates the individualism which lies at the heart of much Christian theology. To oppose individualism it is necessary to redefine Christology itself. Only in this way is there a chance of overcoming the wrong kind of individualism.

'Christa/Community' thus becomes a way of pointing out that 'Christ' is so often too heavily defined by 'Jesus', in ways that are androcentric and individualistic. Brock's linguistic strategy contributes to the overcoming of a number of the distortions of Christocentrism identified in Chapter 3, including Jesusology, androcentrism and egocentrism.

Brock's Christology: four questions

To test the robustness of Brock's Christology, and to see whether there are elements from elsewhere in Christian tradition which may critique, support or develop her main thesis, I shall consider four aspects:

- the interplay between the method and content of her Christology;
- the basis within Christian tradition out of which Brock works;
- the doctrine of God in relation to which Brock develops her thesis;

---

28 E.g. the example provided by Thistlethwaite: see Ch. 3 n. 22 above.

- the nature of Christ, given Brock's understanding of 'Christa/ Community'.

Method and content

The first area of enquiry can be formulated as a direct question: does Brock simply identify a set of good, ethical practices and call them 'Christa/Community'?[29] That is to suggest that human experience may not only have shaped the concerns which drive Brock's theological argumentation, but also have provided its content.[30] Whether Brock is open to this charge will need to be determined.

The converse of this line of enquiry is undoubtedly true: human praxis is shaped by whatever Christology is formulated. Bad conduct produces bad Christology; better Christology can help people live better. This is clearly the framework for Brock's work.[31] But does this functional-sounding Christology then become merely a linguistic tool for a reading of reality, and the formulation of a philosophy for life, which could easily be labelled quite differently? How constitutive, in other words, for the communal, relational ethic (and Christology, and theology) which Brock proposes is 'the person of Jesus/Christ', 'the story of Jesus', 'the narrative/s of Jesus/Christ', or the 'being of Christ' – to offer just

---

29 The same question was asked of Tom Driver's ethical Christology over two decades ago: Driver, *Christ in a Changing World: Towards an Ethical Christology*, London: SCM Press, 1981.

30 E.g. The 'rightness' of such commitments, and even Christian support for their development, may, however, not necessarily lead to the conclusion that they require a theological foundation. Participation in a more general, post-Enlightenment (even if in part Christianity-inspired) concern for individual human rights, or for equality between the sexes could be the issue here.

31 The ethical focus of theological reflection appears confirmed by such statements as: '"Religion" is more how one lives, and less what one believes' : R. N. Brock, 'Shape-Shifting Disturbances as Divine Presence' in M. D. Chapman (ed.), *The Future of Liberal Theology*, Aldershot and Burlington: Ashgate, 2002.

four possible ways in which much traditional Christian theology would speak of Jesus/Christ?

There can be little doubt that Brock's method means that she is unlikely to offer her Christology in a way that will satisfy many orthodox theologians. She does not begin with the Bible or aspects of Christian tradition, reinterpreting them for the present, even if such reflection is clearly part of her procedure. If her reflections on Mark are either an imposed theology, or ultimately merely illustrative of a theological judgement reached on other grounds, then it will be possible to question how necessary it is to speak of Christ (even as 'Christa/Community') at all. The basic question is: how does Brock know what she is looking for, both in the examples of good human community she seeks, and in the biblical material relating to Christa/Community?

It is possible to argue on two fronts. The first recognizes that Brock's identification of non-patriarchal power relations as manifestations of erotic power, and thus as examples of Christ/Community, is made possible on ethical grounds which are not specifically Christian. The analysis of power that Brock conducts (e.g. much use of the work of Alice Miller), because it is not initially or explicitly theological, could suggest that it is feminism, not Christianity, which controls Brock's whole presentation. Similarly, second, the passages to which Brock is drawn in her use of the Bible are the result of her feminist concerns.

However, for such observations, even if accurate, to be considered as *objections*, either to Brock's procedure or to her conclusions, requires that the objector be opposed in principle to the notion that feminism and Christianity can be compatible. Moreover, the second observation overlooks the fact that *all readers* approach biblical texts with particular interests and concerns.[32] At issue, then, is not by what means Brock first stumbled upon

---

32 This feature of hermeneutics has been known in New Testament studies at least since Bultmann, and has become prominent through respect for reader-response methods of reading texts.

the ideas with which she works as Christian ideas, nor how she lays out her exposition, but whether the interplay of biblical, psychological, sociological, feminist and theological components in her integrated analysis of Christology is tenable as Christian theology.

In my view, Brock is not ultimately guilty of merely labelling a particular practice as theological, although it can be claimed that she did not explain her thinking enough to avoid that charge. Brock genuinely finds 'Christ' (as 'Christa/Community') in a range of examples of human community, but she needs to highlight more fully the grounds on which Christ is identified. The reason why Brock looks for, and seeks to promote, non-patriarchal relationships is that good ethical practice and Christian insight coincide at that point. As well as being able to perceive bad Christian practice and bad Christian theology, she finds materials in Christianity which enable her to identify and promote non-patriarchal community. It is for this reason that she can remain within the Christian faith. Her intent is simple but bold: 'I seek both to salvage and transform Christianity.'[33]

Within the interplay, then, of biblical, psychological, sociological, feminist and theological inquiry, there is a theological driving force which enables experience, ethical insight and intention, and theological judgement to coincide. This interplay, rather than ethical or feminist preference alone, shapes the framework of Brock's Christology. If it is accurate to say that she comes to the Gospel of Mark with feminist-ethical insights already in place, then it must also be said that these feminist-ethical insights have already been informed by Mark (or by another part of Christian tradition).

---

33 Brock, *Journeys*, p. xv.

Brock's use of Christian tradition

To press this point further, a second line of enquiry can be followed: the question of the basis *within Christian tradition* out of which Brock works. If the tradition can be said to have provided materials with which Brock can work, what conclusions must be drawn about the method she follows, and/or the possible existence of a theological *a priori* in her approach? According to her praxis-based method,[34] Christ should not be defined until reflection upon experience has been undertaken. But a further question is what, from the tradition, predisposes her to criticize the individualism of much Christology, past and present? It need not be claimed that she has drawn on non-theological material here; but she may be being influenced in her Christology by considerations from elsewhere within the theological enterprise. Does her statement that 'the church ... [is] ... the community of heart, of courage, and of hope'[35] mean that ecclesiocentrism has come to play a dominant role in her thought? Is the Kingdom of God, as a corporate idea, the leading edge of her thinking and practice, thus aligning her closely with the social gospel?[36] Either may ultimately prove to be the case. I do not wish to spend time and space establishing this one way or the other here.[37] At issue

---

34 See e.g. Brock, 'Shape-Shifting Disturbances'.

35 See above, n. 26.

36 The value of which is recognized in Brock, 'Shape-Shifting Disturbances': 'Christian voices and practices resisting forces of injustice have existed alongside them [i.e. churches supporting injustice], creating social movements such as abolition, women's suffrage, the Social Gospel movement, the Civil Rights movement, and the sanctuary movement' (p. 172).

37 For to prove such a claim – if it were even possible – would do no more than provide evidence of a different centre to Brock's theology than the one she claims to hold (bearing in mind that Brock is seeking to define a centre to her theology different from the way the centrality of Christ is usually conceived; Brock, *Journeys*, p. 69). It would not, in fact, of itself undermine either her method or her conclusions in Christology. Christology could, in other words, still be communally conceived as 'Christa/Community', even while the focal point of Brock's theology could be identified as 'Church' or 'Kingdom of God'.

is whether Brock is right in her christological reflection. The key question is: is it accurate to conceive of Christ in such corporate terms as Brock is suggesting?

As far as Brock's method is concerned, it need simply be noted that every theology relates experience and tradition to each other in some way, and it is unlikely that any theologian – however sophisticated their method – can truly answer the question of where they start from. Post-liberal responses to experiential method in theology, while they highlight helpfully the all-pervasiveness of tradition/s in theological discourse, cannot adequately challenge Brock's confrontation of orthodoxy. Whether or not Brock has *actually* begun to develop her Christology with an *a priori* liberation Christology derived from who knows where, with a doctrine of the Church or of the Kingdom of God, or with a set of experiences which have led her to some parts of Christian tradition (the liberative aspects) and not others, does not alter the force of the resulting Christology. And it is that with which we must deal. In short, Brock may be beginning, methodologically or theologically, from a different place than where she thinks she is beginning, but that does not invalidate the results.

Brock's doctrine of God

The third issue to examine in her Christology is her understanding of God: what doctrine of God is Brock working with as she develops her thesis? Four interlocking themes require brief comment here: power, freedom, transcendence and Trinity. Much of Brock's work entails the examination of the use and abuse of power and how this has informed and shapes Christian thought and practice. The nature of God's power must be explored within such an enquiry. Brock's exposition of divine power in terms of 'erotic power', together with a Christology articulated in terms of 'Christa/Community', is the result of her attempt to wrestling with the positive and negative aspects of Christian handling of the question of God's power.

It is important to state immediately that Brock is not guilty of making generalized or sentimental statements in favour of the powerlessness of God. In the face of the evident abuse of power in Church and society, in opposition to deemed misunderstandings of the 'sovereignty of God', and aware of the devotional power of meditation upon the cross, she does not succumb to the temptation to praise powerlessness. On the basis of her exploration of women's experience, she is critical of the ease with which powerlessness is supported and promoted in Christianity. Brock recognizes: 'Power is essential to self-esteem, to freedom, and to well-being.'[38] She is not therefore dodging the inevitability of power. Rather: 'We need, I believe, alternative ways to understand power and values that enhance community, healing, and justice – that unleash the life-giving energy necessary for just and sustainable life in human communities and on the earth.'[39] Her concern is to establish a positive, life-enhancing understanding of power (hence the attention to 'erotic power'), believing that clarification of this power will prove to be a clarification of the power of God. Christological reflection – redefining Christ as Christa/Community – is, in Brock's view, crucial to that exploration.

It may be objected that Brock does not deal adequately with the extent to which Christian theology has consistently asserted the independent freedom of God, over against human power. Brock takes pains at several points to stress how damaging has been the Christian desire to emphasize the independence of God from human affairs, and the dependence of the human being upon God and/or Christ. This lies behind Brock's opposition to many of the ways in which the transcendence of God has been used in Christian theology.[40] The intent here is clear: to affirm and promote full

---

38 Brock, *Journeys*, p. 33.

39 Brock, 'A New Thing in the Land: The Female Surrounds the Warrior' in C. L. Rigby (ed.), *Power, Powerlessness and the Divine: New Inquiries in Bible and Theology*, Atlanta: Scholars Press, 1997, pp. 137–59, here p. 141.

40 E.g. Brock, *Journeys*, pp. 54, 56.

attention to human responsibility. But this could be thought to put too much into human hands. Because of her emphasis upon present contexts and actions, Brock also stresses immanence over transcendence. But this emphasis may be leading her astray. Despite Brock's greater attention to immanence and to mutuality and responsibility in the exercise of power in human relationships, it is still necessary to denote the power referred to (even as erotic power) as the power *of God*. To make such a claim is more than of theoretical significance, or mere employment of a linguistic tool. Without recognition of the overcoming of patriarchy *as an action of God*, then the power exercised in human relationships – as human power – runs the risk of obscuring the persistence of fallibility and frailty within human agents. Such activity needs to be seen as the action of God in order to respect the evident fact of human frailty, *even if it may also need to be claimed that God's own self is caught up in that same frailty and fragility.* It is, in short, recognition of sin which requires that the transcendent freedom of God be upheld. Though Brock expounds her understanding of sin at some length, the significance of that exposition for her attention to God's transcendence is, in my view, underplayed.[41]

Brock's observation and analysis of how the power of God is so frequently misconstrued in Christian thought and practice lead her into further problematic territory. She notes how the power of God has been construed in the light of, and in defence of, patriarchal power structures in Church and society.[42] Upheld by patriarchal understandings of the doctrine of the Trinity, these renderings of the power of God do not correspond to the relational Christology which Brock is able to find in Mark's Gospel, and which therefore forms the bedrock of her own attention to

---

41 Discussing Heyward and Brock's work, L. S. Bond notes the need at the very least for 'some kind of imaginative transcendence', *Trouble with Jesus: Women, Christology and Preaching*, St Louis: Chalice Press, 1999, p. 97.

42 Brock, *Journeys*, p. 57.

'Christa/Community'. How is Brock's critique of the Trinity to be evaluated?

At one level, her references to the doctrine of the Trinity could be said to be out of date. Exploration of the doctrine since 1988, when *Journeys by Heart* was first published, could be said to have undermined Brock's statements about the way in which 'classical trinitarian formulas' or 'the unholy trinity' perpetuate patriarchy. Many studies, some undertaken by feminists, have sought to argue that the doctrine preserves the potential to overcome the unequal, patriarchal relationships (within God and among human beings) which it has so often fostered.[43] This potential is realizable in the present, whatever may have been made of the doctrine in the past, and even despite the language in which the doctrine was formulated.

Are things really so simple, however? Though I agree with the inevitability of using the doctrine of the Trinity in Christian theology,[44] I am far from convinced that we should be looking primarily at that doctrine for the overcoming of patriarchy in relation to the doctrine of God. It seems more likely that what happened historically – exploration of doctrines about Christ resulted in the doctrine of the Trinity – will continue to happen. And though we have glimpsed something more of God via the doctrine of the Trinity (and therefore carry it with us in Christian tradition), we have yet more to discover about God, inspired

---

43 E.g. Jane Williams, 'The Fatherhood of God' in A. I. C. Heron (ed.), *The Forgotten Trinity Vol. 3*, London: BCC/CCBI 1991, pp. 91–101; S. Coakley, 'Why Three? Some Further Reflections on the Origins of the Doctrine of the Trinity' in S. Coakley and D. Pailin (eds.), *The Making and Remaking of Christian Doctrine*, Oxford: Clarendon Press, 1993, pp. 29–56; C. M. LaCugna, *God For Us*, Edinburgh: T. & T. Clark, 1991; E. A. Johnson, *She Who Is: The Mystery of God in Feminist Theological Discourse*, New York: Crossroad, 1997, ch. 10. An (in my view unsuccessful) attempt to counter the tendencies of such discussion can be found in many of the essays in A. K. Kimel (ed.), *Speaking the Christian God: The Holy Trinity and the Challenge of Feminism*, Grand Rapids: Eerdmans, 1992.

44 Ch. 3 above, pp. 71–2.

again and again by reformulations of the doctrine of Christ (such as Christ as 'Christa/Community').

We are thus left with one main objection to the doctrine of God with which Brock works in her Christology: she insufficiently respects the need for the notion of the transcendent freedom of God. In Brock's understanding, it seems, God has no being out-side of the appropriate, enriching exercise of human power.[45] God, being who God is (so far as we know), will be *within* appropriately construed, affirming power relations. Yet it is the notion of the transcendent freedom of God that preserves the recognition of the limitation of human possibility to construct such relation-ships. Admittedly this may be a case of a male theologian still working too much with a notion of sin as pride or assertion, rather than one of sin as damaged or lack of relationship.[46] Theo-logical defence of the transcendent freedom of God may keep humans 'in their place' too much and stifle the human potential which Brock seeks to assert and to promote, especially among women. But if the transcendent freedom of God is understood *in fact* in terms of the knowledge that people are co-constituted in the midst of the frailty and fragility of the created order, then the divine presence is identified as powerfully at work in the midst of human affairs. The divine power works as an Otherness which it is not within human capacity to create, but it is not a power alien to what human beings at their best can contribute to bringing about. I would argue that this insight better enables the divine (erotic) power to be experienced as the power *of God*, especially as God is known to us in the form of Christ.

---

45 Interestingly, the point at which much current trinitarian exploration, some of which is not directly sympathetic to feminist insights, has come to (as e.g. in the work of Zizioulas and Gunton).

46 Brock's – and many other feminists' – use of V. Saiving's influential work is pertinent here.

Defining Christa/Community

The fourth and final angle of critique must deal directly with the content of Brock's Christology. What is 'Christa/Community', and is it a legitimate, contemporary restatement of who Christ is? To translate Brock's insights into more traditional terminology, we may say that Christ today is constituted *as* a group of people. Christ is not 'beyond', 'behind', 'within' or 'beneath' believers. It is even possible to say that those who co-constitute Christ may not 'believe' at all. It is certainly not their believing which qualifies them to co-constitute Christ, but the quality of their interrelationship and the nature of their commitments. Nor is Christ present 'in' or 'among' the group thus defined as Christ. If we are to find a preposition at all, then 'between' is the most appropriate; but even here, this may lead us to assume (wrongly) that Christ is a disembodied spirit drawing people to each other. Even this will not do, for Christ is clearly, for Brock, *embodied* relationality; and this is neither 'in' the individuals nor 'in' the groups, but existing where people in non-patriarchal power relations *create community*. Such communities are manifestations of 'Christa/Community' in that they enable their members to face past hurts, live with 'broken-heartedness' and yet give and receive mutual affirmation through participation in divine power.[47]

I have noted already the possibility that Brock may, in practice, be striving to reconceive 'church'. Perhaps any corporate emphasis in Christian theology ultimately leads to ecclesiology. Therefore, when Brock sees the need to shift to a 'different center', she is perhaps simply moving from Christology to ecclesiology, rather than redefining Christology.[48] Is her construal defensible

---

47 It is perhaps striking that the notion that Brock may have reduced Christ to an idea or principle does not even arise as a possible objection. This is a mark of the difference between theologies in the past which raised radical questions about the relationship between 'Jesus' and 'Christ' (e.g. Tillich), and Brock's contemporary feminist form of such questioning.

48 I shall take up this point in the next section.

as Christology? In at least two respects it is; in one respect, it is not.

First, it is defensible in it sheer concreteness. Too often, Christologies turn Christ into a disembodied spirit, lose touch with the incarnate aspect of Christ's contemporary presence in the world, and require Christ to be unmoved by the harsh realities and injustices of human living. Brock's method, and the content of the particular human experience she weaves into her theology, will not permit this. The communities she seeks to describe and promote *are* Christ. Second, Brock's Christology is defensible in its corporateness. Her consistent opposition to individualism, expressed in her noting of the weaknesses in any Christology too closely linked to the life of a solitary male figure, has borne fruit here. If God's power is to be enjoyed and participated in corporately, then Christ can only be understood in corporate terms. Any Christology which collapses Christ into a divine manifestation in any one individual, even Jesus of Nazareth, has reduced the range of the self-revelation of God, and refuses the task of interpreting the nature of the embodied presence of the divine Logos in the world.

But despite these evident strengths, the question 'what, then, has happened to Jesus?' remains. Despite her clear intent to develop 'a christology not centered in Jesus' is it not still the case that an interpretation of Jesus in some form is vital for Brock's Christology, even when understood in terms of Jesus and his followers? Jesus remains an important figure for Christians, Brock included. We must therefore ask not whether Brock's Christology is (in fact) centred in Jesus, but what role Jesus plays. In the context of his immediate social circle, Jesus becomes something of an exemplar. 'Jesus is like the whitecap on the wave.'[49] We must, says Brock, resist giving attention to that whitecap lest we fail to discern the restless energy of the oceans beneath. This is true in so far

---

49 Brock, *Journeys*, p. 50.

as individualistic Christologies, solely focused on Jesus or on the reception of Christ in the life of the individual believer, must be resisted. But how are the movements of the restless ocean discernible? It is a mistake to focus on the whitecap, but it is essential to know what is being looked for in the midst of the ocean's chaotic depths. It is here that Brock needs 'Jesus' more than she realizes.

The 'Jesus' she needs, though, is not the 'historical Jesus' – either in the Jesus of history or the Jesus recovered by historians. The 'Jesus' she needs is certainly the Jesus of Mark, in relation to which she expounded her reading of Christ as Christa/Community. More precisely: the Jesus she needs is a narrative theological construct derived from a liberationist reading of the Bible. Such an observation does not undermine her position. It supports her undertaking and conclusions, while offering one negative critical insight: that is, that in her understandable reluctance to develop a Christology too closely tied to the figure of Jesus, she has underplayed the role that a narrative Jesus must inevitably play in any Christian theology.

Theology must inevitably be based on a sacramental view of history. Historical change is a catalogue of events (including eruptions, disruptions or 'disturbances'[50]) which demand theological reflection, and which then become, in narrative form, the means by which human life as lived within God is then experienced and interpreted. In Christian terms, the Jesus narratives function in this way and become a norm, even the norm of norms, for Christian God-talk. Brock rightly continues this essential Christian practice even while critiquing some of the ways in which Jesus has featured in Christian thought and practice.

To summarize: Brock's Christology develops Christian theological reflection about Christ in the present through her attention to the corporate embodiment of Christ in the world today. In so doing she strives towards good ethical practice without

---

50 Brock, 'Shape-Shifting Disturbances', pp. 170–4.

reducing Christology to ethics. Because of its corporate emphasis, her Christology arguably gives way to a greater than recognized concern for a form of ecclesiology: she is keen to promote particular forms of human community. However, her desire to stress the human dimension in the right ordering of interpersonal power relations restricts the extent to which she can retain a sense of the independent freedom of God. Brock's resistance to individualizing Christ in terms of a single saviour figure offers a powerful critique of much traditional Christology. She does, however, in effect underestimate the importance of the narrative Jesus in her understanding of the interplay of experience, Bible and theology in the Christian task.

Brock's Christocentrism: an assessment

My appraisal of Brock's view of the centre of her theology takes two forms: what are we to make of her claim that she seeks a 'different center' for Christian faith? and is Brock's form of Christocentrism to be recommended for Christian theology today? Brock's statement of her position is undoubtedly clear: 'The feminist shift in standards creates new visions that are moving toward a different center for Christian faith.'[51]

With these words, Brock highlights how feminism has enabled her to redefine Christ. The 'different center' which results is, as we have seen, a combination of narrative tradition and ethical practice: Christ as Christa/Community as read in and from the Gospels; Christ as Christa/Community as experienced, lived and promoted in communities of non-patriarchal relationships. But what is Brock's centre different from? Has she, *in fact*, moved away from a christological centre in theology? Or has she shifted the focus *within* a Christocentric approach to faith and theology? I conclude the latter, for a number of reasons.

---

51 Brock, *Journeys*, p. 69.

First, though *Journeys by Heart* makes references to 'church', it is clearly not a study in ecclesiology. Furthermore, though Brock refers to *basileia* (kingdom) as she expounds the gospel texts, she is, again, not working primarily to redefine the Kingdom of God. Redefinitions of Church and Kingdom could rightly follow on from her christological enquiry; but they certainly do not control it. Christ is being redefined on the basis of the interplay of Bible, theological tradition and lived practice, with communal practice (good and bad) at the fore because of Brock's and other women's life experience. Second, what is criticized throughout is not Christology itself, but inadequate Christologies and soteriologies. It is Brock's desire to 'salvage and transform Christianity', on the basis of the impact and experience of Christ in the context of liberative praxis. What she calls Christa/Community may thus appear to move some distance from traditional Christologies. By the linguistic link between 'Christa/Community' and 'Christ' Brock reveals her intent to develop the tradition, while distancing her redefinition from inadequate understandings of Christ drawn from Christianity past and present. Her proposal of Christa/Community is, then, a proposal for the redefinition of Christ for the present. The 'different center' proposed by Brock produces a different centre for Christology, not a relocation of the centre of theology as a whole. Given her recognition of Christology's importance, however, Brock's christological enquiries cannot but affect the shape of her theology as a whole. She remains, in short, more Christocentric than she acknowledges.

Is Brock's form of Christocentric theology to be recommended? Undoubtedly; but to return to points raised at the start of the previous section, two qualifying comments must be made. First, the experiential method followed means that Brock is prone to disregard theological lines of enquiry which initially appear unfruitful. I think of two areas: all doctrines of the atonement are rejected ('The doctrines of salvific death do not make sense'[52]);

---

52 Brock, *Journeys*, p. xiii.

all trinitarian speculation is disregarded. Although Brock rejects many formulations of these doctrines, it doesn't follow that reflecting on these formulations has nothing to contribute to contemporary christological exploration.[53]

The second qualification concerns the points at which Brock's Christocentrism can be informed from other themes of Christian theology. The close links between her Christology and understandings of Church and Kingdom suggest that what can be gained for Christology *from* ecclesiology and eschatology would be a fruitful enquiry. A Christocentric approach to theology ensures, on theological grounds, that Christology takes the lead over ecclesiology. But it is in ecclesiology that the 'body of Christ' is spoken of in corporate terms. Further critical interaction with the ways in which this christological aspect of the doctrine of the Church has been handled throughout the history of the Christian tradition may therefore be a creative addition to Brock's enquiries.[54]

Brock's is, then, still a Christocentric theology. She has already been engaged in part of the task undertaken in summary form in Chapter 3 of this present study. She has seen distortions of Christocentrism and sought to correct them. She has endeavoured to replace a bad Christocentrism with a good one. I have suggested ways in which her Christology and Christocentrism may be challenged and developed. Such critical observations are, however, merely pointers towards the third part of this book.

---

53 The way in which recent work on the Trinity coincides in many respects with where Brock wants to get to confirms this point.

54 Not to mention the earlier versions of corporate Christology, contained in works such as J. A. T. Robinson, *The Body: A Study in Pauline Theology*, London: SCM Press, 1952; and C. F. D. Moule, *The Origin of Christology*, Cambridge: Cambridge University Press, 1977. These studies have certainly informed the direction this present study will take.

Part Three

Who (and What) is Christ for Us Today?

7

What is Christ Today?

It is twenty years since I first read John B. Cobb Jr's *Christ in a Pluralistic Age*.[1] On first reading I was perturbed. Here was a theologian who, in my view, was undermining Christian faith. It seemed to me that, in his keenness to attend to the world around him, and in particular to the challenge of other faiths to Christianity, he had diluted Christianity. My main criticism of his work, in a paper I produced as a new graduate student, was that he depersonalized Christ in speaking of Christ as a 'process of creative transformation'. Two decades later, having wrestled in the meantime with the same issues in many different forms, I find myself more sympathetic to Cobb's text. My main criticism remains, but I understand better what Cobb was trying to do. Perhaps there is no better tribute to his work than to say that I have spent the past twenty years trying to find adequate answers to the questions that his book left in my mind. For Cobb's enquiries helped me to recognize that, important though Bonhoeffer's question was to all those who ventured to speak of Christ ('who is Christ for us today?'), this was not the only question which had to be addressed.

The conversations in Part Two, with Schleiermacher, Rauschen-busch and Brock, have produced a number of telling insights for the tasks of constructing a contemporary Christology and

---

1 John B. Cobb Jr, *Christ in a Pluralistic Age*, Philadelphia: Westminster Press, 1975, esp. chs. 1–3.

working out the meaning of Christ in Christian practice today. In this chapter, these insights will be distilled under three headings in relation to the question '*what* is Christ for us today?' Bonhoeffer was reluctant to pose that question and his insistence on asking the personal question '*who?*', has had long-lasting effects. But it is urgent to ask the more basic question 'what?' because Christians can assume even less than Bonhoeffer that people in wider society are interested in *either* question at all. Three answers can be given in response to the question 'what?'

Christ as embodied in relationships

First, Jesus/Christ takes the form of particular configurations of relationships. The commitment of Christianity to the con-creteness (incarnation) of God's presence in the material world requires that the presence of God be identified in material terms. The presence of God in Jesus/Christ must be understood as a 'continuing incarnation' and hence in embodied terms. Other-wise, the reality of Jesus/Christ becomes spiritualized, and con-fession of Jesus/Christ's presence is either wholly internalized (and thus privatized) or 'transcendentalized', so that the 'mind' or 'spirit' of Christ becomes an overarching, dominant category which neglects reference to the rough edges of concrete, human living. The conversations with Schleiermacher, Rauschenbusch and Brock indicate that exploration of this 'continuing incarna-tion' may best occur through critical scrutiny and promotion of Christ in the form of particular kinds of human relationships.

Attention to the reality of Jesus/Christ as the presence of God in the world today in such terms contains within it a profound respect for particularity. There is no non-contextual confession of belief in God. There is no context-less Jesus/Christ. The recognition that Jesus/Christ is embodied in particular configurations of embod-ied relationships means that it is inevitable that Jesus/Christ will be spoken of in specific, contextual terms. This coheres well with Christian conviction about the importance of the particularity of God's presence in the figure, Jesus of Nazareth. There is, however, a double irony in Christianity's commitment to the 'scandal of particularity' constituted by the centrality of Jesus/Christ. First, Christianity has too easily narrowed its focus to the isolated individual Jesus and become so preoccupied with that figure that it has overlooked the full consequences of the scandalous attention to the broader history of Christ. Second, Christianity has risked ignoring the ways in which God has always been scandalously, particularly present in the world, and continues to strive to be present in people's relationships to each other and to the world around them.

What, though, of the view that such an emphasis upon human relationships inevitably leads to anthropocentrism? The charge cannot stick so long as it is ensured that human beings are not the measure or focus of all things. The approach will undoubtedly seem anthropocentric in so far as Christology is being undertaken in relation to human experience. (How can Christology undertaken by human beings be otherwise?) However, this is the inevitably experiential dimension of theology, not anthropocentrism. Such an experiential theology would become anthropocentrism in a negative sense, as defined in Chapter 3, only if no mechanism were found for critique of experience lest Jesus/Christ be wrongly identified with *any* form of human relationship. This is where the contributions of the three theologians studied become clear.

That 'not any relationship will do' has become evident throughout this study. The presence of God in Jesus/Christ in the world is locatable in specific types of relationships, not in all. Schleiermacher spoke of 'living fellowship with Christ' and noted the community-creating activity of the God-conscious redeemer. He sought to identify the form of a 'new humanity in Christ' on the basis of the reception of Christ by believers in the context of living fellowship. The 'Christ-piety' which he explores throughout his work proves to be the means for identifying the embodied relationships that constitute Christ today. Such relationships will clearly intersect with 'church' without being simply one and the same. Rauschenbusch spoke of the 'composite personality' of Christ, which he sought to interpret in relation to the concrete forms of the Kingdom of God. Brock's term 'Christa/Community' denotes a pattern of non-patriarchal relationships which embody Christ today. All are ways of locating and expounding the presence of Christ in specific, concrete terms.

Where justice is being sought in the context of human inter-relationships,[2] then Christ is present, and people are participating in living fellowship with Christ. Where hierarchies that use rank to demean people are challenged, then Christ is active as an agent of change at the centres and margins of the political life of human structures and organizations. Where human relationships across generations do not stifle, but allow young to teach old, and old to teach young, in a rich tapestry of human creativity, then Christ is present as God's dynamic person-forming energy. There are, as we shall see, no words about Jesus/Christ worth saying or images worth fashioning which do not recognize that God is present in embodied form in Jesus/Christ in the world. There is likewise no attention to the spiritual presence of Jesus/Christ worth paying, which fails to recognize that Jesus/Christ's spirit lives in real bodies, and between real people, in very concrete settings.

A more active way of expressing this understanding of Christ is via the term 'network of living'. Christ is a network of living,

---

2 To use Mary Hunt's helpful term: 'justice-seeking' (in *Fierce Tenderness*). The Kingdom of God may also better now be referred to as the 'kinship of God'. I do not now recall where I first encountered the use of the term 'kinship' as an alternative to 'Kingdom' in the phrase Kingdom of God, though it is frequently used within feminist theology. The term 'kin-dom' is also used (see e.g. Bond, *Trouble with Jesus*, discussing 'Mujerista Options' in Christology, pp. 85–90, here p. 86).

because the emphasis when exploring what *Christ* means, and what it means to believe, always needs to be on what it means to *participate* in Christ. Identifying who Christ was and is cannot be a disinterested task. To accept that the task has more than historical value discloses its inevitably existential quality. Commitment to the quest to clarify Christ's identity may sometimes be less orthodox and more nebulous than many Christian churches might wish. Yet the urge to find out what Christ means and who Christ is, and the thrill and risk of following, are closely allied. To be a follower of Christ ultimately means to participate in the network of relationships – past and present – which Christ creates.

The term 'network of living' is helpful in two respects. First, it picks up the notion of the interdependence between the believer or searcher and other believers or searchers, within Christ's sphere of influence. There is no solitary believer 'in Christ', just as the salvific work of Jesus the Christ cannot be confined to the activity of Jesus of Nazareth alone but includes the continuing work of God within those who receive the benefits of salvation. Second, the move away from reception of Christ by the individual in turn shifts the focus away from the *imitation* of Christ by the individual.[3] This has the advantage of preventing participation in Christ being seen first of all as a moral matter. The question of a follower's ethical practice is important. But following Christ is neither initially nor primarily ethical. Being 'in Christ' means first and foremost receiving from God in and through others, and discovering who one is in and through others. Though the 'imitation of Christ' tradition has been a strong feature of Christian spirituality, its drawbacks are its individualism and its tendency to overemphasize the significance of ethical practice.

---

3 As recognized by Schleiermacher, *The Christian Faith*, Edinburgh: T. & T. Clark, 1928, p. 438.

A spiritual presence

Jesus/Christ is, second, also a spiritual presence. Relationships do not exist without bodies, but they do not exist only as bodies. More precisely, and in order to overcome an unnecessary and misleading body/spirit dualism, though in one sense bodies are all we are, we are *living* bodies and account always has to be given of the source of the life that makes bodies live. If God gives life and God is spirit (John 4.24), then it is in turn no surprise that Christianity has made much of the spiritual presence of Jesus/Christ. Nor is it surprising that emphasis has been placed, even throughout the modern period, on the 'mind' or 'personality' of Christ.[4]

In what way, though, can Christ be identified as a spiritual presence without that meaning of Christ becoming dominant? Christ's presence unites people in their common Christian experience but is much more than may be implied by references to 'spirit' or even to 'Holy Spirit'. We can therefore speak of Jesus/Christ as a spiritual presence *within* and *between* particular human bodies, existing in particular kinds of relationship. Only such a definition does justice to the way in which, in order to speak of Christ today, we must speak not only of the kinds of relationships which people form, but also how relationships are shaped and who it is who resources them.

As suggested earlier, however, it must be acknowledged that there is a real danger of 'transcendentalizing' Jesus/Christ. There is a tendency for any christological vision to link an emphasis upon the spirit or mind of Christ with the interpretation of Christ which emerges from a particular culture. In this way, with a profoundly damaging irony, rather than respecting particularity and concreteness, a Christology results which can seek to exert a hegemony over all others (e.g. in the form of the White

---

4 As noted in Rauschenbusch's work, above pp. 128–31.

Christ, the Anglo-Saxon Christ or the male Christ).[5] Prioritizing the relationships in which Jesus/Christ is claimed to be embodied, which is a particular strength of feminist Christologies, is a way of trying to guard against that tendency. But as the examples given show, stress upon embodiment does not of itself necessarily achieve such a corrective. Focus on particular bodies may merely introduce a different version of spiritual superiority.

There is, however, no avoiding the 'spiritual dimension' to the experience of participating in Christ through human relationship. Only through the presence of Jesus/Christ as spirit is it possible to speak *of Christ*, rather than just ourselves, in comparing and contrasting the articulations of our understandings of Jesus/ Christ in relation to our life experience. Some of us may speak of 'the inner Christ' and others of 'the transcendent Christ' – I suggest we can continue to speak of both. Both of these ways of handling Christian convictions about the presence of Jesus/Christ are necessary to support the conviction that Christ is really present in particular kinds of human relationships.

For example, what Schleiermacher describes as the 'pervasive influence' and 'pervasive activity' of Christ is more than the mere continuing, lingering influence of a past historical figure. Christ's is a 'person-forming' work occurring in the social context in which a person allows him- or herself to come under the influence of the redeemer.[6] And this 'total effective influence of Christ' is nothing less than 'the continuation of the creative divine activity

---

5 The points explored in this paragraph form the substance of Alan Davies' *Infected Christianity: A Study of Modern Racism*, Kingston and Montreal: McGill-Queen's University Press, 1988. There are now many surveys of the variety of Christologies which exist (see e.g. Anton Wessels, *Images of Jesus: How Jesus is Perceived and Portrayed in Non-Western Culture*, London: SCM Press, 1990; Priscilla Pope-Levison and John R. Levison, *Jesus in Global Contexts*, Louisville: Westminster/John Knox Press 1992; Volker Küster, *The Many Faces of Jesus Christ: Intercultural Christology*, London: SCM Press, 2001, but the critical edge of Davies' is especially helpful.

6 Schleiermacher, *The Christian Faith*, p. 427.

out of which the Person of Christ arose'.[7] Rauschenbusch's focus on 'personality', despite its limitations, and Brock's identification of the 'eros' energy which drives the relationships at the heart of Christa/Community, address similarly this 'creative divine activity'. Both are dependent upon some sense of Christ being a spiritual presence.

It can, of course, be argued that at this point Christology gives way to pneumatology. We are now talking about God as Spirit rather than God as Son. As will be clear by now, however, I am convinced that to lose the christological reference implicit within understandings of the spirit of God could render the spirit too diffuse a concept. God's presence and action as spirit can be more easily conceived in a concrete way when Christology is kept in view. As Harold Wells notes: 'it is mistaken to think of the Spirit apart from Jesus, since it is through the concrete visibility of Jesus that we can discern the presence and work of the Spirit'.[8]

'Inner' and 'transcendent' forms of the presence of Jesus/Christ admittedly become problematic, as Brock recognized, if the non-material dimension of Christology is absolutized. If the concrete particularity of the relationships within which the presence of Jesus/Christ is discovered and celebrated is negated or over-looked, then the 'inner Christ' fails to relate to the 'real world' of concrete human relationships and is correlated too easily with an escapist form of Christianity. Christians cease to locate Christ in the world, or to have their lives transformed into lives lived in their entirety with and for God. Conversely, this 'inner Christ' can also become a cover for a failure to assess how specific, existing relationships have shaped and shape the understanding of Jesus/ Christ with which any believer works. There is, in other words, a process of 'working back' from the practices of human relation-ships to understandings of Christ which needs to be built into the

---

7 Schleiermacher, *The Christian Faith*, p. 427.
8 H. Wells, *The Christic Center: Life-Giving and Liberating*, Maryknoll: Orbis, 2004, p. 119.

christological task. Things can be learned about Christ through what one learns about oneself and others in the context of actual human relationships in all their messy ambiguity.[9] The spirituality inherent in human relating feeds Christology.

Both embodiment in relationships and spiritual presence are forms of Christ's presence. Each needs and critiques the other. And working from past interpretations of Christ in dialogue with current experiences of Christ in relationships and as spiritual presence is the way that ongoing doctrinal criticism in Christology can proceed.

Words and images

Third, Jesus/Christ is words and images. Though present in and through relationships and as spiritual presence, Jesus/Christ must still be brought to expression. If this did not happen there would be no way of interpreting the presence of God in Christ in the world, as there would be no tradition about Jesus/Christ with which to work. Tradition is handed on through both word and image. Theologians' persistent problem is that their vocation seems to imply that it is in this third answer to the question 'what is Christ?' that the main substance of the matter lies. Within their *job* as theologians, this may well be true. But it cannot be true of the whole of their lives.[10] Christo*poesis* – the fashioning of interpretations of Jesus/Christ[11] – is vital for both Church and society. Only through the fashioning of images (in words, paint, clay, in film and as dramatic presentation) can the particularity of

---

9 This point will be developed more fully in *Christ in Practice*.

10 Or if it is, then they of all people are most to be pitied. For if word-spinning is all they do, then they have lost touch with the reality of Christ and their words will not be trustworthy anyway.

11 That is, in the broadest sense of fashioning interpretations of the Christ, thus acknowledging that interpretations are not always in words.

the presence of God in Jesus/Christ in the world be encountered, respected and critiqued.

Human beings live within imaginative, imagined, narrative worlds. The plausibility of such cognitive worlds depends upon the extent to which they can enable human beings to under-stand themselves and their context, to decide how to act, and to envision a future for themselves and others which focuses upon human flourishing. 'The Christian narrative' is one such world.[12] Narratives about Jesus Christ (the canonical Gospels especially) are crucial within the Christian narrative world. Such narratives always say something both about Christ and about their speak-ers/writers. The latter write as participants in Christ in their acts of expression. Christ existing in the form of words and images, then, is the means by which Christ is carried from culture to culture, diachronically and synchronically. Christ as words and images holds the testimony of those who encounter Christ, and provides the means through which others can test their experi-ence of Christ, in a constant christological conversation through time and across the diversity of human cultures.

Every interpretation of Jesus/Christ is rooted in concrete experience. But each interpretation also invites an 'other' to interpret it. Furthermore, if the approach to Christology adopted throughout this book is accepted, then every Christology already reflects a context in which Christ is experienced as 'other' through others. A Christology is thus always more than the autobiog-raphy of the one who speaks, however deeply existential their Christology or Christo*poesis* might be. The Otherness of Christ

---

12 Whether Christianity can be held to have such a single, unified narrative is a moot point, but it can function as helpful shorthand here. For explorations of narrative theology, and the role of narrative in theology, see e.g. George W. Stroup, *The Promise of Narrative Theology*, London: SCM Press, 1984; or William C. Placher, 'Postliberal Theology' in David F. Ford (ed.), *The Modern Theologians*, Oxford: Oxford University Press, 1997, and the secondary literature cited there.

is thus reflected in word and image on two fronts: through the encounter with Christ, through others, on the part of the one who articulates the Christology, and through the 'word' addressed to the hearer through the Christology produced (whether as word or image). This aspect of Christology as words and images forms a creative dynamic at work at the heart of Christology. Interpretations of Christ reflect their creators and yet resist being confined to the limited worlds of those who fashion them. If such interpretations fail, however, to transcend the particularity of those who create them, and to seek to foster justice-seeking relationships, then they cannot be considered adequate as Christologies. Because it is images of Jesus/Christ which are being fashioned, it is a 'corporate person' who is presented:[13] more than an individual, more than an individual can express, and caught up in a network of similar images which sometimes clash but which demand public comparison and scrutiny. Jesus/Christ existing as words and images always reflects embodied, justice-seeking relationships which do more than project onto the figure of Jesus/Christ the struggles and aspirations of those who speak, write, paint or sculpt. A range of images, then, constitutes a form of the presence of Christ in the world today, through which God addresses the world.

Jesus/Christ cannot, however, be confined to a particular, insular group. Nor is any one group's understanding of Jesus/ Christ automatically superior to that of another. But important questions remain. Are all Christologies, then, equally valid? How can Christologies be critically compared and evaluated? What would be the point of such critical comparisons? At this point the importance of the interplay of the three understandings of Christ

---

13 Even an abandoned Jesus on the cross demands to be understood as a corporate figure because of the cross's significance as a means of interpreting God's radical inclusiveness: despite the deficiencies present in all theories of atonement, their intention is to proclaim that God was in Christ reconciling all people to God.

(as words and images, as particular patterns of relationship and as spiritual presence) becomes clear. Words and images express who Christ is considered to be, and what Christ is believed to do in and through those who participate in Christ. But without an understanding of the particular kinds of relationship which constitute Christ and without a sense that dignity-respecting, justice-seeking, person-forming relationships are fashioned through Christ's spiritual presence, words about and images of Christ may prove to be no more than forms of self-expression. Not all relationships which claim to be 'in Christ' or 'Christ-like' may actually be so. This applies to churches too. Consideration of 'Jesus/Christ as words and images' therefore reminds us that the task of interpreting Jesus/Christ entails constant simultaneous monitoring of the criteria which operate as words and images of the Christ are presented. (Is this a Christian image? Why/why not? Is this a biblical portrayal? Does this matter? Is this an orthodox interpretation?) Only in this way do Christians have a hope of acting and speaking responsibly in faith.

In this book, I am suggesting as the primary criterion for the evaluation of Christologies: do human beings flourish in the way they relate to each other? All other criteria (whether a Christology is biblical or traditional, for example) are secondary to this.[14] Christian attention to 'human flourishing' does, however, need careful exposition. As noted in Chapter 3, Christianity has too easily adopted an ecclesiocentric approach to humanity as if the only way in which human beings truly flourish is by being (in) church. Noting that Jesus/Christ takes form as words and images serves as a reminder that the Church does not own Jesus/Christ. Jesus/Christ speaks and acts in society beyond churches via a wide cultural tradition of words and images, which seek reflection in relationships formed not only as churches. In this way, Jesus/

---

14 For a fuller discussion of this point see Wells, *Christic Center*, esp. Part III.

Christ is seen to be alive in the world. Christological controversy arises inside and outside the Church because of this fact. 'Where is Christ?' must always be a question which accompanies the question 'who is Christ?'

Some of the sharpest christological controversy occurs where context-specific Christologies rub up against each other. It is precisely at such points where the challenge of constructing authentic empowering Christologies is truly faced. Contextual Christologies which empower those who articulate them are challenged to show how they might also empower others through being adapted and 'owned' in a different context. It is only in this way that Christologies can serve *human* flourishing, as opposed to serving a particular interest group. The context-specific nature of Chalcedonian Christology has been exposed on these grounds (whom was it actually serving?). It has proved useful beyond its fifth-century context, but it does not help equally well the cause of all who seek to discover and explore what it means to believe in God as known in Christ. The challenge now is whether the fifth-century attempt to clarify what God was doing in the person of Christ can be heard and enacted in other contexts. Likewise, contemporary African Christologies (e.g. Jesus as ancestor [15]) challenge Western versions to review the categories through which they portray the way in which Christ forms human persons. [16]

We have noted that Jesus/Christ as 'words and images' means that Christ as relationships and spiritual presence can be expressed in a variety of forms of human speech and pictorial expression. A number of insights emerge from respect for the sheer variety of media in which experiences of Christ are conveyed. First, interpreters can detach their handling of the

---

15 See e.g. F. Kabasélé, 'Christ as Ancestor and Elder Brother' in R. J. Schreiter (ed.), *Faces of Jesus in Africa*, Maryknoll: Orbis, 1991, pp. 116–27.

16 On the tensions between static and dynamic understandings of Christ and the challenges of critical reception and appropriation of biblical and patristic material, see e.g. Wells, *Christic Center*, pp. 148–56.

reality of Jesus/Christ from their own experience: in their words, they seek to speak of Jesus/Christ, not just of themselves, even if they are also articulating a relationship (being 'in Christ') in which they participate. Second, interpreters use words and pictures in a way that makes public their understanding of Jesus/Christ. This means that others can see if they agree. Interpreters from different cultures and theological persuasions can wrestle respectfully with differing understandings of Jesus/Christ in the hope that Jesus/Christ becomes clearer to each. Third, across the many ways in which Jesus/Christ is interpreted, it becomes possible to say that there may be some interpretations that are simply unacceptable *as Christian readings*. Discovering these indicates what kinds of relationships cannot, in Christian perspective, be deemed manifestations of Jesus/Christ. A Nazi reading of Christ is, for example, illegitimate as a Christian reading of Jesus/Christ. A 'White Christ' is unacceptable if the whiteness is caught up within a view of Jesus/Christ or human relationships which promotes apartheid of any kind.[17]

Fourth, words about and images of Jesus/Christ become a crucial way in which Christians try to explain what they grasp of God's eschatological vision for the created order. If Jesus is 'Christ' (Messiah – the one who comes at the end of time), then Christians have within their belief-system, and in the midst of their attempt to fashion a way of living, a vision of what they believe God wants ultimately for humanity's future. The way in which a Christology is expressed is therefore always based on an interpretation of current experience in tension with a future imagined with the help of God in Jesus/Christ. A relationally conceived Christology is always a way of expressing an interpretation of human relation-

---

17 Though, obviously, the portrayal of Jesus as White need not in itself be seen as wrong even if it is historically inaccurate. But in these terms, an interesting (and challenging) criterion for the Christian adequacy of so much Western art emerges: does a white-faced Jesus in a crucifixion scene necessarily promote justice-seeking, Kingdom/kin-ship of God-related relationships?

ships standing in tension with a vision of what it is possible for human relationships and society to become (eschatologically) 'in Christ'. The particularity of Jesus/Christ in words and images is thus a reminder that no interpretation wholly grasps the reality of Jesus/Christ either as an expression of a wholly fulfilled relationship or as a spiritual presence. Every interpretation is particular, contextual, exploratory and, as a vision of who Christ is and will be, provisional.

Christianity needs the stories and images of Jesus in order to be able to do its work of identifying what, who and where God in Christ is present. But it is crucial in the midst of the task of interpreting and reinterpreting words and images portraying Jesus/Christ that this provisionality be recognized. Otherwise, Jesus/Christ could collapse, in understanding and experience, into a Christ of our own making, either spun directly or indirectly out of the experience of a particular group. The Christian tradition carries a range of stories and images which are always being added to and which ask questions of each other. Jesus/Christ as spiritual presence and embodied in relationship depends upon our attempts to articulate who Jesus/Christ is in these varied forms, in and for the world today, within and across a diversity of groups. The variety is crucial. Jesus/Christ is claimed wholly by none, but accessible to all. To express this differently: only through ideology-critique of all Christologies – relational Christologies included – can Christ be who Christ is: God among us, where 'us' means the whole of humanity.

One final aspect of 'Christ as words and images' must be addressed. What about images that come from beyond the Christian faith community? It should be clear by now that the origin of any image of Jesus/Christ is not at all a cause of concern. The task of interpreting and reinterpreting Jesus/Christ is to serve the cause of human flourishing. In Christian understanding, such human flourishing happens 'in Christ', and the Church – understood both as a collection of concrete communities and as a carrier of the Christ tradition – has the task of continually reinterpreting Christ so that the work of Christ in enabling human beings to flourish is better understood in every age. It is the Church's task, but not the Church's task alone, to undertake such interpretation. As has already been recognized, many, including critics of the Church, join in. The origin and intention of extra-ecclesial interpretations of Jesus/Christ may be significant, but they are not necessarily decisive as far as the function and usefulness of an interpretation are concerned. For, the moment that anyone has ventured to offer an interpretation of Jesus/Christ, they have placed themselves within Christ's sphere of influence. Even if they stand at the margins of the Church and its theology, because it is *Jesus/Christ* who is being interpreted, then the Church cannot but listen, for God may be speaking.[18]

An example will illustrate this well. The red-tinged photograph *Piss Christ* by the New York-based artist Andres Serrano has proved controversial since its first showing in 1987. It shows a plastic crucifix floating in urine mixed with cow's blood. The very idea seems blasphemous, even if, on first glance, the image looks like a fairly typical example of religious iconography. Serrano acknowledges that he works with 'Catholic obsessions' and that he is drawn to Christ, while having problems with the Catholic Church.[19] What may appear blasphemous can, however, be shown to have a quite traditional interpretation, whatever the intention behind the piece:[20] the figure on the cross is immersed in a world of waste, wastefulness and suffering and the value and purpose of

---

18 The 'marginal' location links back to Ch. 1 and anticipates the significance of seeing Jesus/Christ at the borders of cultures.

19 In an interview with Coco Fusco, first published in *High Performance*, Fall 1991, now available on the Internet at http://www.communityarts.net/readingroom/archive/ca/fusco-serrano.php

20 And it must now be acknowledged of any work of art (written, painted or sculpted) that authorial intention may not always either be clear or decisive for the task of interpretation.

his role are questionable. If the figure is to be seen and respected as a hopeful figure, then the enormity of the challenge must not be underestimated. One of the main symbols with which the figure of Jesus/Christ is associated – the cross – can, then, prove to be even more powerful than expected.

As the study of signs and symbols has shown, symbols that endure must be contextualized to do their work, yet they also rise above their context in order to function symbolically. This is why and how Christ as words and images enables Christ as spiritual presence to foster relationships worthy of being identified as a form of Christ in the world today.

To sum up: Christ, then, *is* a particular form of relationship, spiritual presence, and words and images. Christ is not reducible to one of these three components without the other two, but is graspable only in terms of all three simultaneously. Whoever encounters an interpretation of Christ in a visual image, or via a story about Jesus, remains at some distance from attaching a meaning to Christ until they engage in the task of bringing their supposedly 'objective' reading into interplay with their understandings of the inner life of a human being, and of how human beings are to relate to each other. The task of identifying Christ, I repeat, is an existential matter. Whoever works from the context of their primary relationships (family, friends, work, political) towards what and who they believe Christ to be requires the tradition of words and images which both Church and culture carry with them in order to evaluate their patterns of relationship. Christ is not simply to be 'read off' from what purport to be good human relationships. Whoever works outwards from the inner (spiritual) life, believing themselves to have experienced Christ at the core of their being, cannot remain isolated in their conviction. They will cross-check their experience with words and images of Christ used through history. They will also scrutinize the interplay between their personal experience and traditional images with respect to the impact on their understanding of how they relate to others. The triad of dimensions of Christology thus produces a trinity of tasks: to relate each of the dimensions constantly to the other two, lest Christ be narrative or image alone, matter alone or spirit alone. None by itself will do. The incarnate God lives in and among humankind and is carried by its culture. This is the only way we can encounter such a God, even while also believing that God cannot be bound by the way that God has chosen to be.

8

Who is Jesus/Christ for Us Today?

A Contemporary Christology

If my critique is to stand that John B. Cobb Jr 'depersonalized Christ',[1] then I should make it constructive by now offering a substantive answer to Bonhoeffer's question: *who*, then, *is* Christ for us today? The relational Christology to be expounded in this chapter is an attempt to speak about God via the story of Jesus, as (Christocentric) Christian theology must. I introduce eight theological statements, each in the form 'Jesus/Christ as God . . .'.[2] The conviction upheld throughout is: when we have to do with Jesus/Christ, we really have to do with God.[3]

As in Chapter 7, the sections that follow are the result of my sustained engagement with the work of the thinkers discussed in Chapters 4–6. Though my eight statements are not correlated point for point with those earlier chapters, the essential part played by my conversations with the three thinkers will be evident

---

1 See above, p. 169.

2 This wording resists being interpreted along the lines of Jesus/Christ is 'like' God, or behaves 'as if' God were present with Christ (but 'isn't really'). Equally, the form of the statements does not collapse God into Christ without remainder (which would amount to Christomonism).

3 Another form I refrain from using is 'Jesus/Christ is the one who . . .', in order to prevent us from focusing on the solitary, heroic action of a single figure.

throughout. I explore the corporate figure of Jesus/Christ in the following ways:

- as God the inspiring life-giver
- as God the co-sufferer
- as God the friend of sinners and the sinned-against
- as God who saves
- as God embodied in love
- as God's person
- as God's challenging, judging voice
- as the accessible God.

Jesus/Christ as God the inspiring life-giver

The proclamation of Jesus/Christ as risen expresses the conviction that God is a God of life, the source of all life. In formulating this conviction in terms of the resurrection of Jesus, the earliest followers were not saying that Jesus did not die. They were not in denial about the death of their close companion, however traumatic their experience must have been. They were declaring their belief in the life-giving God, despite the death of Jesus of Nazareth, and linking that belief directly to Jesus' life and mission. The sense that Jesus was 'still with them' was clearly confusing – as the not-to-be-harmonized gospel accounts of the resurrection testify. The belief that Jesus was still *with* them asserts a belief that God was active and present with them. The conviction that Jesus was still with *them* is a significant pointer to the corporate way in which the message of resurrection should be received and understood.

The question whether the resurrection was an event for Jesus or an event for his disciples presents a false dichotomy. If it was only an event for Jesus, then it is of no real relevance to anyone, for there were no witnesses, and it carries no necessary consequences for anyone. If it was only an event for his disciples, then God was presumably not involved in any other way than to provoke something in their minds, or their emotional lives. This is not a minor point. In Christian understanding, belief in the resurrection is belief in the *bodily* resurrection of Jesus. In other words, resurrection affects material circumstances and is bound up with the being of Jesus Christ, and not merely with the inner lives of Jesus' followers. Despite the clear implication of some of the early narratives that resuscitation and resurrection were not always as sharply distinguished as might have been helpful,[4] belief in the bodily resurrection of Jesus does two things: it affirms resurrection as an action of God; it asserts resurrection as not merely a spiritual event.

To proclaim Jesus/Christ as risen is thus to affirm belief in the continuing action of a life-giving God as a transforming power in the midst of the material world. The resurrection is therefore best understood as an event for the followers of Jesus/Christ *because* it is an event brought about by God. If God is to be understood christocentrically, and is believed to have being independent of the experience of God's followers, then the action of God the life-giver must be grasped in relation to the figure of Jesus/Christ. The action of God is continuous with the action of Jesus of Nazareth, though resists being construed in terms of the action of an individual working in isolation. This being so, the continuing activity of the resurrecting God needs likewise to be seen as a communal event.[5] Wherever God's transforming, life-giving power is present, a communal setting for the recognition and enjoyment of that life-giving presence will be evident.

---

4 That is, the resurrection narratives in the Gospels do not directly address a question which most contemporary readers inevitably want to ask: was this the same body revivified, or a new, different body which was somehow identifiable as Jesus?

5 A point pressed nearly three decades ago in Peter Selby, *Look for the Living: The Corporate Nature of Resurrection Faith*, London: SCM Press, 1976.

It can be claimed that the resurrection of Jesus is the starting point for all Christian thought and practice.[6] But this should not be understood in the sense that the Church stands or falls on whether a particular past event which happened to Jesus could, or could not, have been caught on video. The resurrection is the starting point for Christian theology because God is a God who goes on giving life in the face of death, and because an understanding of how and why that happens is best channelled through the telling and retelling of the story of Jesus of Nazareth and his many followers.

This continual life-giving power of God is understandably spoken of in early Christianity in terms of the life of, and life in, the spirit of God. Jesus of Nazareth participated in the life of God's spirit, as do his followers. All those who do the will of God embody the spirit of God. For Christians, all understandings of the spirit's work and presence are stamped by the mark of Jesus. In trinitarian terms, the Spirit is forever also the spirit of the Son sent by the Father (and, in Western Christianity, also by the Son). Attention to the spirit's presence and activity in this way must always be a recognition that the spirit is a living, emobodied presence. Belief in the bodily resurrection of Jesus gives birth to a Christocentric doctrine of the spirit. Such a Christocentric pneumatology is thus always also an enfleshed (incarnational) pneumatology.[7]

Jesus/Christ can thus be declared as risen in embodied form where the life-giving presence of God is found. We know about the nature of that presence because of the activity of Jesus of Nazareth among his companions, and through reflection upon his life and impact. That reflection takes place most fully, however,

---

6 H. Wells, *The Christic Center: Life-Giving and Liberating*, Maryknoll: Orbis, 2004, p. 138, though I differ from Wells' emphasis.

7 And we should admit that there is no *de facto* difference between a Christocentric pneumatology and a pneumatological Christology, so long as 'Jesus/Christ' and 'Spirit' are allowed each to interpret the other; Wells, *Christic Center*, p. 119.

with respect to the human contexts in the present in which the presence of the risen Jesus/Christ is celebrated.

Jesus/Christ as God the co-sufferer

Christocentrism is not crucicentrism.[8] There is, however, in Christian terms, no resurrection without crucifixion. This insight is not to be popularized in the slogan 'no pain, no gain', as if the cultivation of pain will bring automatic gain as for an athlete stretching to the limits of physical exertion in order to succeed. Much ascetic practice in Christianity appears to have assumed this, but it is a distortion of the relationship between crucifixion and resurrection. Followers of Jesus/Christ may come to expect suffering. This is to be seen as a consequence of belief or action consistent with proclamation of the presence of God in Jesus/Christ, and is not a matter of seeking to suffer in order to be 'Christ-like'.[9] Jesus/Christ is available to, and present with, all those who suffer. But how is this to be understood?

'Jesus/Christ is present with those who suffer' means that God is really present with *anyone* who suffers. The simple message of the gospel traditions, which take note of and accentuate Jesus of Nazareth's embarrassing inclusiveness, is that those whose humanity is negated, denied or stunted in any way are of special interest to God. This does not merely mean those on the edge of the Church, though Christians are prone to think in such terms. We are dealing with the whole of humanity here.[10] This means that

---

8 Above, pp. 48–9.

9 On which, see e.g. the helpful recent discussion in Deanna Thompson, *Crossing the Divide: Luther, Feminism and the Cross*, Minneapolis: Augsburg Fortress Press, 2004, ch. 4, esp. pp. 111–14.

10 Indeed, with the whole of creation. To explore the implications of what it might mean for Jesus/Christ to be present in the suffering of the whole of creation would take us into important territory, but into areas which there is not space to deal with adequately here.

Jesus/Christ is present not merely with those who are conscious of that presence.

Schleiermacher expressed well the intensity and scale of Christ's suffering in relation to all those who experience suffering.[11] More recently, liberation theologies have taken much further the recognition that God in Christ participates in the suffering of humanity.[12]

God 'co-suffering' means that because of the extent of God's participation in the created order God can be said to experience what his creation experiences. Human suffering is not taken away, but God is so closely active in creation as an ongoing project, that when God's creatures suffer, God does too. God transposes the way in which human beings speak easily to each other of being 'with you in your time of suffering' to a new level of participation in the experience of another. This is the insight resulting from reflecting on incarnation, and the full significance in particular of reflecting on the death of Jesus.

The Church has a vital role to play in highlighting from a Christian perspective the nature and form of this co-suffering presence of God in Christ. The task is, however, one of *identifying*, not controlling it. For God is where God chooses to be present. God is also present where God is called upon. It is part of the Church's collective memory of the God in whom it believes that God in Christ chooses to be present even when and where this is a cause of embarrassment and challenge to the Church itself. Jesus/Christ was not present in Dunblane only when the suffering gathered for worship after the murder of so many of the city's children.[13]

The Church's task, then, is to locate suffering within a dynamic

---

11 Above, pp. 91, 99–100.

12 E.g. C. S. Song, *Jesus, the Crucified People*, Minneapolis: Fortress Press, 1996, esp. ch. 10.

13 I refer here to the shooting of sixteen children and their teacher at their school in Scotland on 13 March 1996.

of crucifixion and resurrection. The words and images used to interpret who Christ is today must, in other words, narrate the full story of Jesus/Christ, from birth to death and beyond. Only by the telling of the full story can God be proclaimed as the life-giver. Only in this way can God's desire and capacity to promote life even in the face of suffering and death be made plain. The Church can certainly be viewed itself as a 'suffering community' in so far as it supports those who suffer, and gathers together those who know their need. But its job is not to foster suffering, even if its role includes helping people to recognize their sinfulness.[14] Nor is its task to claim to understand it. It participates with the rest of humanity in bearing the pain which is part of creation, knowing that God suffers with creation and seeks to enable the created order not to be overwhelmed by suffering.

Jesus/Christ as God the friend of sinners and the sinned-against

Suffering is not the same as sin, although we can see from biblical accounts how and why the two are easily related, and why God is often seen as the cause of suffering.[15] Suffering may bring people together, but suffering is often the result of the denial of humanity. Where humanity is denied, people become isolated, marginalized or are treated as non-persons. Sin can be understood as lack of relationship, fundamentally with God, but also reflected in a lack of relationship to others. It is therefore not surprising to find close correlations both between sin and suffering, and between

---

14 As is often pointed out, the Church clearly does often promote immense suffering through the guilt it induces in people. Guilt need not, of course, always be a bad thing. The Church's job is often bigger and more exacting than it recognizes, in its handling of sin, guilt and God's forgiveness and redemption. As Bonhoeffer recognized, free grace is costly, not cheap.

15 E.g. Gen. 3.16–19; Isa. 45.7, Luke 13.1–5; John 9.1–2.

sin as separation from God and sin as human isolation.[16] Here, the presence and action of God as the friend of those who experience isolation – either as sinner or sinned-against – comes to centre stage. It is not, of course, the case that those who suffer are necessarily any more or less 'sinful' than those who do not suffer. But the suffering, the negated, the nameless are those made conscious of sin: their own and others'. They are aware of what they lack, what they regret or the nature of their exclusion. They are conscious of limitation. They can often see the reasons and causes of their lack of relationship.[17] It is precisely because of this consciousness of sin and its consequences that God's gracious availability and God's power to work on their behalf are clear to them.

A number of understandings of 'sin' are needed in order to tease out what is entailed here. Liberation theologies of many types have drawn attention to the way in which the primary form of sin that people experience may, contrary to much traditional Christian thinking, be that of being 'sinned against'. Those in poverty are often poor because the wealthy exploit and inadequately reward people for their labour. Those who experience racial discrimination do so because of the effortless superiority displayed towards them by other racial groups. Women are (still) often treated as inferior as a result of the patriarchal structures which shape most societies. Throughout the modern period theological developments in understanding sin have emphasized its structural nature.[18] All human beings live within a 'kingdom of

---

16 On sin as separation/lack of relationship, see e.g. M. Grey, 'Falling into Freedom: Searching for New Interpretations of Sin in a Secular Society', *Scottish Journal of Theology* 47, 1994, pp. 223–43, here esp. pp. 230–2.

17 Though often, equally, they cannot. At this point, systematic theology interweaves with the demands of pastoral practice and insights drawn from politics, sociology and psychology.

18 It is a feature of Rauschenbusch's thought and a *sine qua non* of liberation theologies. It should, however, be noted that even Schleiermacher had referred to the impact of 'vital fellowship with Christ' upon 'the disappearing corporate life of sinfulness' (*Christian Faith*, p. 437), an early precursor of Ritschl's 'kingdom of sin' which was to prove so influential on Rauschenbusch.

sin', even while some may strive to live also within the 'kingdom of God'.[19] The drawback of such an emphasis, of course, is that it can lead to a failure to respect the universality of sin.[20] In other words, in (rightly) drawing attention to sins of others, such an emphasis can leave personal, individual forms of sin ill-explored. Sin, however, remains a universal reality, even though it takes a variety of forms.

Structural sin and notions of 'being sinned against' focus upon unjust behaviour within complex webs of relationships. Attention to sin's universality in personal, individual terms dwells more upon each human being's propensity to desire to be free of all forms of dependence and interaction with God and creation in the orientation of their life, as if complete autonomy is possible.[21] Both forms of sin operate as if God were not the life-giving source of our very being. Therefore, to speak of Jesus/Christ in terms of God's friendship with sinners needs unpacking in at least two ways.

First, God is available to all people in the recognition of their own incompleteness, and their need of others and of God. While God is available as the friend even of those who oppress, God is no friend of their oppressive action. As friend of the oppressed, the excluded – those made all too aware of their own unworthiness – Jesus/Christ is the friend of those who are sinned against.[22]

19 Though, it should be noted, this terminology is not meant to imply some specific kind of Lutheran 'two kingdoms' theology.

20 This is not an intention of any of the forms of theology mentioned, all of which affirm the universality of sin, even while drawing out one often overlooked aspect.

21 For a contemporary exposition of 'original sin' which takes seriously both individual/personal and structural forms of sin, see A. McFadyen, *Bound to Sin: Abuse, Holocaust and the Christian Doctrine of Sin*, Cambridge: Cambridge University Press, 2000.

22 There is not space to investigate the full theological implications of the historical proposals suggested by E. P. Sanders in ch. 6 ('The Sinners') of *Jesus and Judaism*, London: SCM Press, 1985. Suffice to say that 'sinners' and 'the common people' are not to be equated in Sanders' judgement and that,

Jesus/Christ has come, after all, to call not the righteous but sinners (Mark 2.17).[23] The righteous are likely to be a satisfied people. Sinners, by contrast, are those who know their need. The righteous are those who need to be made aware of their need. Jesus/Christ is risen both among those who know their own need, sense their incompleteness, and who seek relationship with others and with God, and among those who are blocked from seeing the possibility of relating to God.[24] In this (relational) sense, Christ was 'made . . . to be sin . . . so that in him we might become the righteousness of God' (2 Cor. 5.21).

Second, Jesus/Christ is for us God the *friend* of sinners and the sinned-against. Friendship is a surprisingly underdeveloped concept in Christian thought and practice.[25] It will be examined further in *Christ in Practice*. Suffice to say at this point that Brock's insights on the Gospels are particularly helpful here: Jesus is to be understood in the context of his friends and is dependent on people around him. This aspect of the biblical tradition accentuates the fact that God implicates Godself within the plot of human history. We may even go so far as to say that God is

---

furthermore, Jesus may have welcomed people (even 'sinners' in the technical sense of transgressors of the Jewish Law) without requiring them to repent. The point, of course, is to stress how bound up the Jesus movement was with opposing social exclusion in any form, in the interests of embodying in practice the inclusivity of a gracious God.

23 One intriguing aspect of the gospel traditions' transmission of this saying is Luke's (or Luke's source's) adding of 'to repentance' to the Marcan wording (Luke 5.32). One might have expected this more of Matthew, who retains the Marcan wording in Matt. 9.13.

24 Jesus/Christ does not take away what people feel, but feels what people feel in being risen among them. In this sense, Christ is with them.

25 Though see now E. D. H. Carmichael, *Friendship: Interpreting Christian Love*, London and New York: T. & T. Clark International, 2004. Earlier studies include G. Meilaender, *Friendship: A Study in Theological Ethics*, Notre Dame: University of Notre Dame Press, 1981; M. E. Hunt, *Fierce Tenderness: A Feminist Theology of Friendship*, New York: Crossroad, 1992; E. Stuart, *Just Good Friends*, London: Mowbray, 1995; and E. Moltmann-Wendel, *Rediscovering Friendship*, London: SCM Press, 2000.

subject to the whims and decisions of the characters acting in the plot of Christian history. God does not ultimately control them. Such is the risk of friendship and the risk that God in Christ takes as the friend of sinners and the sinned-against.

A Christocentric concept of God makes clear why God cannot coerce people to act in ways to which they do not assent. As friend, God relies on people's willingness to act. As friend, God is dependent upon those sought as friends in friendship. God desires to be a friend to all, but cannot be if those sought in friendship refuse God's friendship, and refuse to participate in God's friendly, friend-making project. Wherever friendship emerges, however – often at the edges of identifiable 'church' – Jesus/Christ, the bearer of God's friendship, is present.

Friendship understood in this way invites theological exploration and interpretation. For to be Christ-like, a friendship needs to be more than a relationship between 'like and like'. A friendship which reflects that of a gracious, generous God spills over beyond the safety of a relationship between similar people and desires to include others. The practice of such friendship, and theological reflection upon that practice, then combine to deepen and enhance the experience of friendship. In turn, more of God in Christ is discovered. Such exploration contributes to the disclosure of the real presence of divine friendship, identified through the recognition of Jesus/Christ among friends. Theology is then a form of language for expressing the fact that sinners and the sinned-against can make the best of friends, for only true friends are able to acknowledge sinfulness.

Jesus/Christ as God who saves

'[O]nly the suffering God can help.'[26] This was Bonhoeffer's conclusion in 1930s and 1940s Germany. His conclusion has been echoed ever since. But the suffering of God is itself not enough. Bonhoeffer maintained that God was always a resurrecting God, while also emphasizing the suffering endured by God within the suffering of God's people. Perhaps, though, even the suffering and resurrecting God is not enough. For what is to be made of the 'saving God'? In what sense, if any, can we claim today that 'Jesus saves'? Christianity would not be Christianity without claiming the saving significance of Jesus/Christ. It is not attention to Christian doctrine alone which requires such a conclusion.[27] When Christians claim that they have 'experience' of Jesus/Christ, they refer to the saving power of God in Jesus/Christ. But what is this, and how does it work?

Jesus/Christ 'saves', first of all, as God the forgiving companion. In the context of friendship, where sin and sins are acknowledged and named, God's forgiveness can be present too. In much Christian thought and practice it has been implied that we need to be forgiven for who we are, as if human nature itself were flawed. But even if there remains a need for a notion of 'original sin', in order to stress the human propensity to seek to be self-sufficient and self-reliant, it is also true that Christianity must risk the charge of Pelagianism in believing in the goodness of creation. In maintaining a conviction that when God created human beings, God looked and saw that humanity was good, Christians have to stress, alongside the universality of sin, the constant possibility

---

26 D. Bonhoeffer, *Letters and Papers from Prison: The Enlarged Edition*, London: SCM Press, 1971, p. 361.

27 That is, the knowledge that any Christian theology worthy of the name 'Christian' would have a chapter on soteriology within it.

of God's goodness being visible in the world.[28] In Christian understanding, then, each individual needs forgiving in a deep, existential sense for their sin, in order to be reoriented towards the God upon whom their very existence depends. This feature of soteriology is unevenly treated both in the New Testament and in later Christian tradition though is prominent in the writings of the apostle Paul and in all branches of Christendom directly influenced by his understanding of salvation.

Locating the forgiving activity of God in the context of a Christology of friendship reminds us that an individual(istic), existential understanding of forgiveness can lead to a tendency to overlook the covenantal context within which such forgiveness is discovered and worked out. Paul would have frowned upon the way his understanding of forgiveness and salvation has become detached from a consideration of the relationship between God and God's people. He might have been equally bemused by the shift which now seems necessary to a variety of social contexts within which such forgiveness has to be discovered: work, family, friendships.[29] It is, however, thoroughly in continuity with the Judaism of Jesus' and Paul's day to offer an extended interpretation of the forgiving companionship of God, so that the Church (even when the Church is understood in continuity with 'Israel' understood as the people of God) is not the only corporate setting within which the discovery of Jesus/Christ can be made.

---

28 As has been rightly expressed: 'the Pelagian assessment of the effects of Adam's fall and understanding of grace cannot be squared with Scripture, although the church, in decisively rejecting Pelagian views, did not wholly endorse Augustine's refutations' (D. F. Wright, 'Pelagianism' in S. B. Ferguson and D. F. Wright (eds.), New Dictionary of Theology, Downers Grove and Leicester: IVP, 1988, p. 501). In other words, Christian thought has remained caught on the horns of a dilemma about whether humans really are basically bad or basically good, even though it seems to have resolved the problem by siding with Augustine.

29 Allowing for the fact also that work relationships, being often 'contractual', could therefore also be considered not to be 'covenantal' at all.

If forgiveness is to be relationally conceived, in a communal context, then the presence of Jesus/Christ, as the forgiving friendship of God, must be identified within a variety of settings. Jesus/Christ is really present when a parent forgives a child, and a child a parent. Jesus/Christ is really present when an employee forgives an employer and vice versa.[30] Jesus/Christ is really present when friend forgives friend, or church member a minister. If it is felt necessary for this somewhat anecdotal, 'ordinary' understanding of forgiveness then to be rooted in the deeper, more existential understanding already described, then so be it.[31] But the latter (theological-existential) understanding cannot do without the former, and the former (ordinary) understanding locates the action of the saving God firmly in the concrete world of everyday life.

The term 'companionship' also invites further reflection. A companion is one with whom one eats bread.[32] It is far from coincidental that historical research into Jesus and the doctrinal, doxological and ecclesiastical developments of the religious and theological appropriation of Jesus' life should have made so much of Jesus' eating habits. The Last Supper has to be read in the light of Jesus' shared meals (large and small) or else it is misunderstood. It should not be interpreted only as a sacramental meal, appropriate though that is.[33] Evangelistic campaigns constructed around

---

30 It is striking how easily it is assumed in employment contexts (not to mention church) that to apologize is seen as a sign of weakness (and to refuse to apologize a sign of 'strong leadership'). Nothing could, of course, be further from the truth, though this may not alter the fact that people who seem unable to apologize nevertheless remain in managerial positions!

31 The interplay between theological reflection and daily living is explored more fully in *Christ in Practice*.

32 A link can also be forged here with J. D. Crossan's recent presentation of Jesus' eating habits, in terms of 'open commensality' in *The Historical Jesus: The Life of a Mediterranean Jewish Peasant*, New York: HarperSanFrancisco, 1991, pp. 261–4.

33 There is, of course, insufficient space to begin an excursus into the nature of the presence of Christ at the mass/eucharist/communion. Suffice it

shared meals may be criticized for bribing potential converts with free food. They have also recognized something fairly basic: people loosen up over (and after) meals; they talk, relate, connect. Equally, cultures reveal a great deal through their eating habits. It is of profound significance that the variety of ways in which people shared food was important for the Jesus movement. Meals among friends, meals of invitees, hillside gatherings, begging were all significant and require careful attention in the reception of the Jesus tradition. Forgiveness features at the heart of such a daily occurrence as a shared meal.

Relationships between regular companions would not be sustainable without the thanksgiving expressed in the saying of 'grace' and in the practice of confession and absolution which can occur in the contexts of meals shared with friends. If mass/eucharist/communion may be felt to have institutionalized this dynamic of forgiveness,[34] then the ritualized Last Supper at least points to the potential of every shared meal to be a context in which the forgiveness of God can be offered and received. Because Jesus/Christ is present in the world as the saving God who forgives, the presence of Jesus/Christ can be enjoyed in the context of shared meals among friends.[35]

Attention to the saving action of God in Jesus/Christ cannot avoid one further crucial issue: *how* 'Jesus saves'. All that has been said so far suggests the answer that Jesus/Christ 'saves' by being the continually life-giving, forgiving presence of God in the midst

---

to say that the fact that I do not begin there commits me to neither a 'high' nor a 'low' understanding of this sacrament! The sacrament, however, focuses the nature of the presence of Christ throughout the world (though not equally in all things). It is not a presence of Christ distinct in kind from where Christ is elsewhere present.

34 Ironic at a time when modernity gets flak for having secularized Western culture.

35 A point I address in 'Did You Say "Grace"?: Eating in Community in *Babette's Feast*' in C.Marsh and G. Ortiz, *Explorations in Theology and Film*, Oxford: Blackwell, 1997, pp. 207–18.

of people's deepest relationships. Though this is true, it may still not say enough. For has not the 'how?' question been clearly addressed throughout the Christian tradition by referring to the Jewish sacrificial tradition, leading to a doctrine of atonement? And even if the Christian appropriation of that sacrificial tradition has been substantiated, and yet also in part undermined, by such writings as the Letter to the Hebrews,[36] the question remains about what sense is to be made of the appropriation of the doctrine of atonement today. In line with the relational Christology being worked out here, I need to make sense of the doctrine of the atonement in relational, communal terms.

The doctrine of the atonement is the main way in which Christian theology has addressed the question of the continuing salvific effect of the death of Christ. It is clearly not the whole picture of salvation as far as Christian thought and practice are concerned.[37] Nor has Christianity ever placed its trust in a single theory of atonement. The extent to which doctrinal formulations are time-bound is perhaps nowhere more apparent than in relation to this doctrine.[38] But the sense that 'Jesus died for our sins' is deeply rooted in Christian thought and practice, however many different answers there are to the question of *how* that death achieves this. Twentieth- and twenty-first-century criticism of versions of the

---

36 By interpreting Jesus as the sacrifice to end all sacrifices (Heb. 9.11–14). The portrayal of Jesus quoting Hosea 6.6 – 'I desire mercy not sacrifice' – in Matt. 9.13 is also relevant here.

37 See e.g. the many models of soteriology presented in J. McIntyre, *The Shape of Soteriology*, Edinburgh: T. & T. Clark, 1992, ch. 2.

38 There are different accounts of how many theories exist in Christian tradition and how they should be interpreted. See e.g. G. Aulén, *Christus Victor*, London: SPCK, 1931; P. Fiddes, *Past Event and Present Salvation*, London: Darton, Longman & Todd, 1989, and C. J. den Heyer, *Jesus and the Doctrine of the Atonement*, London: SCM Press, 1998, which stresses again the culturally conditioned nature of the different theories. For the most recent discussions of the atonement, see e.g. J. D. Weaver, *Non-Violent Atonement*, Grand Rapids and Cambridge: Eerdmans, 2001; and H. Boersma, *Violence, Hospitality and the Cross: Reappropriating the Atonement Tradition*, Grand Rapids: Baker Academic, 2004.

doctrine which have held sway in Christian tradition (especially penal and sacrificial theories, including versions of the substitutionary theory of atonement) have been prominent in recent discussions about the atonement. Whatever value is contained within such theories, the understandings of God which they imply are profoundly problematic. God needed, and needs, no sacrifice; that is a basic Christian (and Jewish-prophetic) insight (Amos 5.21–22). To add that God does not even need the sacrifice of Jesus is a challenging but not inconsistent extension of that insight, however necessary it has proved for Christian tradition to reflect on the meaning of the death of Jesus in sacrificial terms.[39]

To accept therefore that Brock and other critics of the understanding of atonement so often used in Christian thought and practice are justified in their criticisms raises two main questions. What is to be done with the fact that the doctrine of the atonement is nevertheless *there* in Christian tradition (and used very heavily in Christian liturgy)? How can a relational Christology inform the reception and reworking of the doctrine?

The doctrine is simply there, so it has to be made sense of in some way. But it must be critiqued. In fact, attention to the death of Jesus does not inevitably send us towards a doctrine of atonement, any more than it requires us to adhere to one particular version of that doctrine.[40] It is better to relocate the death of Jesus within a relational Christology so that the death is understood

---

39 For some account of why Jesus died is bound to be called for.

40 Grayston's meticulous study of understandings of the death of Jesus, as handled in the New Testament, is especially useful here, and his overall conclusions very salutary. There are many features of his conclusion which are compatible with this whole study, not least his statement: 'I stress these social connexions of the death of Christ ... in order to counter the impression that his death belongs chiefly to a transaction with God carried out on our behalf, that it is primarily a feature of atonement theology concerned with the removal of guilt. To act on that impression is to deprive Christ's death of a great deal of its significance' (*Dying, We Live: A New Enquiry into the Death of Christ in the New Testament*, London: Darton, Longman & Todd, 1990, p. 367).

within the continuum of life, death and resurrection of Jesus, and so also that the continuum of Jesus' life history is viewed in the context of those around him. At this point, the insights of all three thinkers discussed in Part Two converge. The redemptive power of Christ is contained in living fellowship with Christ. Christ is a social reality. The isolation and abandonment of Jesus on the cross are not overlooked. They are transformed through God's acting in and among Jesus and his followers. Despite their initial denial of Jesus, his immediate followers came to be carriers (in word and presence) of the Kingdom he proclaimed and celebrated.

The isolation and abandonment of Jesus on the cross, and of any who experience such desolation through sin or being sinned against, are conquered by the social solidarity and connectedness of participation in the social reality of Christ. The inevitable death of Jesus remains a shocking event.[41] But it attracts to itself huge significance because it stands as a stark example of the costliness, in human terms, of God's quest for right relationships within the created order. God's self-expenditure in Christ puts at risk God's redemptive project, because it is subject to being taken up within the ongoing life of Jesus/Christ as embodied in the lives of Jesus' followers. But this is clearly the risk God was prepared to take. It is a risk wholly consistent with the way in which God created a free world.

God does not, then, require the sacrifice of Jesus, but participates in Jesus' self-offering with full recognition that this is the cost of loving. Atonement theories are understandably woven around Jesus' death because of the realization of the cosmic significance of the event in so far as the project of God – for God's Kingdom to come – is obstructed by the fracture of the body of Christ. Here we see the value of the discussion so far: Christ's body is

---

41 'Inevitable' not in the sense of being directly willed by God, but in the sense that that is the kind of things that human beings do, given the 'kingdom of sin' within which we all live.

not Jesus' alone. If the body of Christ is understood relationally (as a concrete example of the patterns of relationship willed by God for God's Kingdom), then obstructions to the establishing of such relationships are brought into sharp relief. The obstruction caused by the disruption of a primary example of that sought-for relationship (as manifest in Jesus and his movement) is a challenge to the potential success of the freedom of God to act in the world. Jesus' death was thus not 'willed by God'. It was accepted as a costly consequence of freedom. The resulting brokenness of the body of Christ has also to be lived with. Yet its brokenness does not deter the life-giving will and power of God. The saving struggle of God to reconstitute the body of Christ in the world is the resurrecting God's activity to go on creating life.

How then does God save in Jesus/Christ? God saves by overcoming the death of Jesus through the resurrection, and through seeing that resurrection reflected in lively, life-enhancing fellowship of those who live 'in Christ'. The death of Jesus is constantly re-enacted in the death wish of forms of human (lack of) relationship which stifle humanity. Such stifling of relationship constantly needs transforming into the new relationality of the body of Christ. The God who co-suffers within the human realm bears within Godself the pain of the failure of relationship – and thus the pain of the death of Jesus is felt by God – and the pain of the cost of forgiveness within any human relationship where relationships are twisted or broken. But the death of Jesus is not 'needed' by God. It has only been 'needed' by Christian interpreters, in the sense that the life, death and resurrection of Jesus have enabled Christians to see the kind of God with whom we are dealing.[42]

God saves in Jesus/Christ, then, by incorporating people within Christ's body. If we are not to understand what it means to be 'in Christ' ecclesiocentrically, however, then we must be reminded again that church and the body of Christ are not identical. While

---

42 See previous note.

the Church has a crucial, prophetic and educational role in seeking to clarify who, what and where Christ is, Christ's body must be identified in terms of where God in Christ is present and active, not where any form of church would like Christ to be. Christ's body is where forgiveness happens and where new life is found. If that seems to happen primarily in various patterns of relationships with which forms of 'church' intersect – family, friendships, work, nation/state, race – then these are the forms of Christ's body which need to be investigated to find the form that salvation takes.[43]

Discussion about atonement does, however, keep in view one very significant aspect of God's saving activity in Jesus/Christ, which a relational, christological approach is always likely to downplay. Such discussion keeps alive the tension between objective and subjective poles of salvation – the giver and receiver of salvation. In so doing, it reminds us that the salvation effected by God within the context of human relationships is always enfleshed divine activity, and never simply human action, even as human response to a divine act or initiative.[44] So, however inadequate past atonement theories prove to be, their intent to pinpoint the objectivity of divine action within the course of human events needs maintaining. For the objectivity of God's action is paramount even when the emphasis of that action is shifted from a single past, historical action to the in-betweenness of human interrelationships past and present. In the same way that relatively adequate atonement theories always need to combine subjective and objective dimensions,[45] so also participation in the

---

43 This is explored further in *Christ in Practice*.

44 On subjective and objective aspects of atonement, see e.g. Fiddes, *Past Event*, pp. 26–30.

45 I am adapting here the use of the term 'relative adequacy' from David Tracy, *The Analogical Imagination*, London: SCM Press, 1981, thereby respecting the provisional nature of all theological formulations.

saving work of Christ recognizes divine and human initiative synergistically at work.[46]

Jesus/Christ as God embodied in love

A relational Christology cannot speak of relationship in an unspecific sense, for, as has already been noted, not all relationships are necessarily good. God is love (1 John 4.16), and therefore Jesus/Christ is a loving body. Both aspects of the presence of God – love and embodiedness – need addressing.

The presence of Jesus/Christ cannot be reduced to spiritual or to material presence alone. But it is of profound importance that those standing in relationship to each other 'in Christ' are embodied – that is, living and tangible in today's 'real world', particularly given the tendency throughout Christian tradition to overemphasize the spiritual nature of the presence of Jesus/Christ. This is one of the main reasons why the historicity of Jesus of Nazareth remains crucial in a Christian exploration of the contemporary body of Christ. Jesus' actual historical existence requires Christians to keep embodiment – messy incarnation and concreteness – at the heart of their exploration into the being and presence of God. Where reflection on the figure of Jesus isolates him from his own context and from his immediate followers, it is not possible for the social nature of the being and presence of Christ to be fully understood.

An attempt to interpret the love of God in light of this, then, will need to tease out the theological significance of the dependence of Jesus on those around him (and not merely on the basis of Jesus' relationship to his Father). Love is expressed in interdependence.

---

46 Such a statement will always be treated with suspicion by Reformation-inspired theologians, as it makes salvation in part a human work. Divine initiative is, of course, not denied here. This is neither Pelagianism nor anthropocentrism. It is merely a recognition that human reception of divine salvation is a dynamic process.

The continuing presence of God in the world in the form of the body of Christ renders God in a clear sense dependent upon creation by God's own choice. This is itself an expression of God's action as a loving God. It is through the interdependence of all those upon whom God depends that God hopes and trusts that just, true, authentic and loving relationships will emerge.[47]

A relational Christology compels us to attend to how loving relationships take place in concrete, embodied terms. Relational Christology does not allow us to get away with personal (individual) attention to the spiritual life, either in interpreting Jesus' life or in understanding our own. Furthermore, recognition of the fact that Jesus/Christ is present in the world as embodied love invites Christians to reflect upon the possibility of 'working back' from human experience of embodied love to a deepening understanding of God in Jesus/Christ. 'Embodied love' here includes but is not confined to sexual love.[48] All forms of love are embodied in the sense that it is people, as bodies, who love. Different forms of love are expressed physically in different ways, including by a handshake or an embrace, as well as in sexual intimacy.[49] When Brock draws our attention to the 'erotic' aspects of human,

---

47 I do not wish to seek to clarify who God depends on, i.e., whether they are *conscious* of working for God or not. It may even be said that God actively depends on *all* creatures. I do not see how an answer to such questions is possible. The most we can say is that God seeks to be interdependent with the whole creation in the hope that all choose to work for the well-being of all.

48 Nor, of course, is all sexual activity included in the reference, for not all sexual activity is loving. Sexual relations do, however, offer one of the most profound expressions of embodied love in human affairs. What sexual activity 'counts', why and in what ways, would need to be the subject of another book.

49 'Saying the peace' in the context of Christian worship is an intriguing and sometimes problematic example of how the embodiment of the body of Christ is respected in Christian faith: people actually touch each other (via a handshake or embrace), possibly someone they do not know. This constitutes an unusual public action in Western cultures. This ritual practice is, of course, sometimes abused by participants, and is understandably a difficult ritual for survivors of sexual abuse. It can, however, also be a small and significant ritual of the celebration of embodiment.

embodied interrelationship, she is stressing the extent to which love will not ignore the material, the enfleshed.[50]

This has two important implications. It means, first, that the loving presence of Jesus/Christ in the world can only take enfleshed form. Bonhoeffer may have proved too ecclesiocentric in his insistence on the concreteness of Christ. His recognition of the form of Christ as loving relationship in the most concrete of terms cannot, however, be sidestepped. As will be shown in *Christ in Practice*, though Bonhoeffer does not answer adequately for our purposes all questions about the concrete forms of Christ's presence in the world, his stark demand that concrete social forms of Christ be identified is persuasive. You cannot, in other words, get away with pointing out that Christ is a social reality without specifying what forms that social reality takes.

Second, focusing on the enfleshment of love therefore has socio-political implications. The social reality of Christ will need to be identifiable in particular structures of human community. If love is to be made manifest in concrete form in particular kinds of human relationship, then it is important to create structures that foster such relationships. Not only do you have to specify the social forms in which Christ is present, you also have to clarify how such social forms take shape.

While recognizing its imperfection, the Church seeks to be one example of such a structure. But it is a body that is *conscious* of its participation in Christ, and aware of its faltering ability to identify who and where Christ is in the world. To be fully 'in Christ', the Church must see as part of its task the role of influencing other 'bodies', via its collective impact and the influence of its individual members in an explicitly political manner.[51] It is also to take a lead

---

50 Brock is not referring here simply to sexual activity, though her definition of 'erotic' is not unconnected.

51 On which, see e.g. D. Forrester, *Theology and Politics*, Oxford: Blackwell, 1988, esp. ch. 5. This relates also to the task of 'Christianizing' which Rauschenbusch was exploring, though his discussion must now be

in the task of identifying who and where Christ is clearly present in other social forms. What is the form of a family in which Christ is seen to be present? What is a Christ-like friendship? When are working relations able to be characterized as being 'in Christ'?

In exploring this political dimension of the presence of Jesus/ Christ in the world as God's embodied love, a tension between the crucified and risen Christ will always be apparent. The frailty and incompleteness of all social forms of Christ will be evident. The Church and all other social approximations of the body of Christ are, like Christ, broken and awaiting full consummation of the (eschatological) promise of resurrection.

It is thus appropriate for Christian thought and practice to relate the notion of the body of Christ more to the Kingdom of God than to the Church as we now know it.[52] This far from plays down the importance of the Church. But it acknowledges the Church's limited place in the world and also the freedom of God in Jesus/ Christ to work both within and outside it. 'The community of the baptized' is always bigger than the Church as usually conceived; Christ's body always reaches further than Christians usually recognize. This community is therefore already an extension of the political shape of the body of Christ in the world. As such, the

---

recast, in the light of critique of his own position, away from assumptions about the superiority of Christianity and about the potential equation of Christianizing and Americanizing (see above, p. 137).

52 The Pauline references to 'Kingdom of God' are notoriously slender (8 references in Romans, 1 Corinthians, Galatians and 1 Thessalonians; 6 more in Ephesians, Colossians and 2 Thessalonians). With some possible exceptions (e.g. Rom. 14.17 and Col. 1.13) nearly all are future-oriented eschatological references. It is hard to adapt Paul's words in the way that some gospel texts can be used (above all Matt. 12.28/Luke 11.20 and Luke 17.21) for a present understanding of the Kingdom of God, related to the quality of relationship which exists between people in this life. Paul's exploration of 'body of Christ' language (esp. from 1 Cor. 12) can, however, be used in this way, so long as we banish current notions of what constitutes 'church' from our minds. And as one eminent New Testament scholar reminded me not so long ago: 'We must not forget that Paul did not, in fact, belong to what we might call a "local church".'

'community of the baptized' invites fuller realization in publicly identifiable form through those who participate in it living lives which embody more and more the love of God individually and communally.

Members of the community of the baptized, as those who symbolize but do not exhaust the reach of God's presence in Jesus/Christ in the world, thereby contribute to the fulfilment of God's Kingdom in the world. They are not alone in this. But they are empowered to do so by the spirit of God at work in them by virtue of their baptism. The body of Christ – as the embodied love of God – is thus the crucial christological image for linking the Church to the desire of God that the whole world become God's Kingdom.

Jesus/Christ as God's person

If the doctrine of the atonement needed revisiting in the light of attention to relational Christology, then the same applies to the Chalcedonian definition of Jesus/Christ as 'truly God, truly human'. Reached in AD 451, after political and theological wrangling and the application of insights drawn from pastoral practice across many generations of Christian experience, the Chalcedonian definition was always doing more than merely saying something about Jesus of Nazareth. Definitions of God, salvation and what it means to be human were also bound up in it. By then, the doctrine of the Trinity had also emerged as the conceptual framework within which the person and work of Jesus Christ were to be understood. We are, then, to receive the Chalcedonian definition in the context of the 'differentiated theism' which the doctrine of the Trinity sought to express.[53]

---

53 This has been one of the focal points of recent trinitarian discussion, as a result of the need to clarify how and why the doctrine of the Trinity is an understanding of God so different from other monotheistic traditions' views of God. In some cases, e.g. the work of J. Moltmann in *The Trinity and the Kingdom of God*, London: SCM Press, 1981, the apologetic purpose sometimes appears to have gone so far that his phraseology begins to sound tri-theistic.

211

The Chalcedonian definition displays the tendency to separate Jesus/Christ from the rest of humanity, despite what it professes to state. However, rereading Chalcedon in the light of a shift towards a relational Christology invites us to consider how Christology always attempts to clarify what a human being is meant to be. In seeking to understand Jesus/Christ as 'God's person', we address the question of what God wants humanity to be like. The challenge is how to respond to that question without descending into anthropocentrism.

The first step is to grasp the components that make up Christian understanding of Jesus/Christ as the 'image of God', and how therefore human beings themselves may be understood as also made in God's image. The interplay between Genesis 1.26–27 and Colossians 1.15 is particularly important. For the writer of Colossians, it is Christ who gives us insight into what God is like, for Christ bears (is!) God's image. It is clear that Christ has more than a salvific significance, though this is present in Colossians 1.20. It is more accurate to say that because Christ carries a salvific significance, therefore something fundamental is being claimed about Christ's shaping of what it means to be human. The very relationship between creator and created, reflected in Genesis 1 is affected by what happens 'in Christ'. The reconciliation of 'all things' in Christ is the purpose of salvation (Col. 1.20).

Whichever way one approaches the matter, there is, then, a link between a relational understanding of God (Trinity), a relational understanding of the human being (the human being as a social animal) and a relational understanding of Jesus/Christ. All three cohere within Christian thought and practice. Overemphasis upon the solitariness of Jesus/Christ as divine and human in one person can thus mislead. It is therefore imperative that Christology develop a relational understanding of Jesus/Christ as God's person. Humanity and divinity are found in perfect interaction in the person of Jesus/Christ. Embodied in Jesus and his followers, and embodied in all relationships that embody love and thus reflect the life-giving, transforming power of God, Jesus/Christ is the continuing revelation of what it means to be fully human. The goal of studying the person of Christ is thus the full formation of persons made in God's image, because Jesus/Christ is for Christians the way in which what it means to be a person is made evident in the world.

Jesus/Christ as God's challenging, judging voice

What place is there in a relational understanding of Christ for the prophetic edge of Jesus of Nazareth? How can an understanding of Jesus/Christ which could easily become all too comfortable, and lazily affirm existing relationships, also reflect the way in which Christ can be critical of the Church, and can challenge human beings in their attempt to live humanly, individually and communally? Jesus of Nazareth's criticism of over-dependence upon family invites us to reflect on where the primary relationships that contribute to the Kingdom's emergence are to be located (Mark 3.31–35). There is further such prophetic speech in the traditions about Jesus, whether or not all of it derives directly from Jesus himself: the Matthean woes against the scribes and Pharisees (23.1–36), the criticisms of the wealthy (Mark 10.17–22; Luke 6.24–25), the challenge to the disciples who sought rank (Mark 9.33–37 and parallels; Mark 10.35–45). What is to happen to such sharp-edged tradition within a communal, relational understanding of Jesus/Christ?

It need not be softened or tamed. If friendships are best when sin is acknowledged and the firm rebuke of another occurs in a constructive way within an existing relationship, then prophecy has not been excluded from a relational Christology: Jesus/Christ is both supporter and critic of the way that people live. But where, then, is the voice of the stranger, the outsider, in this rather all-encompassing world? How is Jesus/Christ to speak 'from the outside' when the main thrust of relational Christologies will always be that Jesus/Christ is to be discovered in and through the complex and intricate network of living human relationships?

We confront here a further aspect of what our critical questioning of Brock's work revealed: that a downplaying of transcendence runs the risk of preventing Jesus/Christ from speaking over against our attempts to discover and shape Christ within the patterns of our relationships.[54] A sense of the transcendence of Christ is necessary even when the focus of who, where and what Christ is today is placed on embodied relationships. Transcendence is experienced within the networks of relationships in which Christ is discovered to be present. Experience of Christ's otherness occurs not simply in aesthetic, experiential or even mystical forms (e.g. as awe or joy or fear). 'Otherness' is also experienced as a word of challenge or criticism. So it is through respect for transcendence (as a means of acknowledging that it is God who is present in Christ in the midst of human relationships) that Christ can function as the judge of human complacency and comfort.

In their study *Being in Communion*, Stephen Fowl and Gregory Jones develop this point in relation to the Church as the 'person-forming' community. Chapter 5 of their study focuses on the way that the Church learns from 'outsiders'. They comment:

> Any community that cuts itself off from engagement with outsiders deprives itself needlessly of a crucial resource for living and interpreting faithfully ... If we are to listen to the voices of outsiders, we need to be able both to recognize outsiders and to learn how to listen to their strange voices.[55]

In the same way that the Church does not exist in isolation but is

---

54 Appeal to Bond's 'imaginative transcendence' is again important. See above, Ch. 6 n. 41.

55 S. E. Fowl and L. G. Jones, *Reading in Communion: Scripture and Ethics in Christian Life*, London: SPCK, 1991, pp. 110–11.

challenged 'from outside', so also all concrete communal contexts in which God in Christ struggles for presence need to receive the challenge of other communities. In general terms, Fowl's and Jones' view of the Church might be considered overly optimistic.[56] Nevertheless, their study acknowledges that Christ is not consumed by the Church, however important the notion of the Church as a manifestation of Christ's body in the world proves to be.

Attention to the way in which God speaks through outsiders thus provides a theological rationale for respecting the limits of the Church as the sole collection of communities in which God in Christ is embodied. If the presence of Jesus/Christ is never exhausted by any particular, concrete human community then it must also be possible to understand Christ to be present across and through a diversity of concrete forms. Only in this way can Jesus/Christ play fully the role of the prophetic, challenging voice of God in the world.[57] Christian communities are judged by the fact that other communities exist (in other religious traditions, or as neighbourhood groups, or as political campaigns) which sometimes more clearly embody God in Christ than does the Church.

A second example of the need for Jesus/Christ to continue to play this critical role can be found through conversation with the work of Jackie Grant. Grant observes the ways in which words are

---

56 Their account is an attempt to be inspirationally prescriptive for church life even while presented as exposition (so that the Church 'might become what it is').

57 Another way of expressing this would be to say that any theology needs a theology of culture, thus clarifying the relationship between Church and world/Church and society in relation to which that theology deems its subject-matter to be found. Any Christian (or Jewish) theology which finds no place for what I call the 'Cyrus of Persia Principle' (according to which God can be seen to be at work in the world from outside God's identified people, cf. Isa. 44.28; 45.1) ceases to be plausible. In contemporary terms we could say that God befriends God's own supposed critics.

easy to use in theology yet they sometimes cloak injustices and play down the challenges which theologically informed action entails. She notes, for example, the easy use of the term 'partnership' in theological discourse, even though 'partnerships are neither necessarily equal nor necessarily healthy'.[58] This insight should be used to examine carefully calls for a relational Christology, for not all relationships are necessarily healthy. At issue is what *kind* of relationship is being commended through appeal to a relational Christology. In her critique of White women's easy adoption of the language of partnership Grant writes: 'From a Black woman's vantage point . . . the language of partnership is merely a rewording of the language of "reconciliation", which proves to be empty rhetoric unless it is preceded by liberation.'[59] The relationships which Christ brings about are just and loving. For them to become a reality judgement may therefore be involved: a critique of bad practice en route to a better relationship; repentance for past actions, and forgiveness, so that a relationship may begin again. Liberation can be a struggle. Susan Bond affirms this insight by Grant: 'Relational approaches imply a "make-nice" policy of "Can't we all just get along?" that run the risk of reducing social justice to group therapy.'[60] The message is clear: a concern to develop a relational Christology may conceal a desire to smooth out the rough edges which encounter with Jesus/Christ in the context of living, embodied relationships actually entails. Cheap grace, forgiveness without cost, reconciliation without liberation will not be participation in the body of Christ. Fostering such a relational Christology would be like trying to seek resurrection without crucifixion.

---

58 J. Grant, *White Women's Christ, Black Women's Jesus*, Atlanta: Scholars Press, 1989, p. 191.

59 Grant, *White Women's Christ, Black Women's Jesus*, p. 191.

60 L. S. Bond, *Trouble with Jesus: Women, Christology, and Preaching*, St Louis, MO: Chalice Press, 1999, p. 33.

Jesus/Christ as the accessible God

If focusing the presence of God in the world on a single individual has had its drawbacks, it has also had its payoffs: the presence of God becomes manageable, simplified and able to be portrayed more easily than would be possible with an abstract thought or belief. Incarnation, availability and accessibility hang together. Christian theology has, though, been weak in supporting a notion of God's 'continuing incarnation', save when it has lazily read too much into the institutional forms of the Church. Relational Christologies have the responsibility of contributing to the exploration of God's continuing incarnation in Jesus/Christ in the world, while at the same time seeking to maintain the sense of the accessibility of God which has come from concentrating on Jesus of Nazareth as the Christ.

Because it is *Jesus* who has been called Christ, then it is Jesus who becomes the means through which the accessible God is portrayed: in words and images, as well as in embodied relationships and as spiritual presence. It is only because all of these dimensions are at work in Christian thought and practice that Christians saying 'Jesus is here' can begin to make any sense. It is upon this basis that christological art, literature, film and sculpture do their work. God cannot be visually portrayed. But Jesus *is* God as far as Christians are concerned, in the sense that it is through portrayal of Jesus as God that Christians can talk to and about God, and relate to God, at all. ('No one has ever seen God. It is God the only Son, who is close to the Father's heart, who has made him known', John 1.18.) Jesus/Christ makes God accessible by being God for us. It became clear in Chapter 3, however, how easily the complexity of the christological task can be short-circuited, and so Christianity itself fails to fulfil its broader brief: to communicate what it knows of *God* in Christ.

Given the way that Christianity works, the accessible God will be spoken of via the story of Jesus/Christ. To consider that the task of Christology is to strive to offer better, context-related, versions of the story of Jesus is to acknowledge that the goal of theology is to honour the God who is available to those who seek God and to contribute to the task of stimulating and shaping the relationships which express what it means to be 'in Christ'.

Summary

The eight simple statements in this chapter are intended as suggestions of the ways in which Christians can speak about God in Christ, in a manner which takes Christocentrism seriously in thought and practice, and moves constantly between reflection and living. Admittedly, many readers will feel that the argument of this book has been conducted far too much at the level of theory throughout. However much readers may have been willing to trust that I seek to live what is reflected upon here, this remains a work of 'systematic theology' rather than one of 'practical theology'. Though this is true, it is also important to stress that a book of methodology alone (Part One of this present text) and a book solely exploring the practice of being Christian (which is addressed in the companion volume *Christ in Practice*) would have been inadequate too. I wanted to find out what it is possible to say about God in Christ today, taking account of some of the challenges to Christian faith which modern theologians have had to wrestle with. That has been the simple purpose of Parts Two and Three. Part Three has, however, provided a clear, practical, theological platform on which to build. If Christ is as I describe in Chapter 8, and if we must today think of Christ in terms of embodied relationship, spiritual presence and words and images (Chapter 7), then what are the consequences for Christian life? That is explored in *Christ in Practice*.

Bibliography

Adams, D., 1993, 'Review of *Learning about Theology from the Third World*, by William A. Dyrness', *Interpretation* 47, pp. 103–4

Allen, C., 1998, *The Human Christ: The Search for the Historical Jesus*, New York: The Free Press

Altizer, T. J. J. and Hamilton, W., 1968, *Radical Theology and the Death of God*, Harmondsworth: Penguin

Amaladoss, M., 1993, 'The Pluralism of Religions and the Significance of Christ' in R. S. Sugirtharajah (ed.), *Asian Faces of Jesus*, Maryknoll: Orbis/London: SCM Press, pp. 85–103

Arnal, W. E. and Desjardins, M. (eds.), 1997, *Whose Historical Jesus?* Waterloo, Ontario: Wilfrid Laurier University Press

Aulén, G., 1931, *Christus Victor*, London: SPCK

Baillie, D. M., 1961, *God Was in Christ*, London: Faber & Faber

Barbour, R. S. (ed.), 1993, *The Kingdom of God and Human Society*, Edinburgh: T. & T. Clark

Barth, K., 1981, *Die protestantsiche Theologie im 19. Jahrhundert: Ihre Vorgeschichte und ihre Geschichte*, 4th edn, Zürich: Theologischer Verlag (ET *Protestant Theology in the Nineteenth Century: Its Background and History*, Grand Rapids: Eerdmans/London: SCM Press, 2002)

—— 1982, *The Theology of Schleiermacher*, Grand Rapids: Eerdmans

Baugh, L., 1997, *Imaging the Divine: Jesus and Christ-Figures in Film*, Kansas City: Sheed & Ward

Begbie, J., 1991, *Voicing Creation's Praise: Towards a Theology of the Arts*, Edinburgh: T. & T. Clark

Bennett, C., 2001, *In Search of Jesus: Insider and Outsider Images*, London and New York: Continuum

Berkey, R. F. and Edwards, S. A. (eds.), 1993, *Christology in Dialogue*, Cleveland, OH: The Pilgrim Press

Berkhof, H., 1989, *Two Hundred Years of Theology*, Grand Rapid: Eerdmans

Best, E., 1955, *One Body in Christ*, London: SPCK

Boersma, H., 2004, *Violence, Hospitality and the Cross: Reappropriating the Atonement Tradition*, Grand Rapids: Baker Academic

Boff, L., 1980, *Jesus Christ Liberator*, London: SPCK

—— 1988, *Trinity and Society*, Maryknoll: Orbis/London: Burns & Oates

Bond, L. S., 1999, *Trouble with Jesus: Women, Christology, and Preaching*, St Louis, MO: Chalice Press

Bonhoeffer, D., 1954, *Life Together* (7th impression: 1968), London: SCM Press

—— 1955, *Ethics*, London: SCM Press

—— 1959, *The Cost of Discipleship*, London: SCM Press

—— 1962, *Act and Being*, London: Collins

—— 1965, *No Rusty Swords: Letters, Lectures and Notes 1928–1936*, London: Collins

—— 1966, *The Way to Freedom: Letters, Lectures and Notes 1935–1939*, London: Collins

—— 1971, *Letters and Papers from Prison: The Enlarged Edition*, London: SCM Press

—— 1978, *Christology*, London: Fount Paperbacks

—— 1998, *Sanctorum Communio: A Theological Study of the Sociology of the Church (Dietrich Bonhoeffer Works, Volume 1)*, Minneapolis: Fortress Press

Bonino, J. M. (ed.), 1984, *Faces of Jesus: Latin American Christologies*, Maryknoll: Orbis

Bosch, D., 1991, *Transforming Mission*, Maryknoll: Orbis

Bowden, J., 1977, *Voices in the Wilderness*, London: SCM Press

Braaten, C. E., 1992, *No Other Gospel!: Christianity among the World's Religions*, Minneapolis: Fortress Press

Brock, R. N., 1984, 'The Feminist Redemption of Christ' in J. L. Weidman (ed.), *Christian Feminism: Visions of a New Humanity*, San Francisco: Harper & Row, pp. 55–74

—— 1988, *Journeys by Heart: A Christology of Erotic Power*, New York: Crossroad

—— 1989, 'On Mirrors, Mists and Murmurs: Toward an Asian American Theology' in J. Plaskow and C. P. Christ (eds.), *Weaving the*

Visions: New Patterns in Feminist Spirituality, San Francisco: Harper & Row, pp. 235–43

—— 1989, 'And a Little Child Will Lead Us: Christology and Child Abuse' in J. C. Brown and C. R. Bohn (eds.), *Christianity, Patriarchy and Abuse: A Feminist Critique*, New York: Pilgrim Press, pp. 42–61

—— 1994, 'Dusting the Bible on the Floor: A Hermeneutics of Wisdom' in E. S. Fiorenza (ed.), *Searching the Scriptures: A Feminist Introduction*, London: SCM Press, pp. 64–75

—— 1995, 'What Is a Feminist? Strategies for Change and Transformations of Consciousness' in R. N. Brock, C. Camp and S. Jones (eds.), *Setting the Table: Women in Theological Conversation*, St Louis: Chalice Press, pp. 3–21

—— 1995, 'The Greening of the Soul: A Feminist Theological Paradigm of the Web of Life' in R. N. Brock, C. Camp and S. Jones (eds.), *Setting the Table: Women in Theological Conversation*, St Louis: Chalice Press, pp. 133–53

—— 1997, 'A New Thing in the Land: The Female Surrounds the Warrior' in C. L. Rigby (ed.), *Power, Powerlessness and the Divine: New Inquiries in Bible and Theology*, Atlanta: Scholars Press, pp. 137–59

—— 1998, 'Interstitial Integrity' in R. Badham (ed.), *Introduction to Christian Theology: Contemporary North American Perspectives*, Louisville: Westminster/John Knox Press, pp. 183–96

—— 2002, 'Shape-Shifting Disturbances as Divine Presence' in M. D. Chapman (ed.), *The Future of Liberal Theology*, Aldershot and Burlington: Ashgate, pp. 170–90

Brock, R. N. and Parker, R. A., 2001, *Proverbs of Ashes: Violence, Redemptive Suffering, and the Search for What Saves Us*, Boston: Beacon Press

Brock, R. N. and Southard, N., 1987, 'The Other Half of the Basket: Asian American Women and the Search for a Theological Home', *Journal of Feminist Studies in Religion* 3, pp. 135–50

Brock, R. N. and Thistlethwaite, S. B., 1996, *Casting Stones: Prostitution and Liberation in Asia and the United States*, Minneapolis: Fortress Press

Brown, C., 1988, *Jesus in European Protestant Thought: 1778–1860*, Grand Rapids: Baker Book House

Brown, D., 1985, *The Divine Trinity*, London: Duckworth

Brown, F. B., 2000, *Good Taste, Bad Taste and Christian Taste: Aesthetics in Religious Life*, New York: Oxford University Press

Burnham, J. (ed.), 2004, *Perspectives on the Passion of the Christ: Religious Thinkers and Writers Explore the Issues Raised by the Controversial Movie*, New York: Miramax Books

Called to Love and Praise, 1999, A Report by The Faith and Order Committee of the Methodist Church (of Great Britain), Peterborough: Methodist Publishing House

Cardenal, E., 1977, *Love in Practice: The Gospel in Solentiname*, London: Search Press

Carlson, J. and Ludwig, R. A., 1994, *Jesus and Faith: A Conversation on the Work of John Dominic Crossan*, Maryknoll: Orbis

Carmichael, E. D. H. (Liz), 2004, *Friendship: Interpreting Christian Love*, London and New York: T. & T. Clark International

Chilton, B. D. (ed.), 1984, *The Kingdom of God*, London: SPCK/Philadelphia: Fortress Press

Chilton, B. D. and Evans, C. A. (eds.), 1994, *Studying the Historical Jesus: Evaluations of the State of Current Research*, Leiden/New York/Köln: Brill

Coakley, S., 1993, 'Why Three? Some Further Reflections on the Origins of the Doctrine of the Trinity' in S. Coakley and D. Pailin (eds.), *The Making and Remaking of Christian Doctrine*, Oxford: Clarendon Press, pp. 29–56

Cobb, J. B. Jr, 1975, *Christ in a Pluralistic Age*, Philadelphia: Westminster Press

—— 1988, 'Critique of J. Hick "An Inspiration Christology for a Religiously Plural World"' in S. T. Davis (ed.), *Encountering Jesus: A Debate on Christology*, Atlanta: John Knox Press, pp. 27–9

Cone, J. H., 1972, *The Spirituals and the Blues*, New York: Seabury Press

—— 1975, *God of the Oppressed*, San Francisco: HarperSanFrancisco

—— 1986, *My Soul Looks Back*, Maryknoll: Orbis

Corley, K. E. and Webb, R. L. (eds.), 2004, *Jesus and Mel Gibson's* The Passion of the Christ, London and New York: Continuum

Cragg, K., 1986, *The Christ and the Faiths: Theology in Cross-Reference*, London: SPCK

Cross, F. L. and Livingstone, E. A. (eds.), 1997, *The Oxford Dictionary of the Christian Church*, Oxford: Oxford University Press

Crossan, J. D., 1991, *The Historical Jesus*, San Francisco: HarperSanFrancisco/Edinburgh: T. & T. Clark

—— 1994, *Jesus: A Revolutionary Biography*, San Francisco: HarperSanFrancisco

—— 1999, *The Birth of Christianity*, Edinburgh: T. & T. Clark

Crossan, J. D., Johnson, L. T, and Kelber, W. H., 1999, *The Jesus Controversy: Perspectives in Conflict*, Harrisburg: TPI

Daly, M., 1973, *Beyond God the Father*, Boston: Beacon Press

Davies, A., 1988, *Infected Christianity: A Study of Modern Racism*, Kingston and Montreal: McGill-Queen's University Press

Davies, H., 1963, 'The Expression of the Social Gospel in Worship', *Studia Liturgica* 2, pp. 174–92

Davis, S. T. (ed.), 1988, *Encountering Jesus: A Debate on Christology*, Atlanta: John Knox Press

Day, T., 1982, *Dietrich Bonhoeffer on Christian Community and Common Sense*, Lewiston: The Edwin Mellen Press

D'Costa, G. (ed.), 1990, *Christian Uniqueness Reconsidered: The Myth of a Pluralistic Theology of Religions*, Maryknoll; Orbis

De Gruchy, J. (ed.), 1999, *The Cambridge Companion to Dietrich Bonhoeffer*, Cambridge: Cambridge University Press

Del Colle, R., 1994, *Christ and the Spirit: Spirit Christology in Trinitarian Perspective*, Oxford: Oxford University Press

——1999, 'Schleiermacher and Spirit Christology: Unexplored Horizons of *The Christian Faith*', *International Journal of Systematic Theology* 1, pp. 286–307

Dorrien, G. J., 1990, *Reconstructing the Common Good: Theology and the Social Order*, Maryknoll: Orbis

Douglas, K. B., 1994, *The Black Christ*, Maryknoll: Orbis

Driver, T. F., 1981, *Christ in a Changing World: Towards an Ethical Christology*, London: SCM Press

Dunn, J. D. G., 2003, *Jesus Remembered*, Grand Rapids and Cambridge: Eerdmans

Dyrness, W. A., 2001, *Visual Faith: Art, Theology and Worship in Dialogue*, Grand Rapids: Baker Academic

Eckardt, A. R., 1992, *Reclaiming the Jesus of History: Christology Today*, Minneapolis: Fortress Press

Evans, C. H., 2001, 'Gender and the Kingdom of God: The Family Values of Walter Rauschenbusch' in C. H. Evans (ed.), *The Social Gospel Today*, Louisville, London and Leiden: Westminister John Knox Press, pp. 53–66

——2004, *The Kingdom Is Always But Coming: A Life of Walter Rauschenbusch*, Grand Rapids and Cambridge: Eerdmans

Fiddes, P. S., 1989, *Past Event and Present Salvation: The Christian Idea of Atonement*, London: Darton, Longman & Todd

Finaldi, G. *et al.*, 2000, *The Image of Christ: The Catalogue of the Exhibition Seeing Salvation*, London: National Gallery

Fiorenza, E. S., 1983, *In Memory of Her*, London: SCM Press

——1995, *Jesus: Miriam's Child, Sophia's Prophet*, New York: Continuum/London: SCM Press

——1999, 'To Follow the Vision: The Jesus Movement as Basileia Movement' in M. A. Farley and S. Jones (eds.), *Liberating Eschatology: Essays in Honor of Letty M. Russell*, Louisville: Westminster/John Knox Press, pp. 123–43

Fiorenza, F. S., 1975, 'Critical Social Theory and Christology: Towards an Understanding of Atonement and Redemption as Emancipatory Solidarity', *Proceedings of the Catholic Theological Society of America* 30, pp. 63–110

——1994, 'The Jesus of Piety and the Historical Jesus', *Proceedings of the Catholic Theological Society of America* 49, pp. 90–9

Fishburn, J. F., 1981, *The Fatherhood of God and the Victorian Family: The Social Gospel in America*, Philadelphia: Fortress Press

——2003, 'Walter Rauschenbusch and "The Woman Movement": A Gender Analysis' in W. J. Deichmann Edwards and C. De Swarte Gifford (eds.), *Gender and the Social Gospel*, Urbana and Chicago: University of Illinois Press, pp. 71–86

Fisher, S., 1988, *Revelatory Positivism?: Barth's Earliest Theology and the Marburg School*, Oxford: Oxford University Press

Folkenflik, R., 1991, 'biography' in J. W. Yolton *et al.* (eds.), *The Blackwell Companion to the Enlightenment*, Oxford: Blackwell, p. 63

Ford, D. F., 1999, *Self and Salvation: Being Transformed*, Cambridge: Cambridge University Press

The Forgotten Trinity, 3 vols. (1989–91), London: BCC/CCBI

Forrester, D. B., 1988, *Theology and Politics*, Oxford: Basil Blackwell

Forsyth, P. T., 1909, *The Person and Place of Jesus Christ*, London: Independent Press

Fowl, S. E. and Jones, L. G., 1991, *Reading in Communion: Scripture and Ethics in Christian Life*, London: SPCK

Fox, M., 1988, *The Coming of the Cosmic Christ*, San Francisco: HarperSanFrancisco

Frei, H., 1992, *Types of Christian Theology*, New Haven and London: Yale University Press

——1993, *Theology and Narrative: Selected Essays*, New York and Oxford: Oxford University Press

Fusco, C., 1991, 'Interview with A. Serrano' (first published in *High*

Performance, Fall 1991) available at http://www.communityarts. net/readingroom/archive/ca/fusco-serrano.php

Galloway, A. D., 1951, *The Cosmic Christ*, London: Nisbet

Gerrish, B. A., 1982, *The Old Protestantism and the New: Essays on the Reformation Heritage*, Edinburgh: T. & T. Clark

—— 1984, *A Prince of the Church: Schleiermacher and the Beginnings of Modern Theology*, London: SCM Press

—— 1985, 'Friedrich Schleiermacher' in N. Smart *et al.* (eds.), *Nineteenth Century Religious Thought in the West Vol.1*, Cambridge: Cambridge University Press, pp. 123–56

—— 1993, *Continuing the Reformation: Essays on Modern Religious Thought*, London and Chicago: The University of Chicago Press

Grant, J., 1989, *White Women's Christ and Black Women's Jesus*, Atlanta: Scholars Press

Grayston, K., 1990, *Dying, We Live: A New Enquiry into the Death of Christ in the New Testament*, London: Darton, Longman & Todd

Green, C., 1972, *The Sociality of Christ and Humanity: Dietrich Bonhoeffer's Early Theology 1927–1933*, Missoula: Scholars Press

Greenwood, R., 1994, *Transforming Priesthood: A New Theology of Mission and Ministry*, London: SPCK

Grey, M., 1989, *Redeeming the Dream; Feminism, Redemption and Christian Tradition*, London: SPCK

—— 1994, 'Falling into Freedom; Searching for New Interpretations of Sin in a Secular Society' *Scottish Journal of Theology* 47, pp. 223–43

Guenther-Gleason, P. E., 1997, *On Schleiermacher and Gender Politics*, Harrisburg: TPI

Gunton, C. E., 1983, *Yesterday and Today; A Study of Continuities in Christology*, London; Darton, Longman & Todd

—— 1988, *The Actuality of Atonement: A Study of Metaphor, Rationality and the Christian Tradition*, Edinburgh: T. & T. Clark

—— 1991, *The Promise of Trinitarian Theology*, Edinburgh: T. & T. Clark

Gunton, C. E. and Hardy, D. W. (eds.), 1989, *On Being the Church*, Edinburgh: T. & T. Clark

Haight, R., 1996, 'The Impact of Jesus Research on Christology', *Louvain Studies* 21, pp. 216–28

—— 1999, *Jesus: Symbol of God*, Maryknoll: Orbis

Hamilton, W., 1993, *A Quest for the Post-Historical Jesus*, London: SCM Press

Hampson, D., 1990, *Theology and Feminism*, Oxford and Cambridge, MA: Blackwell

Handy, R. T. (ed.), 1966, *The Social Gospel in America 1870–1920*, New York: Oxford University Press

Hardy, D. W., 1989, 'Created and Redeemed Sociality' in C. E. Gunton and D. W. Hardy (eds.), *On Being the Church*, Edinburgh: T. & T. Clark, pp. 21–47 (= D. W. Hardy, *God's Ways with the World: Thinking and Practising Christian Faith*, Edinburgh: T. & T. Clark, 1996, pp. 188–205)

Hauerwas, S., 1981, *A Community of Character: Toward a Constructive Christian Social Ethic*, Notre Dame and London: University of Notre Dame Press

—— 1997, *Wilderness Wanderings: Probing Twentieth-Century Theology and Philosophy*, Boulder and Oxford: Westview Press

—— 1998, *Sanctify Them in the Truth: Holiness Exemplified*, Edinburgh: T. & T. Clark

—— 2000, *A Better Hope: Resources for a Church Confronting Capitalism, Democracy, and Postmodernity*, Grand Rapids: Brazos Press

—— 2001, *With the Grain of the Universe: The Church's Witness and Natural Theology*, Grand Rapids: Brazos Press

Henaut, B. W., 1997, 'Is the "Historical Jesus" a Christological Construct?' in W. E. Arnal and M. Desjardins (eds.), *Whose Historical Jesus?* Waterloo, Ontario: Wilfrid Laurier University Press, pp. 241–68

Henry, C. F. H., 1992, *The Identity of Jesus of Nazareth*, Nashville: Broadman Press

Herrmann, W., 1972, *The Communion of the Christian with God* (German original: 4th edn, 1903), London: SCM Press

den Heyer, C. J., 1996, *Jesus Matters*, London: SCM Press

—— 1998, *Jesus and the Doctrine of the Atonement*, London: SCM Press

Heyward, C., 1989, *Speaking of Christ: A Lesbian Feminist Voice*, Cleveland: Pilgrim Press

—— 1998, 'Jesus of Nazareth/Christ of Faith: Foundations of a Reactive Christology' in S. B. Thistlethwaite and M. P. Engel (eds.), *Lift Every Voice: Constructing Christian Theologies from the Underside*, Maryknoll: Orbis, pp. 197–206

—— 1999, *Saving Jesus from Those Who Are Right: Rethinking What It Means to Be Christian*, Minneapolis: Fortress Press

Hick, J., 1993, *The Metaphor of God Incarnate*, London: SCM Press

Hick, J. and Knitter, P. F. (eds.), 1987, *The Myth of Christian Uniqueness*, Maryknoll: Orbis (= London: SCM Press, 1988)

Hodgson, P. C., 1989, *God in History: Shapes of Freedom*, Nashville: Abingdon Press

—— 1994, *Winds of the Spirit: A Constructive Christian Theology*, Louisville: Westminster/John Knox/London: SCM Press

Horsley, R., 1987, *Jesus and the Spiral of Violence*, San Francisco: Harper & Row

—— 1994, *Sociology and the Jesus Movement*, 2nd edn, New York: Continuum

—— 2003, *Jesus and Empire: The Kingdom of God and the New World Disorder*, Minneapolis: Fortress Press

Houlden, J. L. (ed.), 2003, *Jesus in History, Thought and Culture: An Encyclopaedia*, Santa Barbara, Denver and Oxford: ABC-CLIO

Hunsinger, G., 1991, *How to Read Karl Barth*, Oxford: Oxford University Press

—— 2000, *Disruptive Grace: Studies in the Theology of Karl Barth*, Grand Rapids: Eerdmans

Hunt, M. E., 1992, *Fierce Tenderness: A Feminist Theology of Friendship*, New York: Crossroad

Hurtado, L. W., 1997, 'A Taxonomy of Recent Historical-Jesus Work' in W. E. Arnal and M. Desjardins (eds.), *Whose Historical Jesus?* Waterloo, Ontario: Wilfrid Laurier University Press, pp. 272–95

—— 2003, *Lord Jesus Christ: Devotion to Jesus in Earliest Christianity*, Grand Rapids and Cambridge: Eerdmans

Jasper, D., 1989, *The Study of Literature and Religion*, Minneapolis: Fortress Press

Johnson, E. A., 1993, 'Redeeming the Name of Christ: Christology' in C. M. LaCugna (ed.), *Freeing Theology: The Essentials of Theology in Feminist Perspective*, Edinburgh: T. & T. Clark, pp. 115–37

—— 1997, *She Who Is: The Mystery of God in Feminist Theological Discourse*, New York: Crossroad

Johnson, L. T., 1996, *The Real Jesus: The Misguided Quest for the Historical Jesus and the Truth of the Traditional Gospels*, San Francisco: HarperSanFrancisco

Johnston, R. K., 2000, *Reel Spirituality: Theology and Film in Dialogue*, Grand Rapids: Baker Academic

Kabasélé, F., 1991, 'Christ as Ancestor and Elder Brother' in R. J. Schreiter (ed.), *Faces of Jesus in Africa*, Maryknoll: Orbis, pp. 116–27

Kähler, M., 1964, *The So-Called Historical Jesus and the Historic Biblical Christ* (German original: 1892), Philadelphia: Fortress Press

—— 1966, *Die Wissenschaft der christlichen Lehre von dem evangelischen Grundartikel aus im Abrisse dargestellt*, Neukirchen-Vluyn: Neukirchener Verlag (first published 1905)

Kam-Weng, N., 1996, *From Christ to Social Practice: Christological Foundations for Social Practice in the Theologies of Albrecht Ritschl, Karl Barth and Jürgen Moltmann*, Hong Kong: Alliance Bible Seminary

Käsemann, E., 1971, 'The Theological Problem Presented by the Motif of the Body of Christ' in *Perspectives on Paul*, London: SCM Press, pp. 102–21

Kee, H. C., 1995, 'A Century of Quests for the Culturally Compatible Jesus', *Theology Today*, 52, pp. 17–28

Kelber, W. H., 1999, 'The Quest for the Historical Jesus: From the Perspectives of Medieval, Modern, and Post-Enlightenment Readings, and in View of Ancient, Oral Aesthetics' in J. D. Crossan *et al.*, *The Jesus Controversy: Perspectives in Conflict*, Harrisburg: TPI, pp. 75–115

Kennedy, L., 1999, *All in the Mind: A Farewell to God*, London: Hodder & Stoughton

Kimel, A. F. (ed.), 1992, *Speaking the Christian God: The Holy Trinity and the Challenge of Feminism*, Grand Rapids: Eerdmans

Knitter, P., 1985, *No Other Name? A Critical Survey of Christian Attitudes Toward the World Religions*, London: SCM Press

—— 1996, *Jesus and the Other Names: Christian Mission and Global Responsibility*, Oxford: Oneworld

Krauss, R., 1992, *Gottesoffenbarung und menschliche Religion: eine Analyse des Religionsbegriffs in Karl Barths Kirchlicher Dogmatik mit besonderer Berücksichtigung F. D. E. Schleiermachers*, Lewiston: Edwin Mellen Press

Krieg, R. A., 1988, *Story-Shaped Christology: The Role of Narratives in Identifying Jesus Christ*, Mahwah: Paulist Press

Kuitert, H. M., 1999, *Jesus: The Legacy of Christianity*, London: SCM Press

Küster, V., 2001, *The Many Faces of Jesus Christ*, London: SCM Press

LaCugna, C. M., 1991, *God For Us*, Edinburgh: T. & T. Clark

Lage, D., 1990, *Martin Luther's Christology and Ethics*, Lewiston, Queenston and Lampeter: Edwin Mellen Press

Lee, J. Y., 1995, *Marginality: The Key to Multicultural Theology*, Minneapolis: Fortress Press

Link, H-G., 1975, *Geschichte Jesu und Bild Christi*, Neukirchen-Vluyn: Neukirchener Verlag

Lyden, J., 2003, *Film as Religion: Myths, Morals and Rituals*, New York and London: New York University Press

Lynch, G., 2002, *After Religion: 'Generation X' and the Search for Meaning*, London: Darton Longman & Todd

——2005, *Understanding Theology and Popular Culture*, Oxford: Blackwell

McCarraher, E., 2000, *Christian Critics: Religion and the Impasse in Modern American Social Thought*, Ithaca and London: Cornell University Press

McCormack, B. L., 1995, *Karl Barth's Critically Realistic Dialectical Theology: Its Genesis and Development 1909–1936*, Oxford: Clarendon Press

McFadyen, A., 2000, *Bound to Sin: Abuse, Holocaust and the Christian Doctrine of Sin*, Cambridge: Cambridge University Press

McIntyre, J., 1992, *The Shape of Soteriology*, Edinburgh: T. & T. Clark

——1998, *The Shape of Christology* (2nd edn; 1st edn, London: SCM Press, 1966), Edinburgh: T. & T. Clark

MacKinnon, D., 1972, '"Substance" in Christology – A Cross-Bench View' in S. W. Sykes and J. P. Clayton (eds.), *Christ, Faith and History*, Cambridge: Cambridge University Press, pp. 279–300

Macquarrie, J., 1990, *Jesus Christ in Modern Thought*, London: SCM Press

Marsh, C., 1992, *Albrecht Ritschl and the Problem of the Historical Jesus*, San Francisco: Edwin Mellen Press

——1997, 'Did You Say "Grace"?: Eating in Community in *Babette's Feast*' in C. Marsh and G. Ortiz, *Explorations in Theology and Film*, Oxford: Blackwell, pp. 207–18

——1997, 'Quests of the Historical Jesus in New Historicist Perspective', *Biblical Interpretation* 5, pp. 403–37

——2002, art. 'Religion and the Arts' in C. Partridge (ed.), *Dictionary of Contemporary Religion in the Western World*, Leicester and Downers Grove: Inter-varsity Press, pp. 65–8

——2002, *Christianity in a Post-Atheist Age*, London: SCM Press

—— 2002, 'The Experience of Theological Education: Maintaining a "Liberal" Agenda in a Post-Liberal Age' in M. D. Chapman (ed.), *The Future of Liberal Theology*, Aldershot: Ashgate, pp. 139–59

—— 2004, 'Black Christs in White Christian Perspective: Some Critical Reflections', *Black Theology* 2.1, pp. 45–56

—— 2004, 'Appealing to "Experience": What Does it Mean?' in C. Marsh, B. Beck, A. Shier-Jones and H. Wareing (eds.), *Unmasking Methodist Theology*, London: Continuum, pp. 118–30

—— 2004, *Cinema and Sentiment: Film's Challenge to Theology*, Milton Keynes: Paternoster Press

—— 2006, 'Why the Quest for Jesus Can Never Only Be Historical', forthcoming in P. De Mey (ed.), *Sourcing the Quests*, Peeters: Leuven

Marsh, C. and Ortiz, G. (1997) *Explorations in Theology and Film: Movies and Meaning*, Oxford: Blackwell

Meilaender, G., 1981, *Friendship: A Study in Theological Ethics*, London and Notre Dame: University of Notre Dame Press

Milet, J., 1981, *God or Christ? A Study in Social Psychology*, London: SCM Press

Miller, A., 1987, *For Your Own Good: The Roots of Violence in Child-Rearing* (German original 1980), London: Virago

—— 1987, *The Drama of Being a Child: The Search for the True Self*, London: Virago

Minus, P. M., 1988, *Walter Rauschenbusch: American Reformer*, New York: Macmillan

Moltmann, J., 1981, *The Trinity and the Kingdom of God*, London: SCM Press

—— 1990, *The Way of Jesus Christ: Christology in Messianic Dimensions*, London: SCM Press

—— 1994, *Jesus Christ for Today's World*, London: SCM Press

Moltmann-Wendel, E., 2000, *Rediscovering Friendship*, London: SCM Press

Morgan, R. and Pye, M. (eds.), 1977, *Ernst Troeltsch: Writings on Theology and Religion*, London: Duckworth

Morse, C., 1994, *Not Every Spirit: A Dogmatics of Christian Disbelief*, Valley Forge: TPI

Moule, C. F. D., 1977, *The Origin of Christology*, Cambridge: Cambridge University Press

Moxnes, H., 1997, 'The Theological Importance of the "Third Quest" for the Historical Jesus', in W. E. Arnal and M. Desjardins (eds.),

Whose Historical Jesus? Waterloo, Ontario: Wilfrid Laurier University Press, pp. 132–42
—— 2003, *Putting Jesus in His Place: A Radical Vision of Household and Kingdom*, Louisville and London: Westminster John Knox Press

Niebuhr, R. R., 1965, *Schleiermacher on Christ and Religion*, London: SCM Press
—— 1984, 'Friedrich Schleiermacher' in M. E. Marty and D. G. Peerman (eds.), *A Handbook of Christian Theologians*, Cambridge: Lutterworth Press, pp. 17–35
Nowak, K., 2002, *Schleiermacher: Leben, Werk und Wirkung*, 2nd edn, Göttingen: Vandenhoeck & Ruprecht

Ottati, D., 1989, *Jesus Christ and Christian Vision*, Minneapolis: Fortress Press

Pannenberg, W., 1992, *Systematic Theology Vol. 1*, Edinburgh: T. & T. Clark
Parrinder, G., 1995, *Jesus in the Qur'an*, Oxford: Oneworld
Peitz, D. A., 1992, *Solidarity as Hermeneutic: A Revisionist Reading of the Theology of Walter Rauschenbusch*, New York: Peter Lang
Phillips, J. A., 1967, *The Form of Christ in the World: A Study of Bonhoeffer's Christology*, London: Collins
Placher, W. C., 1997, 'Postliberal Theology' in D. F. Ford (ed.), *The Modern Theologians*, Oxford: Oxford University Press, pp. 343–56
Plate, S. B. (ed.), 2004, *Re-Viewing The Passion: Mel Gibson's Film and Its Critics*, New York and Basingstoke: Palgrave Macmillan
Pope-Levison, P. and Levison, J. R., 1992, *Jesus in Global Contexts*, Louisville: Westminster/John Knox Press
Porter, S. E. *et al.* (eds.), 1997, *Images of Christ: Ancient and Modern*, Sheffield: Sheffield Academic Press

Rauschenbusch, W., 1907, *Christianity and the Social Crisis*, Louisville: Westminster/John Knox Press (reprint 1991)
—— 1912, *Christianizing the Social Order*, New York: Macmillan
—— 1916, *The Social Principles of Jesus*, New York: Grosset & Dunlap
—— 1917, *A Theology for the Social Gospel*, New York: Macmillan
—— 1927, *Prayers of the Social Awakening*, London: SCM Press
—— 1968, *The Righteousness of the Kingdom*, Nashville: Abingdon Press

—— 1984 *Walter Rauschenbusch: Selected Writings* (ed. W. S. Hudson), New York, Mahwah: Paulist Press

Redeker, M., 1973, *Schleiermacher: Life and Thought*, Philadelphia: Fortress Press

Riches, J. K., 1972, 'What is a "Christocentric" Theology?' in S. W. Sykes and J. P. Clayton (eds.), *Christ, Faith and History*, Cambridge: Cambridge University Press, pp. 223–38

Ringe, S., 1985, *Jesus, Liberation and the Biblical Jubilee*, Philadelphia: Fortress Press

—— 1999, *Wisdom's Friends: Community and Christology in the Fourth Gospel*, Louisville: Westminster John Knox Press

Ritschl, A. B., 1872, *A Critical History of the Christian Doctrine of Justification and Reconciliation*, Edinburgh: Edmonston and Douglas

—— 1902, *The Christian Doctrine of Justification and Reconciliation: The Positive Development of the Doctrine*, Edinburgh: T. & T. Clark

Robinson, J. A. T., 1952, *The Body: A Study in Pauline Theology*, London: SCM Press

—— 1963, *Honest to God*, London: SCM Press

—— 1980, 'Honest to Christ Today' in *The Roots of a Radical*, London: SCM Press, pp. 59–77

Rogerson, J. W., 1985, 'The Hebrew Conception of Corporate Personality: A Re-examination' in B. Lang (ed.), *Anthropological Approaches to the Old Testament*, London: SPCK/Philadlephia: Fortress Press, pp. 43–59 (= *JTS* 21, 1970, pp. 1–16)

Rousseau, J. J. and Arav, R., 1995, *Jesus and His World*, London: SCM Press/Minneapolis: Fortress Press

Rüegger, H., 1992, *Kirche als seelsorgerliche Gemeinschaft: Dietrich Bonhoeffers Seelsorgeverständnis im Kontext seiner bruderschaftlichen Ekklesiologie*, Bern: Peter Lang

Ruether, R. R., 1981, *To Change the World*, London: SCM Press

—— 1983, *Feminism and God-Talk: Toward a Feminist Theology*, Boston: Beacon Press/London: SCM Press

Samartha, S. J., 1987, 'The Cross and the Rainbow: Christ in a Multireligious Culture' in J. Hick and P. F. Knitter (eds.), *The Myth of Christian Uniqueness*, Maryknoll: Orbis, pp. 69–88

—— 1991, *One Christ – Many Religions: Towards a Revised Christology*, Maryknoll: Orbis

Sanders, E. P., 1985, *Jesus and Judaism*, London: SCM Press

Schaberg, J., 1994, 'A Feminist Experience of Historical Jesus Scholarship', *Continuum* 3, pp. 266–85 (= 'A Feminist Experience of Historical-Jesus Scholarship' in W. E. Arnal and M. Desjardins (eds.), *Whose Historical Jesus?* Waterloo, Ontario: Wilfrid Laurier University Press, pp. 146–60)

Schleiermacher, F. D. E., 1926, *Soliloquies*, Chicago: Open Court (German original: 1800)

—— 1928, *The Christian Faith*, Edinburgh: T. & T. Clark (German original: 2nd edn, 1830)

—— 1958, *On Religion: Speeches to Its Cultured Despisers*, New York, Hagerstown, San Francisco, London: Harper & Row (German original: 3rd edn 1821; ET 1893)

—— 1975, *The Life of Jesus*, Philadelphia: Fortress Press (German original: 1864; of lecture-series from 1832)

—— 1981, *On the Glaubenslehre: Two Letters to Dr. Luecke*, Chico: Scholars Press

—— 1987, *Friedrich Schleiermacher: Pioneer of Modern Theology* (ed. K. W. Clements), London: Collins

—— 1988, *On Religion: Speeches to Its Cultured Despisers*, Cambridge, New York and Oakleigh, Victoria: Cambridge University Press (German original: 1st edn, 1799)

—— 1990, *Christmas Eve: Dialogue on the Incarnation*, San Francisco: Edwin Mellen Press (German original: 1st edn, 1806)

Schreiter, R. (ed.), 1991, *Faces of Jesus in Africa*, Maryknoll: Orbis

Schwarz, H., 1998, *Christology*, Grand Rapids and Cambridge: Eerdmans

Schweitzer, A., 2000, *The Quest of the Historical Jesus*, 1st complete edn, London: SCM Press (German original: 1906; 6th edn, 1950)

Schwöbel, C., 1995, 'Christology and Trinitarian Thought' in C. Schwöbel (ed.), *Trinitarian Theology Today*, Edinburgh: T. & T. Clark, pp. 113–146

Selby, P., 1976, *Look for the Living: The Corporate Nature of Resurrection Faith*, London: SCM Press

Sloyan, G., 1995, *The Crucifixion of Jesus: History, Myth, Faith*, Minneapolis: Fortress Press

Sobrino, J., 1978, *Christology at the Crossroads*, London: SCM Press

—— 1987, *Jesus in Latin America*, Maryknoll: Orbis

Soelle, D., 1975, *Suffering*, London: Darton, Longman & Todd

Song, C. S., 1982, *The Compassionate God*, London: SCM Press

—— 1993, 'Oh, Jesus, Here with Us!' in R. S. Sugirtharajah (ed.), *Asian Faces of Jesus*, Maryknoll: Orbis/London: SCM Press, pp. 131–48

—— 1996, *Jesus, the Crucified People*, Minneapolis: Fortress Press

Soosten, J. Von, 1992, *Die Sozialität der Kirche: Theologie und Theorie der Kirche in Dietrich Bonhoeffers 'Sanctorum Communio'*, München: Kaiser

Spiegler, G., 1967, *The Eternal Covenant: Schleiermacher's Experiment in Cultural Theology*, New York, Evanston and London: Harper & Row

Stalcup, S., 1995, 'What About Jesus? Christology and the Challenges of Women' in R. N. Brock, C. Camp and S. Jones (eds.), *Setting the Table: Women in Theological Conversation*, St Louis: Chalice Press, pp. 107–32

Stern, R. C. *et al.*, 1999, *Savior on the Silver Screen*, Mahwah, NJ: Paulist Press

Stevens, M. (ed.), 1993, *Reconstructing the Christ Symbol: Essays in Feminist Christology*, New York: Paulist Press

Strauss, D. F., 1977, *The Christ of Faith and the Jesus of History: A Critique of Schleiermacher's 'The Life of Jesus'*, Philadelphia: Fortress Press (German original, 1865)

Stroup, G. W., 1984, *The Promise of Narrative Theology*, London: SCM Press

Stuart, E., 1995, *Just Good Friends*, London: Mowbray

Sugirtharajah, R. S. (ed.), 1993, *Asian Faces of Jesus,* Maryknoll: Orbis/London: SCM Press

Suurmond, J-J., 1994, *Word and Spirit at Play*, London: SCM Press

Sykes, S. W. and Clayton, J. P. (eds.), 1972, *Christ, Faith and History*, Cambridge: Cambridge University Press

Tabraham, B., 1995, *The Making of Methodism*, Peterborough: Epworth Press

Tatum, W. B., 1997, *Jesus at the Movies: A Guide to the First Hundred Years*, Santa Rosa, CA: Polebridge Press

Telford, W. R., 1994, 'Major Trends and Interpretive Issues in the Study of Jesus' in B. Chilton and C. A. Evans (eds.), *Studying the Historical Jesus: Evaluations of the State of Current Research*, Leiden, New York and Cologne: Brill, pp. 33–74

—— 1997, 'Jesus Christ Movie-Star: The Depiction of Jesus in the Cinema' in C. Marsh and G. Ortiz (eds.), *Explorations in Theology and Film: Movies and Meaning*, Oxford: Blackwell, pp. 115–39

Thistlethwaite, S. B., 1989, *Sex, Race and God*, New York: Crossroad

Thompson, D., 2004, *Crossing the Divide: Luther, Feminism and the Cross*, Minneapolis: Augsburg Fortress

Tillich, P., 1957, *Systematic Theology* (Vol. 2), Chicago: Chicago University Press

Tracy, D., 1981, *The Analogical Imagination*, London: SCM Press

Vaage, L., 1997, 'Recent Concerns: The Scholar as *Engagé*' in W. E. Arnal and M. Desjardins (eds.), *Whose Historical Jesus?* Waterloo, Ontario: Wilfrid Laurier University Press, pp. 181–6

Van Beeck, F. J., 1994, 'The Quest of the Historical Jesus: Origins, Achievement, and the Specter of Diminishing Returns' in J. Carlson and R. A. Ludwig, *Jesus and Faith: A Conversation on the Work of John Dominic Crossan*, Maryknoll: Orbis, pp. 83–99

Wagner, F., 1989, 'Christologie als exemplarische Theorie des Selbstbewußtseins' in *Was ist Theologie?*, Gütersloh: Gütersloher Verlagshaus Gerd Mohn, pp. 309–42

Wakefield, G., 1999, *Methodist Spirituality*, Peterborough: Epworth Press

Walsh, R., 2003, *Reading the Gospels in the Dark: Portrayals of Jesus in Film*, Harrisburg: TPI

Ward, K., 2000, *Religion and Community*, Oxford: Clarendon Press

Weaver, J. D., 2001, *Non-Violent Atonement*, Grand Rapids and Cambridge: Eerdmans

Weaver, W. P., 1999, *The Historical Jesus in the Twentieth Century: 1900–1950*, Harrisburg: TPI

Welch, C., 1972, *Protestant Thought in the Nineteenth Century: Vol. 1 (1799–1870)*, New Haven and London: Yale University Press

Wells, H., 2004, *The Christic Center: Life-Giving and Liberating*, Maryknoll: Orbis

Wessels, A., 1990, *Images of Jesus: How Jesus is Perceived and Portrayed in Non-European Cultures*, London: SCM Press

Wildman, W. J., 1998, *Fidelity with Plausibility: Modest Christologies in the Twentieth Century*, New York: SUNY Press

Williams, J., 1991, 'The Fatherhood of God' in A. I. C. Heron (ed.), *The Forgotten Trinity Vol. 3*, London: BCC/CCBI, pp. 91–101

Wilson-Kastner, P., 1983, *Faith, Feminism and the Christ*, Philadelphia: Fortress Press

Wolfes, M., 1999, *Protestantische Theologie und Moderne Welt*, Berlin: De Gruyter

——2004, *Öffentlichkeit und Bürgergesellschaft: Friedrich Schleiermachers Politische Wirksamkeit*, Berlin: De Gruyter

Wright, D. F., 1988, art. 'Pelagianism' in S. B. Ferguson and D. F. Wright (eds.), *New Dictionary of Theology*, Downers Grove and Leicester: Intervarsity Press, pp. 499–501

Young, P. D., 1995, *Christ in a Post-Christian World*, Minneapolis: Fortress Press

Index of Names and Subjects